Dreams in Myth, Medicine, and Movies

Dreams in Myth, Medicine, and Movies

Sharon Packer

Westport, Connecticut
London

Library of Congress Cataloging-in-Publication Data

Packer, Sharon.
  Dreams in myth, medicine, and movies / Sharon Packer.
    p. cm.
  Includes bibliographical references and index.
  ISBN 0-275-97243-7 (alk. paper)
    1. Dreams. I. Title.
BF1078 .P28 2002
154.6'3—dc21   2002019625

British Library Cataloguing in Publication Data is available.

Library of Congress Catalog Card Number: 2002019625
ISBN: 0-275-97243-7

First published in 2002

Praeger Publishers, 88 Post Road West, Westport, CT 06881
An imprint of Greenwood Publishing Group, Inc.
www.praeger.com

Printed in the United States of America

The paper used in this book complies with the
Permanent Paper Standard issued by the National
Information Standards Organization (Z39.48-1984.)

10 9 8 7 6 5 4 3

To L.B.B. and P.C.

Contents

Preface

The actual writing of this book began on the Reverend Dr. Martin Luther King's birthday and was completed the Sunday before the World Trade Center tragedy. Each of those events has an indelible connection to dreams and is reflected in the text. However, the lectures this book is based upon were delivered over several years, in a series of courses called *Different Approaches to Dreams; Dreams, Drugs, and Drawings;* and *Dream and Film.* Even those courses on dreams started out as spinoffs of a single lecture included in earlier courses: *Insanity and Psychiatry* and *Psychology of Religion.*

In one of those courses, a student noticed how much dreams were intertwined with the history of psychiatry and the history of religion and suggested that I offer a complete course on the history of dreams. At the time, this request seemed like an impossible task that would involve unending research. But the idea lingered. As I perused the existing literature on dreams, it became apparent just how many connections exist among dreams, art, film, religion, culture, and psychiatry. Dreams were a wonderful way to combine my favorite fields! It was worth a try, and, besides, my lectures on dreams had grown too long to squeeze into a single course.

I was surprised by how well received this arcane and out-of-date topic turned out to be. Each course on *Different Approaches to Dreams* filled beyond capacity and ran for five years longer than expected. The lectures again expanded into two additional courses. Each semester, new students appeared, and added new insights, and inspired me further.

It was odd that courses on dreams were so welcomed in a university at a time when psychiatry had shifted its focus away from dreams and onto the biology of the brain. But that was fine by me, because I was a psychiatrist who had once researched the connections between Freud's *The Interpretation of Dreams* and Biblical, Talmudic, and Cabalistic references to dreams. Perhaps I was waiting for the opportunity to rekindle this never-ending interest, although I admittedly stopped expecting to find this opportunity. But my surprise melted away again when I reflected back on my own clinical experience and recalled how eager my patients were to disclose their dreams, regardless of what they sought treatment for and regardless of how rational they were in "real life." Perhaps there was something timeless about this topic.

While teaching these courses, it became clear that certain people were more attracted than others to the study of dream. Predictably, creative types gravitated to these courses, and sometimes used them to enhance their own creativity, and always added their special knowledge about their special pursuits. What was more striking was that many people who were seriously ill or who were recently bereaved also wanted to study dream. This also made sense, because dreams show that an alternative world exists somewhere, if only in the human psyche, but perhaps also someplace else. For those who recently lost a loved one, dreams provided assurance that this person lives on, if only in the memories that are embedded in the unconscious and released during such sleep visions.

Dreams will have special meaning in the wake of the World Trade Center tragedy. This unforeseen event has left many of us with haunting but temporary nightmares. Hopefully, those recurring dreams will soon turn into dreams of consolation, where only the best and most blissful memories are replayed.

Until that time comes, I want to thank those who made this book possible, including my ever patient and encouraging editor, Debbie Carvalko, the New School University, Mesorah Society for Traditional Judaism and Psychiatry, History of Psychiatry Section of Weill-Cornell Medical College, Jewish Book Council, Israel Journal of Psychiatry, Greek Alliance for the Mentally Ill, Hellenic Medical Society, New York Academy of Medicine, Mount Sinai School of Medicine, International Arts Medicine Association, Hebrew Union College Library, George Higham, Jack Green, Paul Bunten, Caroline Duroselle-Melish, Ed Morman, Mark Banschick, Elliot Gershon, Paul Applebaum, Karen Barton, Rick Lippen, Phil Miller, Elissa Tenny, Gina Luria Walker, Nicole Koschmann, Erinn Kelly, Carolyn Lloyd, Barbara Price, Steven Berman, Joel Steinberg, Len Hausman, Joan Root, Stephanie Spanos, Doris Gold, Fred Rosner, Mel Thrash, Mort Ostow, Arthur Tomases, Nate Kravis, Tim Quigley, Tisha Bender, Gunther Engel, David Greenberg, Robert Rubin, Warren Dotz, Bernard Ackerman, and Joan Kessler.

Before We Begin

Most people have thought about dreams at some point in their lives, if only to wonder how their own dreams compare with other people's. Some dismiss dreams as neurochemical nonsense or as silly superstition. Some praise them as prophetic. Others psychoanalyze them and search for psychological secrets. Many people realize that their personal beliefs about dreams differ profoundly from accepted scientific fact, yet refuse to relinquish their secret suspicions about the meanings of dreams, despite what anyone else has to say on the subject.

Dreams are so commonplace, taking place each and every night and sometimes even invading the waking hours, that it makes sense that they should invite speculation from diverse strata of society, from the most learned scholars to the most simple and sheltered of folk. Supernatural interpretations of dreams were popular in prescientific societies and remain the norm in many parts of the world today. Spiritual explanations are appealing to more and more people in the United States, now that New Age ideas have gone mainstream and have made the transition from counterculture to popular culture. It became even easier to seek solace in such spiritual solutions once those psychoanalytic schools that renounced religious belief lost the authority that they once enjoyed.

The issue of psychoanalysis and dreams is an enormous one. Psychoanalysts such as Freud and Jung had so much to say about dreams. Their writings were so widely read, or rephrased, or misrepresented, by so many more secondary sources, that it can sometimes seem as though nothing else of importance has been said on the subject. Yet nothing could be further from the truth. Many, many different approaches to dreams predated Freud's psychoanalytic ideas and coexisted with his, in other cultures and on other continents. Some of these approaches came from science, some from supernaturalism, some from the arts, and some from the newly emerging field of film. It is fascinating to learn about these different approaches to dream and to see how they interconnect in so many unexpected ways.

Freud himself was fascinated by earlier ideas about dreams. He began his epoch-making book on *The Interpretation of Dreams*[1] by cataloguing ancient attempts to explain these enigmatic events. Freud's review of dream theories was not neutral, however. He was not paying homage to the efforts of those who came before him, so much as he was striving to distinguish his own approach to dreams from the approaches of his predecessors and to discredit his competitors. For instance, Freud refers to the Artemidorus' *Oneirocriticon*,[2] which was written in Greek in the second century. He also spoke about Joseph, the Biblical dream teller, who was his ethnic, and perhaps also professional, ancestor.

Freud had many sources of intellectual inspiration, some of which he cited and some of which he did not cite. Sometimes, those unmentioned sources shaped his theories even more than the sources he acknowledged directly. Freud was accused of owing an uncredited debt to Nietzsche, the influential nineteenth-century philosopher who ultimately died in an insane asylum after suffering from neurosyphilis for years. Yet he seized the opportunity to quote from the classical Greek and Roman writers, as if he were trying to gain credibility for his avant-garde ideas and to link himself with a wider intellectual heritage by riding on the shoulders of these respected sources.

Freud was also suspected (although not completely convincingly) of borrowing freely from the literature and lore of his ancestral religion, Judaism.[3] Several scholars were struck by the similarities between Freud's admiration of dreams and the Jewish Talmud's admonition that "an uninterpreted dream is like a letter, unopened." The Talmud makes another strikingly "Freudian-sounding" statement, when it mentions that "a man is shown in a dream only what is suggested by his own thoughts."[4] But bear in mind that the Talmud was compiled in the second and third centuries of the Common Era, while Freud devised his ideas near the end of the nineteenth century.

Not everyone is so quick to equate Freudianism with Judaism. Some go as far as to say that Freud appropriated his psychoanalytic techniques from the Catholic confessional, which he learned about from his Catholic nanny, who took him to church when he was young. Others say that Freud's dream theories drew upon a best-selling spiritual narrative by Therese Lisieux, which was published in 1898, just two years before Freud's own magnum opus appeared in print.[5] The fact that so many serious scholars attempt to attribute Freud's ideas to other sources proves how convinced they are of his historical importance (which is not the same as academic accuracy).

In spite of its many shortcomings, which have been dissected and defended and dissected ad infinitum, Freud's 1900 book *The Interpretation of Dreams* is still believed to be the most influential book of the twentieth century. Freud's cultural influence on the century is compared with that of Marx, Nietzsche, and Einstein. Even those thinkers who disagree with psychoanalytic ideas about dreams—and there are many—typically start their debates about dreams by disputing Freud's original ideas. Some scholars dispute Freud's turn-of-the-century theories about dreams and other things, without realizing that their own opinions agree with Freud's later revisions.[6]

Conversely, some college psychology textbooks begin their small sections on dreams by reminding readers to "wake up from Freud's interpretations of dreams."[7] By including such a caveat, these authors are paying tribute to Freud's enormous impact. Even sleep physiologists and experimental psychologists, whose careers depend upon disproving Freudian dream theories, nevertheless owe their inspirations to Freud's foundation. The same could be said for Carl Gustav Jung, who had been Freud's favorite student before defecting to start his own psychoanalytic school. Jung conceived his spiritually oriented dream concepts to counter Freud's sex-symbolic approach.[8]

Jung's school of analytical psychology retained closer connections to dream interpretation than its Freudian forerunner. Jung laid the groundwork for the New Age movement in America, without living long enough to see it evolve. Jung's lectures were interspersed with so many anecdotes about dreams that it is difficult to assemble all his speculations on this subject in a single source. Jung paid dreams his own greatest tribute by calling his autobiography *Memories, Dreams, Reflections*.[9] By identifying dreams as one of three essential elements of his existence, he recapitulated Freud's point about the centrality of dreams in human consciousness.

Over the centuries, many professions turned their attention to dreams. It is only in the twentieth century that psychoanalysts became the supreme specialists in dreams. Before then and since then, supernaturalists and social scientists, philosophers and physicians, sleep physiologists and psychopharmacologists, artists and anthropologists have all dissected dreams. Painters and poets and playwrights, dancers and dramatists and designers, cinematographers and cybernauts and songwriters have derived ideas from dreams or have depicted dreams directly. Some important scientific discoveries supposedly arrived via dreams, although these sleep-inspired inventors invariably had vast funds of information already stored in their brains, before their ideas crystallized as they "slept on them." Dream-derived art and drama and music sometimes intertwined with science and psychoanalysis, sometimes more than we like to admit.

Dreams mean different things to different people and to different peoples. Dreams may be religious revelations or personal prophecy or dangerous demons. They can be sexual symbols, unfulfilled fantasies, or the collective unconscious. Dreams are seen as medical miracles or therapeutic tools and as artistic achievements or creativity catalysts. For some, dreams are nothing more than neurochemical nonsense or mental manure. Still others deem dreams to be mind movies or free films . . . and are quite content with that!

Few fields have shown the single-minded devotion to dream studies that psychoanalysis has. Few fields can make the claim that the term *dream* appears in the titles of their "bibles," like a banner, as with Freud's *The Interpretation of Dreams* or Jung's *Memories, Dreams, Reflections*. In the past few decades, scholars of religion and mythology have begun to break down psychoanalysts' century-long stronghold on dreams. Often drawing their inspirations from Jung's *Memories, Dreams, Reflections*, top scholars spun off analytical psychology–inspired titles such as *Myths, Dreams, and Mysteries* (Mircea Eliade),[10] *Myths, Dreams, and Religion* (Joseph Campbell),[11] and *Dreams, Illusions, and Other Realities* (Wendy Doniger O'Flaherty).[12] On the other hand, when we realize that it is only relatively recently—over the past one hundred years—that psychoanalysts wrested control of dream interpretation away from the clergy or the occultists, we can put this rivalry in perspective. It will be interesting to see what happens to dream interpretation in the twenty-first century. It will be especially interesting to see if Jung's combination of psychology, science, and occultism continues to seed New Age ideas and ties science and supernaturalism into a permanently twisted knot.

In the pages ahead, we will not try to prove that dreams are best explained by any single approach and nothing but. Instead, we will present many different approaches to dreams, some of which are strikingly similar to these psychoanalytic ideas and some of which are diametrically different. Some of these approaches represent the idiosyncratic ideas of their inventors. Some reflect the standards of the societies that spawned them. Examining the lives of those dream theorists can be almost as informative as examining the theories themselves. By focusing on the cultural context in which these dream-ideas were conceived, we can see how specific theories simultaneously formed and reflected the values of their parent cultures.

In these pages we will witness the ways that different approaches to dreams developed over two to three thousand years. We will start in ancient Mesopotamia, Egypt, Greece, Rome, and Persia and continue to India, Africa and Australasia. We will explore dream themes in medieval, Renaissance, Enlightenment, Romantic, and premodern Europe, before entering the sleep laboratories and psychoanalytic sessions and social psychology studies of the nineteenth and twentieth centuries. We can compare the public dream interpretations of philosophers, psychoanalysts, and psychopharmacologists and shamans, sorcerers, and supernaturalists to the private dream depictions found in painting and puppetry, prose and poetry, film and photography, and dance and drama. We will see how the secular and the sacred have interacted to create completely new conventions for dealing with dreams at the turn of the twenty-first century.

We will muse about the prognosis for psychoanalytic dream interpretation, at a point in time when psychopharmacology takes center stage in psychiatry and at a time when spiritually-oriented New Age dream quests are in full flower. We will briefly discuss the biological basis of dreams, to see how scientific studies compare with psychoanalytic or supernaturalist hypotheses. We will see how the 1953 laboratory discoveries of REM (rapid eye movement) sleep upset idealist ideas about dreams that stressed the immaterial aspects of dreams over the material. We will see how the latest scientific discoveries—as well as the highly publicized antidepressant Prozac—are forcing us to rethink a half-century's worth of assumptions about the association between dreams and REM sleep.

This may sound like a lot to cover in a single volume, but it represents just a tiny fraction of the different approaches to dreams in existence. This presentation will inevitably be incomplete, because there is so very much to say about dreams. There is even more to say about the diverse cultures that addressed the meaning of dreams and about the many marvelous works of art that deal with dreams. Any exploration of a subject as dynamic as dreams will always be a work in progress and never be more than the next installment in a nonstop series. Before we say another word about dreams and their meanings, let us look at dreams and definitions in chapter 2.

NOTES

1. Freud, Sigmund. *The Interpretation of Dreams*. Trans. J. Strachey. New York: Norton, 1965.

2. Artemidorus. *Oneirocriticon*. Trans. Robert J. White. Park Ridge, NJ: Noyes, 1975.

3. Yerushalmi, Joseph Hayim. *Freud's Moses*. New Haven, CT: Yale Univesity Press, 1991; Rice, Emanual. *Freud and Moses: The Long Journey Home*. Albany: State University of New York Press, 1990; Bakan, David. *Sigmund Freud and the Jewish Mystical Tradition*. Princeton, NJ: Van Nostrand, 1958; Gay, Peter. *Freud, A Godless Jew*. New Haven, CT: Yale University Press, 1989; Klein, Dennis. *Jewish Origins of the Psychoanalytic Movement*. Chicago: University of Chicago Press, 1981; Bernstein, Richard J. *Freud and the Legacy of Moses*. Cambridge Studies in Religion and Critical Thought 4. Cambridge, U.K.: Cambridge University Press, 1998; Ostow, Mortimer, ed. *Psychoanalysis and Judaism*. New York: Ktav Publishing, 1982.

4. *The Babylonian Talmud*. Ber. 55b. Trans. and ed. I. Epstein. London, Soncino Press, 1938.

5. Von Grunebaum, G. E. and Roger Caillois, R., eds. *The Dream and Human Societies*. Berkeley: University of California Press, 1966.

6. Bulkeley, Kelly. *Visions of the Night*. Albany: State University of New York Press, 1999.

7. Myers, David G. *Textbook of Psychology*. 5th ed. New York: Worth, 1998.

8. McGuire, William, ed. *The Freud/Jung Letters: The Correspondence between Sigmund Freud and C. G. Jung*. Princeton, NJ: Princeton University Press, 1974; Donn, Linda. *Freud and Jung*. New York: Collier, 1988.

9. Jung, C. G. *Memories, Dreams, Reflections*. Rev. ed. Trans. Richard Winston and Clara Winston. Recorded and ed. Aniela Jaffe. New York: Vintage, 1961.

10. Eliade, Mircea. *Myths, Dreams, and Mysteries*. New York: Harper, 1967.

11. Campbell, Joseph, ed. *Myths, Dreams, and Religion*. New York: Dutton, 1970.

12. O'Flaherty, Wendy Doniger. *Dreams, Illusions, and Other Realities*. Chicago: University of Chicago Press, 1984.

2

Dreams and Definitions

SEMANTIC SIMILARITIES

How interesting it is that the words *dream, delusion, deja vu, delirium, dementia,* and *depression* all sound so similar. More obscure expressions about doubles—such as *dedoublement* or *doppelganger*—are also uncannily close, as are more mundane terms such as *deceptive* or *devious.*

Before going further, let me stress that this attempt at alliteration *is not* serious philology. It belongs to the province of poets, more than anything else. Most—but not all—of these semantic similarities are coincidences, plain and simple. Yet some of the words above *are* related, often in unexpected but extremely significant, ways. Such semantic relationships can tell us a great deal about unconscious conceptions of dreams in different cultures.

The occasionally outdated Oxford English Dictionary (OED) states that our current term *dream* derives from the Old English word for "deceive," as does the word *delusion.* (Other etymological dictionaries disagree with the OED and trace *dream*'s roots to a word that means "joy" or "mirth" or "song.")

If the English words *dream* and *delusion* and *deceive* share the same linguistic origin, then it is safe to say that Anglophones once conceived of dreams as false perceptions, which literally *deceived* the perceiver. English-speaking peoples' skepticism about dreams becomes more understandable. The same could be said about German speakers, since the German *Traum* is related to the Old English *dream.* German speakers are particularly important to our study, because psychoanalytic ideas about dream were coined by native German speakers, first in Austria by Freud and then in Switzerland by Jung. In fact, the notion that dreams are deceivers was so pronounced that C. G. Jung was moved to stress that the opposite is true. He said, "Dreams . . . are natural phenomena which are nothing other than what they pretend to be. They do not deceive, they do not lie, they do not distort or disguise, but naively announce what they are and what they mean."[1]

The OED also mentions that the old English and German words for dream were related to an antiquated term for ghost. This, too, makes sense. Both dreams and ghosts are *deceptive* perceptions. Both can seem completely real when they appear, but both ultimately evaporate, into thin air, after *deceiving* the perceiver into believing that they existed. This semantic link between dreams and ghosts reveals another reason for the irrepressible link between dreams and the occult.

The continuum between *dream* and *delusion* and *deception* is equally compelling. A *delusion* is "a fixed belief that does not waver in the face of obvious and incontestable evidence to the contrary."[2] Thus, a *delusion* is a form of self-*deception*, which confines the deluded person to his own, personally constructed, *dream* world.

These links between *dream, delusion,* and *deception* may be intuitively obvious to most of us today, but not all cultures across the globe think the same way that we do. Many cultures do not automatically equate dreams with delusions. Some look to dreams for truth and hold dreams in higher esteem than waking perceptions. For the most part, those cultures exist in non-Western, nonindustrialized societies, where value systems and everyday demands and overall outlooks on life differ dramatically from the proverbial mainstream, middle-class America.

However, there were extended episodes in time when the Western World accepted dreams as a higher form of reality. Romanticism, symbolism, surrealism, and the counterculture of the 1960s and 1970s, come to mind, as does the New Age ideology that infiltrates the "fin-de-millennium" mentality. To press the point further, we could argue that America's 20th century has been as saturated with the theme of dream as any supernaturalistic and superstitious preliterate society. That is because of the importance that psychoanalytic thought played in this country during those years.

Because of the (sometimes spurious) promises of psychoanalysis, even educated people were willing to delve into their dreams, with the hope of changing their destinies. Like the supernaturalists of old, who sought out augurers and soothsayers, psychoanalysands thought that they could alter their futures if they chanced upon the right omens. In this case, the dream omens pointed to hidden motivations, which were concealed in the unconscious. The unconscious, in turn, could be accessed through the "royal road" of dreams, according to Freudian and Jungian ideology.

The continuum between psychology and parapsychology becomes even more impressive (or offensive) when we realize that Freud's *Der Traumdeutung* (Interpretation of Dreams) sported nearly the same title as a favorite fortune-telling book of the time. The occult publication was entitled *The Interpretation of Dreams and Magic*.[3] An older dream book, penned by a Jewish medieval mystic named Shlomo Almoli, bore the same title.[4] Almoli's work was written for a world that wholeheartedly believed in demons and dybbuks (recycled spirits described in Jewish folklore).[5] This book circulated among ultrareligious, world-renouncing, rural Hasidic Jewish circles, at the very same time that this ultra-sophisticated, highly educated, uber-urbane Viennese physician Freud wrote a better-remembered book on the same subject.[6]

CROSS-CULTURAL CONNOTATIONS

In a later chapter, we will examine some fascinating Jewish influences on Freud's groundbreaking dream theories. For now, let us just say that the Hebrew term for *dream* (chalom) has an entirely different derivation than the English or German words. *Chalom* is related to the Hebrew word for *window* (chalon), because of the belief that dreams provide a window to another world. This interesting association helps us appreciate why dreams were so highly regarded in the Bible, and why they went hand-in-hand with prophecy and mystical experience.

The modern-day mystic or meditator can readily relate to the idea of dream as an aperture to another reality. A popular meditation poster, on display at the New York Open Center, shows the entranced meditator wearing a sleepshirt, arising from his bed, with one foot poised through the open window, as he is about to step out of his sleep, and into the star-filled skies. The stars themselves stretch out toward the far reaches of infinity, with no end in sight.

Someone who is artistically inclined, who has produced a painting within a frame, or who simply became entranced with a work of art is equally familiar with the "dream as window" and "art as window" concept. The surrealist painter René Magritte developed this idea, when he illustrated cloud-covered skies in the center of a human pupil. Magritte's painting replayed an essential surrealist belief: that the mind's eye and the dreaming mind's eye, in particular, can provide an ordinary person with a portal to another reality. The dream turns the ordinary individual into an artist.

This theme of the dream as window to another reality is often repeated in film. The acclaimed 1999 film *Being John Malkovich* creates a dreamlike impression on its viewers, without ever alluding to a dream. It achieves this effect by portraying literal portals that transport its characters into the experience of another person, the actor John Malkovich, played by himself. Through this phantasmagorical portal, ordinary people see life through Malkovich's eyes. They experience the world as both participant and observer, just as they do in their dreams. They become subject and object, simultaneously. Ironically, this arcane concept was considered so avant-garde and so steeped in pedantic, psychoanalytically informed film theory, that the star doubted that the film would be funded. It was a surprise to everyone when the film won a critical prize at the Sundance Film Festival and gained both a popular and a cult following.

It is not just avant-gardists and intellectuals who develop this ancient idea to the artistic extreme. That perennial children's classic *Peter Pan* is an even better example of the dream as window theme. In this story of the boy who never grew up, Wendy and Peter rise from their sleep to enter a Never-Never Land of perpetual dream and adventure. They accomplish this feat by flying through an open bedroom window. Every child who has ever seen or heard the story of Peter Pan has unconsciously incorporated this concept. Many carry this belief into adulthood, without necessarily being aware of its storybook source.

The French word for dream, *reve,* has an origin very different from its Old English and Germanic counterparts. This distinction makes for another reason why French culture is so unique and so unlike the culture of these neighbors. *Reve* is related to *revelation,* a term with both religious and psychological implications. Both *reve* and *revelation* are traced to the Latin root *revelare,* which English speakers know as the word *reveal.*

Revelare literally means "a drawing back of the veil," to make the hidden apparent, and to uncover previously occluded views of something that was present from the start. This French concept is remarkably close to the approach of William Blake, the British mystic, poet, and painter, who wrote about "cleansing the doors of perception." Those who are more familiar with pop culture than with high culture may recall Jim Morrison's melancholic music of the sixties and his band, The Doors, which he named in tribute to Blake's verse.

Thus, for French speakers (and for exceptional Britons such as Blake), dreams routinely reveal, rather than deceive. For the French, it is the veil that deceives the viewers, rather than the image it obstructs. Religious revelations, like dreams, reveal truths that are otherwise unknown or concealed. Such revelations are essential to living life as it was intended. Even secular revelations induce a sudden insight or shift of awareness and offer critical understanding. This French sentiment sounds strikingly similar to psychoanalytic ideas about dreams and about their function as the "royal road to the [otherwise inaccessible] unconscious." It is also uncannily close to the ethos of the short-lived American counterculture, of which Morrison was a prominent member.

When we recall that the dreamlike nineteenth-century symbolist art began in French-speaking regions of Belgium and France, before spreading to other Catholic countries in Europe, it becomes tempting to speculate about the role the French language played in attuning its painters and poets to the revelatory power of dream. In the chapters ahead, we will discuss Freud's experiences in France, where he studied hypnotism and hysteria with French masters such as Charcot and Bernheim. We will also mention Jung's studies with French philosopher-psychiatrist Pierre Janet, who was renowned for his research on dissociative states and multiple personalities. We will wonder if the French language also alerted Freud and Jung—perhaps unconsciously—to the revelatory power of the *reve*. For now, it is enough to point out that our closest English equivalent to the French word *reve* is the word *reverie*. *Reverie* is used synonymously with the word *daydream*. It is a dismissive term that belittles, rather than bolsters, the importance of daydreams.

The Europeans were not the first to contemplate the importance—or lack of importance—of dreams. The English and Germans arrived rather late in the long line of people who perceived that dreams could be deceptive. Similarly, the French were but one of many peoples who pointed out the perception-enhancing powers of dreams. Such ideas about dreams are very, very ancient.

ATTITUDES FROM ANTIQUITY

Homer is credited with identifying dreams as deceptions, but even he was not the first to offer this insight. In the pre-Hellenic Greek culture that produced the *Iliad* and the *Odyssey*, in the eighth century B.C.E., both gods and mortals could be deceived by dreams. The guilt-free gods were willing to deceive people through their dreams, just as they were willing to deceive people through the waking world. Even Zeus, the head of the Homeric pantheon, sent deceptive dreams to his subjects. The lesser deities followed suit. The deceptive dream that Zeus sent to Agamemnon in the *Iliad* incited the mortal king to enter a battle that he was destined to lose.[7]

It was Penelope, Ulysses' wife, who pointed out in the *Odyssey* that "dreams are hard, and hard to be discerned; nor are all things in them fulfilled for men. Twain are the gates of shadowy dreams, the one is fashioned of horn and one of ivory. Such dreams that pass through the portals of sawn ivory are deceitful, and bear tidings that are unfulfilled. But the dreams that come forth through the gates of polished horn bring a true issue, whosoever of mortals behold them."[8]

Similar ideas were expressed in Latin, in the Roman Empire, shortly before the birth of Christ. Paraphrasing his Greek predecessors, the

Latin poet Virgil (70–19 B.C.E.) depicted the dream as a source of both deception and revelation, through the following verses:

> Two gates the silent house of sleep adorn;
> Of polished ivory this, that of transparent horn:
> True visions through transparent horn arise;
> Through polished ivory pass deluding lies.[9]

Contemporary dreamers are just as concerned with distinguishing dreams of revelation from dreams of deception. Some seek psychiatric treatment to discern the difference, and some consult any of the many dream interpretation books that are available for sale. Documenting this continuity of thought from the first millennium through the third millennium can be consoling. Noting that human experiences remain the same over vast stretches of time is equally reassuring. But we must also consider the changes that have occurred in the ways that people conceive of dreams, over the course of 3,000 years. To get a glimpse of our American attitudes toward dream, we can "free associate" to the word *dream*, to see what comes to mind.

AMERICAN ASSOCIATIONS

When asked to cite the first dream-related phrase that comes to mind, the most common response is *American Dream*. Those who lived through the Great Depression remember the time when one could succeed on "a dime and a dream." Australians associate dreams with the Aboriginal myth about *Dreamtime* or *Dreaming*. Native Americans and admirers of Native Americana conjure up images of the *Dreamcatcher* that is placed over a cradle, to sort bad dreams from good ones and to protect baby from unpleasant sleep spirits. African-Americans and civil rights activists recollect the Reverend Dr. Martin Luther King, Jr.'s epoch-making "dream speech." That speech began with the words, "I have a dream," and prodded the passage of the most extensive civil rights legislation since the Civil War. When the erotically inclined speak of the "wet dream," they reaffirm the age-old association between nocturnal emissions and erotic dreams (even though only one out of eight of men's dreams, and only one out of twenty-five of women's dreams is in any literal way erotic.)[10]

When we want to wish someone well, we say, "may all your dreams come true." We speak of a special someone as a "dream date" and encourage a friend to "dare to dream." We search for a "dream home" and yearn to drive around in a "dream machine." Perhaps these expressions date to the time when the word *dream* was synonymous with "joy" or "mirth." More likely, such slogans are just wishful thinking that mask the fact that pleasant dreams are less common than nightmares. At the same time, we dismiss people who are "just dreamers" or who "live in a dreamworld." We are even more impatient with people who revel in "pipe dreams" that are as unrealistic as the vivid visions that occur to one smoking an opium pipe.

Cinemaphiles may speak of Hollywood's "Dream Factory," or Steven Spielberg's production company named "Dreamworks SKG," or Hans Richter's brilliant 1947 art film, *The Dreams That Money Can Buy*. There is Oliver Stone's autobiographical novel, *A Child's Night Dream*,[11] which did not make it to print until its filmmaker-author made a spectacular splash in cinema, many years after it was first written. The dozens upon dozens of dream film titles include *Field of Dreams, Hoop Dreams, Akira Kurosawa's Dreams*, Bergman's *Dreams, What Dreams May Come*, or the more recent and less memorable, *In Dreams*. Traditional theatre devotees think of Broadway's long-running *Joseph and the Amazing Technicolor Dreamcoat*, or Shakespeare's *A Midsummer Night's Dream*, or Hamlet's contemplating of "sleep: perchance to dream," or "what dreams may come." Others quote Shakespeare's *The Tempest*, saying that "We are such stuff as dreams are made on."

First associations can arrive as a song. There is *Dream Lover*, or *Dream a Little Dream of Me*, or *You Are a Beautiful Dreamer*, the Eurythmics' *Sweet Dreams*, Aerosmith's *Dream On*, or The Monkees' *Daydream Believer*, or *These Dreams of You* by Van Morrison and the Dream Team. Dreams appear in the lyrics of *What a day for a daydream*, or *Whenever I want you, all I have to do, is dream, dream, dream, dream*, or *Dream on*. We can cite *Oh, Mr. Sandman, Bring Me a Dream*, or *Life Is But a Dream*, or Irving Berlin's and Bing Crosby's classic, *(I'm Dreaming of a) White Christmas*.

Acid rock references to *I had too much to dream last night* imply, quite accurately, that LSD dramatically increases REM sleep and dream time. Female vocalists such as Debbie Gibson (*Only in My Dreams*), or Mariah Carey (*Dreamlover*), or Aretha Franklin (*I Have a Dream*) sing soulfully about dreams. *Dreamweaver* surfaced in song form, decades before the arrival of the software by the same name. In that American favorite, *The Wizard of Oz*, Judy Garland sang about "a land where dreams come true." Don Quixote, the hero of Cervantes' novel and its musical adaption, *Man of La Mancha*, fights imaginary windmills while he defends his right to "dream the impossible dream."

The Internet is rapidly producing more associations to dreams. Tony Robbins, the motivation guru who promoted fire-walking as a symbol of self-mastery, started a self-help website, *Dreamlife.com*, to play upon connection between self-actualization and the "American Dream." Webheads are familiar with *Dreamweaver*, the computer software used for building websites, while video game fans play on Sega's video game player, *Dreamcast*. The website "http://www.dreams.com" capitalizes

on the proverbial link between dreams and desire, by flipping unsuspecting dream-seekers onto an alternative online pornography site.[12]

People who prefer paper may think of Freud's *Interpretation of Dreams*
or Jung's autobiographical memoir, *Memories, Dreams, Reflections*.
Dreamland could refer to a poem by Pre-Raphaelite artist and author
Dante Gabriel Rossetti,[13] or to artist-author Alfred Kubin's surrealistic
chapter about the "dream realm" or the "dream kingdom." [14]
Prizewinning poet John Berryman published *The Dream Songs*, before
committing suicide.[15] Controversial anthropologist Carlos Castañeda
included a book about dreams in his extensive collection of fantastic
shamanic stories.[16] Beat writer Jack Kerouac's *Book of Dreams* anticipates
the plots and characters that appear in his far better-known books *The
Dharma Bums* and *On the Road*.[17]

Science fiction and fantasy fans may think about artist Boris Vallejo's
book Dreams, with its lush illustrations of Amazonian women overpowering imaginary galaxies and human males. Others imagine Philip
K. Dick's futuristic novel, *Do Androids Dream of Electric Sheep?*, which
became even better known through its film version, *Bladerunner*.[18]
Stephen King's horror thriller *The Dreamcatcher* goes above and beyond
the original Ojibwa Indian idea about catching nightmares in a web that
hangs over the bed. The list goes on and on.

AN AMERICAN DREAM

It is worth looking into the implications of the "American Dream," if
only because this expression has so little connection to the more ethereal
theme of dream that we will discuss during the rest of this book.

The American dream is not a dream at all and is certainly not a sleep
apparition. Unlike the real dream that appears during sleep or during
altered states of consciousness, the American dream is reality-based. It
requires clear consciousness to bring to fruition and occurs only when
we are fully awake. While it may not be instantly attainable, it is
nevertheless within the reach of reality (for Americans, that is, although
not necessarily for anyone else). The American dream tells us that we
can achieve what others elsewhere only imagine and that we can turn
the ethereal into the material. But the American dream does not appear
by magic, in the way that Rumpelstiltskin wove flax into gold or in the
way that Aladdin's genie transported him through the Arabian nights.
The American dream is accomplished through hard work and dedica-
tion, through a special synthesis of nighttime foresight with daily toil.
The American dream offers the opportunity for material goods, personal acquisitions, and worldly achievement. It is the result of human
efforts, rather than divine or diabolical intervention. Its rewards are

this-worldly, rather than otherwise, making it a polar opposite to
supernatural or superstitious dreams that preceded it.

At its worst, the American dream is the dream of strip malls and
sterile suburbs and of specious sameness and meaningless materialism,
all achieved without accompanying spiritual substance. It is the dream
that clergymen rail against in Saturday or Sunday sermons because it
distracts its pursuers from seeing the "truer" visions described by
Biblical dreamers and utopian visionaries.

At its best, the American dream is testimony to the American pioneer
spirit of endurance, ingenuity, and individualism. It is this American
dream that still lures immigrants to the United States and that promises
that they can rise above their family backgrounds and achieve a com-
fortable earthly existence unencumbered by preset class expectations or
outdated social standing.

On the surface, the whole idea of an American dream sounds so
distinctly different from Freud's Old World ideas, which were conceived in anachronistic, monarchy-ruled Austria, more than a century
before. But people who are familiar with Freud's finer points may
suspect that the concept of the American dream is a restatement par
excellence of Freud's hotly-contested hypothesis about dreams as wish
fulfillment. For both Freud and the dreamers of the American dream,
the dream is a place where fantasies are fulfilled. The difference lies in
the fact that Freud stressed the seamier sexual undertones of those
unfulfilled fantasies. The American "dream come true" materializes
through the physical form of money and the material pleasures that
money can buy (which sometimes include new sex or better sexual
partners).

The American dream is a modern myth. But it is not the only myth
that we carry with us when we think about dream. It may be the
myth that made America so hospitable to Freud's ideas after World
War II, when analysts arrived en masse from Europe. In the next
section, on myth and meaning, we will look at more ancient myths
that invade our everyday vocabulary and contribute to our concepts
of dream.

NOTES

    1. Platania, Joe. *Jung for Beginners*. London: Writers and Readers, 1997; Jung,
C. G. *The Collected Works of C. G. Jung*. Trans. R. F. C. Hull. Princeton, NJ:
Princeton University Press, 1974.
    2. American Psychiatric Association. *American Psychiatric Association's Psychi-
atric Glossary*. Washington: American Psychiatric Press, 1984.
    3. Ellenberger, Henri. *The Discovery of the Unconscious*. New York: Basic, 1970.
    4. Trachtenberg, Joshua. *Jewish Magic and Superstition*. New York: Behrman,
1939.

5. Neugroschel, Joachim, trans. and comp. *Yenne Velte* [The Great Works of Jewish Fantasy and the Occult]. 2 vols. New York: Stonehill, 1976; The Dybbuk was the one of the most popular Yiddish plays produced in America. It gained a second life as silent film by the same name and was immortalized by its Art Nouveau advertising poster.

6. Rice, Emmanuel. *Freud and Moses: The Long Journey Home*. Albany: State University of New York Press, 1991.

7. Homer. *Iliad*. Book 2. Trans. Robert Fagles. New York: Viking, 1996.

8. Homer. *Odyssey*. Book 29. Trans. Robert Fagles. New York: Viking, 1996.

9. Virgil. *Aeneid*, VI. Ed. Ralph L. Woods; *The World of Dreams: An Anthology*. New York: Random, 1947, 349-350.

10. Myers, David G. *Textbook of Psychology*. 5th ed. New York: Worth, 1998.

11. Stone, Oliver. *A Child's Night Dream*. New York: St. Martin's, 1998.

12. 1 Jan. 2000 <http://www.dreams.com>.

13. Rossetti, Christina. "Dreamland." <http://cgfa.kelloggcreek.com/rossetti/p-8d-dream.htm>.

14. "The Decline and Fall of the Dream Realm." Kubin, Alfred. *The Other Side*. Trans. Mike Mitchell. Cambs, U.K.: Dedalus, 2000; "The Downfall of the Dream Kingdom." Kubin, Alfred. *The Other Side*. Trans. Denver Lindley. New York: Crown, 1967.

15. Berryman, John. *The Dream Songs*. New York: Noonday-Farrar, 1982.

16. Fikes, Jay Courtney. *Carlos Castaneda, Academic Opportunism and the Psychedelic Sixties*. Victoria, B.C., Canada: Millenia, 1993.

17. Kerouac, Jack. *Book of Dreams*. San Francisco: City Lights, 1981.

18. Dick, Philip K. *Do Androids Dream of Electric Sheep?* New York: Del Rey-Random House, 1993.

3

Myth and Meaning

DEITIES OF DREAM

Every waking day, each of us invokes the names of several heathen deities, simply by using ordinary, everyday English. The more psychologically astute among us pay the most tribute to the pagan pantheon, because so much psychological jargon stems from pre-Christian Greek and Latin classics. References to the Greek and Roman gods of sleep and dreams are particularly plentiful. Their names were Hypnos, Morpheus, and Somnus.

Hypnos was the god who governed sleep. Morpheus, one of Hypnos' many sons, was the deity of dreams. When the Romans adapted Greek culture, they renamed the Greek Hypnos in Latin "Somnus." Somewhat surprisingly, Morpheus, the deity of Dreams and the son of Sleep, got only a brief mention in Greek mythology. He did not surface in full form until Roman times, when the Latin poet Ovid (43 B.C.E.–17? C.E.) wrote about him in *Metamorphoses*. The same Roman myth that introduced Morpheus also immortalized a Greek queen named Halcyone. Halcyone's husband Ceyx reigned over a kingdom in Greece, but it is Halcyone whom we remember, because her name is preserved by our present-day pharmacopoeia. "Halcion" is now the name of a prescription sleeping pill that is popular in America (but was banned in Britain)!

These mythological characters mutated through many different times and tongues, and each has an interesting story that deserves retelling both for its own sake and for the information it offers about the way different cultures conceive of dreams and sleep and sleep-associated events. If we simply examine the pagan pedigree to see who is related to whom, we immediately begin to understand ancient assumptions about basic life processes.

Hypnos was the oldest of these deities and was the son of Nyx (Night), and the father of Morpheus (Dream). Everyone has heard of Hypnos, in one way or another. His image appears in paintings and sculpture. He has been portrayed as either a naked young man with wings attached to his temples or as a bearded man with wings sprouting from his shoulders.[1] A bust of the young Hypnos is on display in the British Museum. Hypnos also appears in several symbolist paintings from the late nineteenth century. Often, he is standing on the sidelines, behind the central image, to symbolize the fact that the scene was either dream-inspired or the result of an artificial sleep state induced by hypnosis.

Hypnosis was a popular practice among spiritualist and occultist circles of the time and was incorrectly associated with both sleep and occult occurrences. Belgian symbolist Fernand Khnopff's haunting painting entitled *I lock my door upon myself* (1891)[2] incorporates Hypnos' image in this symbolic way. It is typically difficult to describe both these paintings and Hypnos' role in them, but that was intentional; the symbolists were concerned with suggesting, rather than stating, and they valued Hypnos and hypnotism precisely because they offered entree into realms that were even more enigmatic.

Many less esoteric references to Hypnos exist in contemporary culture. For instance, hypnotism was named after Hypnos, the god of sleep, because of a surgeon's mistaken notion that a hypnotic trance resembled sleep. It has since been learned that sleep and hypnotic trances are quite distinct and that hypnotism paradoxically increases arousal, whereas sleep permits rest.[3] Even our everyday speech reminds us of this important distinction. When we describe a performance as "hypnotic," we are saying that it is trance-inducing or mesmerizing and that it draws us in, beyond what our ordinary wills would permit. A "hypnotic" performance is the exact opposite of a "soporific" one that puts us to sleep prematurely.

Pharmacists and physicians refer to sleeping pills as "hypnotics" and use the term exactly as it had been intended in Greek. Hypnos' name appears in two other medical terms, "hypnogogic" and "hypnopompic," which refer, respectively, to hallucinations that occur during the moments before falling asleep or immediately upon awakening from sleep.

Hypnos' Latin name "Somnus" is equally familiar to English speakers. When we refer to sleeplessness as "insomnia," we speak of Somnus or, literally, of the "lack of Somnus." We describe sleepwalking (and related conditions) as "somnambulism." In the nineteenth century, people who were put under the sleeplike "spell" of hypnotists were referred to as "somnambules."[4] "Somnolence" is another condition that is related to Somnus and sleep and often afflicts students who fall asleep in lecture hall. The proper botanical term for the opium poppy—

papaverum somniferum—gives another nod to Somnus, both in name and in legend, for it was said that Somnus and his many sons lived in a cave surrounded by poppy flowers.

Morpheus, the deity of dreams, was one of Somnos' (aka Hypnos') many sons. Morpheus had a brother, Phantasos. (In other words, Phantasos was also the son of Somnus/Hypnos.) Phantasos' name has many interesting permutations. It translates directly into "phantasm," which is an arcane word for "ghost" and a likely sib for the equally ethereal and evanescent dream. This connection recollects the Old English association between dream and ghost as well. *Phantasm* became the name of a low-budget but high-quality 1979 horror film, wherein a dreamlike being endured one horrific ordeal after another.

Phantasos' name eventually evolved into our English "fantasy" and "phantasmagoria," and even Disney's famous animated feature, *Fantasia*. Obviously, fantasy bears a strong family resemblance to dream. Another interesting adaptation of Phantasos' name appears in the works of nineteenth century German physician Louis Lewin. Dr. Lewin identified dozens of hallucinogenic plants and grouped them together, under the rubric *phantastica*. He wrote a book about these botanicals, entitled it *Phantastica*, and published it long before Dr. Albert Hofmann synthesized the most infamous *phantastica* of all, LSD. Author Theophile Gautier, who founded the Hashish Club in the mid-nineteenth century, also included a lavish chapter on "Fantasia" in his visionary, hashish-inspired prose. It was Gautier who inspired French writers such as Balzac, Nerval, Maupassant, Hugo, and others to explore altered states of awareness, through the use of this hemp plant.

The relationship of Phantasos and Morpheus deserves more elaboration. The two were brothers, and each had his own responsibilities. Morpheus was best at imitating human beings, in all their activities. Phantasos turned himself into rocks, waters, woods, and other nonliving objects and made inanimate objects look alive, just as they did in Disney's *Fantasia*.[5] Icelos, the third brother, impersonated birds, beasts, and serpents.

Morpheus, our god of dreams, has a more complex heritage than his father or his brothers, as is befitting a phenomenon as complex as dreams. It is uncertain if Morpheus ever had a mother. When Morpheus first appeared in myth, he was living in a dimly-lit cave, lying on an ebony bed, surrounded by poppy flowers. To this day, Morpheus' name is indelibly linked to this opium-bearing poppy plant, the very same plant that sent Dorothy and company into dream-laden slumber as they waited to enter the Emerald City of Oz. Morphine, the potent pain reliever, was named for Morpheus, because someone erroneously assumed that Morpheus was responsible for sleep.

Morphine was synthesized from the opium produced by the poppy plant, as is the less potent codeine. Medicinal morphine was not manufactured for the expressed purpose of inducing dreams. Instead, it was intended to be a sedative that produced sleep, which would in turn relieve pain. Technically speaking, morphine should have been named for Somnus, rather than for his son. Yet there are so many literary links about opium and dreams, that it is immaterial whether or not this name of "morphine" was the result of a mythological or pharmacological mistake. The association between Morpheus, morphine, and opium was cemented forever, through the memoirs of De Quincy (*Confessions of an English Opium Eater*), the poetry of Coleridge (*Kubla Khan*), and the enigmatic etchings of Gustave Doré. There are many, many more artistic and literary and cinematic sources connected to this double-edged drug.

Morpheus' name literally means "he who forms, or molds." The word "morpheus" comes from the Greek root *morphe* (shape), and for good reason. It was said that Morpheus appeared to humans in their dreams in the *shape* of a man, and that Morpheus *shaped* dreams, and gave *shape* to the beings who appear during dreams. The word "metamorphosis" refers to a transformation into another shape or state of being. Appropriately, the myth of Morpheus first appeared in Ovid's Latin masterpiece known as "*Metamorphoses*."

"Morph" is also a favorite term in medicine. Pathologists and hematologists describe cells in terms of their "morphology," as they screen for changes in cell shape that signal the presence of cancer. "Morph" is an equally relevant expression for the computer age, where CGI (computer-generated imagery) makes images melt and merge and "morph" into one another, to achieve a dreamlike quality of instant transpositions and liquid time.

When the premiere publisher of fantastic art named its company Galerie Morpheus, it, too, saluted Somnus' son and alerted mythologically attuned audiences to the dreamy atmosphere achieved by resident illustrators, such as Giger, Becksinski, Bertrow, and others. Morpheus the mythological character got a well-deserved walk-on role in Disney's *Fantasia* of 1940, but top billing was left for his brother, Phantasos. Unfortunately, Morpheus did not appear in the *Fantasia 2000* remake. Morpheus stars in the more recent and equally acclaimed cyber-sci-fi thriller *Matrix*, where dream, reality, and cyberspace become completely confused and require the wisdom of an anemic-appearing African-American named Morpheus (Laurence Fishburne) to guide the players through the constantly metamorphosizing maze.

THE HISTORY OF HYPNOS

It can be useful to put word derivations aside and turn back time to see how Morpheus came into being on a mythological level. By tracing his lineage, we can see how common unconscious conceptions about sleep and dream evolved since ancient times.

Morpheus' father was Hypnos, the son of Nyx, or Night. That line of descent makes perfect sense. Night begets Sleep, almost automatically. This needs no further comment. It is more intriguing that Hypnos was the twin brother of Death, also known as Thanatos. This kinship demands more reflection, especially since it recurs in the myths of many unrelated cultures.

For the ancient Greeks and Romans, Sleep and Death were not just siblings. They were twins and were intimately and inexorably intertwined. As twins, they are essentially identical, until closely examined. One can mimic the other, effortlessly.

Just as importantly, Dream is the nephew of Death. He is not a direct heir of Death, but he is closer than a cousin. This relationship is intuitively obvious to us today, just as it was to the Greek mythographers who wrote nearly 3,000 years ago. There is a purpose to this fanciful tale. Linking Dream to Death helps humans make sense of the world and allays potentially paralyzing fears of the future. The easiest way to make sense of the world is to frame the most unfamiliar aspects of that world in the most familiar terms. Nothing is more unfamiliar than death, whereas sleep and dream are everyday experiences.

The most terrifying task that people face during their lifetimes is the task of imagining their own deaths and of preparing for what, if anything, will happen afterward. Dreams can ease that transition. Dreams occur every night, whereas death happens but once. Each of us can practice deciphering our dreams whenever we wish, but there is no dress rehearsal for death. Poets have proven that it is preferable to think of death as an eternal slumber than to imagine it as a big blank or the great unknown.

Many people achieve a partial sense of mastery over death, once they realize that they have already dealt with their most dreaded dreams. Those who endured a dreamlike delirium and returned to health can assure themselves that they can face this same fate successfully in the future. Under the worst of circumstances, earlier experiences with bad dreams or D.T.s (delirium tremens) reinforce fears about an afterlife filled with hellfire and brimstone and reptiles and beasts. In the *Odyssey*, Homer situated Hades near "the village of dreams" (24.12) and populated it with shadowy figures, whose substance was said to be similar to dreams.[6]

Today, we can read accounts of near-death experiences whenever we wish. Television talk shows invite resuscitation survivors to describe the visions they experienced after they were declared dead. But before the late twentieth century, advanced CPR (cardiopulmonary resuscitation) and cardiac defibrillation were nonexistent, making it impractical to depend upon survivors of cardiac arrest to provide reliable data about near-death. Fevers and febrile convulsions and secondary delirium were more common, though, and could ferment extra speculation about "almost" adventures in the afterlife.[7] But dreams were a far more efficient double for death, back then and today, because we almost always awaken from our dreams with our sensorium intact, and can get immediate feedback each morning without waiting to recuperate from a consciousness-compromising illness.

When we take all these factors into account, we see that the ancient nephew-uncle relationship between Death and Dream makes perfect sense. This relationship implies that mental or spiritual activity continues after death unabated, albeit in noncorporeal form, just as it does in dreams. Dream may not be a direct descendant of Death, but he is still closer than a cousin. For Death, who bore no sons or daughters, Dream is his nearest living link.

Like dreams, Death can be pleasant, banal, or horrid. Whatever it involves, it involves *something*. Existence does not simply vaporize into nothing after death's arrival, at least not according to ancient lore or popular imagination. One's own life and the lives of one's loved ones can continue in perpetuity, thanks to Dream, who doubled as Death's messenger.

It can be remarkably reassuring for the dreamer to see the dead appear in their dreams, looking and acting as if they are still alive somewhere, possibly even appearing years younger or healthier and happier than they looked at the time of their deaths. It is not rare for dreamers to decide that this nocturnal image of the departed is not simply an illusion, but rather, that it is a message straight from the other side. This semidirect relationship between Death and Dream has played itself out, both in myth and in metaphysics and in normal mourning. It is no coincidence that many people who face death become acutely concerned with their dreams.[8]

Many people who are bereaved also become intrigued with their dreams, because dreams provide an opportunity to maintain "contact" with their lost loved ones and to work out issues and conflicts that were unresolved in real life. In the mid-to-late nineteenth century, the association between sleep, dreams, and death was so strong that an entire movement of spiritualist seances emerged. During such seances, people were hypnotized in order to send them into an artificial sleep state that was said to facilitate communication with the dead. The earliest Greek literature is replete with tales of dead relatives appearing in dreams, standing at the head of the sleeper's bed.

Let us put aside our concerns about the scientific validity of ideas about Dream and Death to consider the ways that myths help people to construct meaning around life's most important moments. It was not just the Greeks and Romans who mused about the relationship between dreams and death. Psychoanalysts such as Freud and Jung and Rank and Ferenczi turned to myth, in the first half of that same century, to excavate eternal truths about this ultimate human experience. In the last decades of the twentieth century, at a time when membership in organized religion dropped to all-time lows, interest in mythographers such as Joseph Campbell exploded.

Poets and philosophers examined the dream-death theme many times over the centuries. Some of the most beautiful literature of the Western world revolves around this motif. Writing early in the fourteenth century, Dante set his *Divine Comedy* in a dream. Early in the first canto, as he sets out on his journey through heaven and hell, he tells us that he "cannot rightly tell how [he] entered there, [he] was so full of sleep at that moment when [he] left the true way. . . ."[9] Dante makes it intentionally ambiguous as to whether death and dreams were one. The reader is equally apt to think that his three-tiered trip through Paradise, Purgatory, and the Inferno was nothing more than a night apparition.

Shakespeare was another illustrious literary figure who described the connection between death and dreams. "For in that sleep of death what dreams my come, when we have shuffled off this mortal coil must give us pause," says Hamlet. Hundreds of years later, the psychologically astute actor Robin Williams starred in a phantasmagorical (and fantastically depressing) film about suicide and death, entitled *What Dreams May Come*. That film plays upon that same well-known speech from *Hamlet*: "To sleep: perchance to dream; ay, there's the rub: for in that eternal slumber of death, who knows what dreams may come. . ." Using lavish, state-of-the-art CGI (computer-generated images) of flowers and valleys and mountain peaks, the film focused on the dreamlike quality of the afterlife.

The Tibetan Book of the Dead is another enduring example of the perceived kinship between death and dreams. Written as a religious text, rather than as literary art, it is the product of a remote mountain culture that could not be accused of incorporating Greek influences. *The Tibetan Book of the Dead* describes the "bardos" that humans pass through after death. There, they confront nightmarish illusions, before their disembodied consciousness attains "illumination" in a noncorporeal state.

The 1990 film *Jacob's Ladder* dramatizes these Tibetan beliefs, through a subtle but suspenseful plot that simultaneously references the Old Testament. It is based on a screenplay by a young American (Bruce Joel Rubin) who spent four months in a Tibetan Buddhist monastery. *Jacob's Ladder* presents itself as an action-oriented horror film, even though it is embedded with metaphysical themes and references to Francis

Bacon's paintings and not-so-subtle allusions to the crossover between drugs and dream states. Hallucinatory special effects recreate the nightmarish transition stage endured by a young soldier who was wounded during the Vietnam War. The young man, played by Tim Robbins, never regained consciousness before dying on the battlefield, but the spectator does not realize this until the end of the film. The protagonist does not recognize the illusory nature of his nightmarish visions either. Only the astute observer notices that Robbins is riding alone, on ordinarily overpacked New York City subways, as menacing faces flash past him and as other trains race along the tracks. It is not until the final minutes of the film that both audience and actor are aware that the action took place in the twilight state between dream and death. The Tibetans know this state as the "bardo."

As interesting as the plot and presentation are, it is even more interesting to note that few viewers realize that *Jacob's Ladder* fuses beliefs from a very foreign culture with very familiar themes. Some people, cued by the film's title and the lead character's name, realize that the film references the Old Testament story about the patriarch Jacob, who saw a starry ladder as he slept in a sacred place. There is a reason why audiences are so ready to believe that the plot comes straight out of Western tradition, why they are so slow to identify Rubin's Tibetan influences. That is because the commonality between dream and death is intuitively obvious to all humans. The plot cuts across cultures and needs no translation into another language. The same kernel of truth is encased in different shells. The viewer sees inside and casts off the casing.

HALCION AND HALCYONE

The Romans had their share of myths also. As a nation, the Romans were never as imaginative or as philosophical or as aesthetic as their Greek mentors. So they borrowed freely from the Greeks, just as they borrowed from the Egyptians and the peoples of Asia Minor, whom they conquered. They discarded anything that did not serve their practical purposes and preserved only the most utilitarian ideas of the Greeks. Where the pragmatic Romans left off, the even more pragmatic marketing departments of modern pharmaceutical manufacturers took over and added new myths about the commonality between sleep, dreams, and sleeping pills. When it came time to name a new benzodiazepine-based sleeping pill, certain drug companies called upon their literary skills and mythopoetic abilities. They gifted us with yet another link to Hypnos, Somnus, Morpheus, Night, and Death, when they conceived of the name of "Halcion."

Halcyone had been the proper name of a Greek queen. She was the wife of Ceyx, King of Thessaly, in northeastern Greece. Halcyone the Queen turned into a bird, which became known as the halcyone bird. She eventually "reincarnated" as Halcion the Sleep Pill. This bird is said to protect sailors from the stormy seas, just as the sleeping pill is said to protect sleepers from stormy nights. Halcyone's sad story appears in the Latin tale about *The Halcyone Birds*. This story is so essential to our understanding of the familial ties between Morpheus, Somnus, Nyx, and Phantasos that I will summarize it here.

Halcyone's story starts when her husband, King Ceyx, was grieving for his dead brother. Seeking solace from his unsettled psychological state, Ceyx decided to journey to consult the oracle of Apollo, the god of healing. When Ceyx told his wife Halcyone of his decision to set sail, Halcyone wrongly concluded that her husband wanted to go on a journey in order to avoid her.

Halcyone said to Ceyx, "What fault of mine, dearest husband, has turned your affection from me? Where is that love of me that used to be uppermost in your thoughts? Have you learned to feel easy in the absence of Halcyone?"

She pleaded to accompany Ceyx on this trip, but he refused, because he feared for her safety on the stormy seas. Ceyx's fears proved to be justified. Shortly after he set sail, the raging seas overturned Ceyx's ship, destroying the ship, and claiming the lives of Ceyx and all his shipmates.

Halcyone, left at home alone, did not know what had happened. She spent many sleepless nights, wondering about the well-being of her spouse. She prayed to the goddess Juno (previously known as Hera) for word about her husband's return.

Of course, the deities knew exactly what transpired. After hearing her repeated pleas, Juno (Hera) took pity on Halcyone and decided to inform her about her husband's demise, by delivering a message to her during her sleep. To do this would require the intervention of other important gods.

Juno (Hera) called upon Iris, the goddess of the Rainbow, saying, "Iris, my faithful messenger, go to the drowsy dwelling of Somnus (Hypnos) and tell him to send a vision to Halcyone in the form of Ceyx, to make known to her the event." Iris immediately put on her robe of many colors and set out in search of the palace of the King of Sleep.

The myth continues, telling us that "A mountain cave is the abode of the dull god Somnus, where clouds and shadows are exhaled from the ground, and the light glimmers faintly.... Poppies grow abundantly before the door of the cave, and other herbs, from whose juices Night (Nyx) collects slumbers, which she scatters over the darkened earth. There is no gate to the mansion, to creak on its hinges, nor any watchman; but in the midst lies a couch of black ebony, adorned with black plumes and black curtains. There the god reclines, his limbs relaxed with sleep. Around him lie dreams, resembling various forms, as many as the harvest bears stalks, or the forest leaves, or the seashore sand grains."

Iris entered this underground abode and "brushed away the dreams that hovered around her." After Somnus asked her about her errand, Iris answered, "Somnus, gentlest of the gods, tranquillizer of minds and soother of careworn hearts, Juno sends you her commands that you dispatch a dream to Halcyone, representing her lost husband and all the events of the wreck."

"Then Somnus called one of his numerous sons—Morpheus—the most expert in counterfeiting forms, and in imitating the walk, the countenance, and mode of speaking, even the clothes and attitudes most characteristic of each. But he only imitates men, leaving it to another to personate birds, beasts, and serpents. Him they call Icelos; and Phantasos is a third, who turns himself into rocks, waters, woods, and other things without life. These wait upon kings and great personages in their sleeping hours, while others move among the common people."

"Somnus chose, from all the brothers, Morpheus, to perform the command of Iris; then laid his head on his pillow. Morpheus flew, making no noise with his wings, and soon came to the Haemonian city, where, laying aside his wings, he assumed the form of Ceyx. Under that form, but pale like a dead man, naked, he stood before the couch of the wretched wife. Leaning over the bed, tears streaming from his eyes, he said, 'Do you recognize your Ceyx, unhappy wife, or has death too much changed my visage? Behold me, know me, your husband's shade, instead of himself. Your prayers, Halcyone, availed me nothing. I am dead. No more deceive yourself with vain hopes of my return.'"

"Halcyone, weeping, groaned, and stretched out her arms in her sleep, striving to embrace his body, but grasping only the air." To test the truth of this dream, Halcyone went to the seashore, the next morning, and sought the spot where she last saw Ceyx.

Looking out onto sea, "she saw an indistinct object floating in the water." When she saw for sure that this object was Ceyx's dead body, Halcyone cried out, "I will not be separated from thee, unhappy husband. This time, at least, I will keep thee company. In death, if one tomb may not include us, one epitaph shall; if I may not lay my ashes with thine, my name, at least, shall not be separated." "Her grief forbade more words, and these were broken with tears and sobs."

Determined to join her beloved forever, "Halcyone leaped upon this barrier [that separated the shore from the sea], and she flew. Striking the air with wings produced on the instant, [she] skimmed along the surface of the water, an unhappy bird. As she flew, her throat poured forth sounds full of grief, and like the voice of one lamenting. . . . When she touched the mute and bloodless body, she enfolded its beloved limbs with her new-formed wings, and tried to give kisses with her horny beak. Whether Ceyx felt it, or whether it was only the action of the waves, those who looking on doubted, but the body seemed to raise its head. But indeed he did feel it, and by the pitying gods both of them were changed into birds. They mate and have their young ones. For seven placid days, in winter time, Halcyone broods over her nest, which floats upon the sea. Then the way is safe to seamen."[10]

After reading this melodramatic myth, we can see how Halcion's heritage helped to promote the pharmaceutical product, and how it helped the drug navigate through its own troubled waters. Serious side effects were linked to this particular sleep medication, to the point that Great Britain pulled the drug from its market. The United States imposted stringent restrictions on dosage.

To be fair, it should be noted that there are other connotations to the name of this medication. The word halcyone also means "peaceful," and a peaceful night's sleep is what insomniacs seek. It is also possible that the name "Halcion" was chosen because it recalls the name of another, previously popular sleeping pill, "Placidyl," whose name in turn stemmed from the word "placid."

How impressive it is that these spectacularly profitable pharmaceutical manufacturers could reach back into nearly forgotten Greek and Roman myths, as they forged new frontiers in psychopharmaceuticals. This is reminiscent of Freud's approach in paving new paths in psychoanalysis. Freud excavated the Oedipus myth from Greek drama, and turned Sophocles' tragedy about Oedipus Rex into the Oedipus Complex, and saved Oedipus from literary oblivion.

The story grows more complex when we consider the commentaries of the late University of Chicago professor Alan Bloom. The world-renowned political philosopher railed against contemporary college students' ignorance of the classics (and other things). He bemoaned the fact that modern knowledge about Greek or Latin ideas is transmitted through the filter of Freudian metapsychology and is no longer studied for its own sake. His best-selling 1988 book *The Closing of the American Mind*[11] provoked comments and condemnation from academics everywhere and opened a lively dialogue among university professors and the public. We can only wonder what Bloom would have said had he lived long enough to write a sequel and to learn that pharmaceutical manufacturers would rival Freud's success in promoting public awareness of classical lore.

With that in mind, we will turn to our "modern myths" and the medium that delivers them best: the movies. In the next chapter, we will see how dream, film, and photography interconnect.

NOTES

1. 1 Jan. 2000 <http://longman.awl.com/mythology/glossaries/phrase_h.asp>

2. Delevoy, Robert, Catherine De Croes, and Giselle Ollinger-Zinque. *Fernand Khnopff*. Brussels: Cosmos Monographie, Edition Lebeer-Hossmann, 1987.

3. Spiegel, Herbert, and David Spiegel. *Trance and Treatment*. Washington: American Psychiatric Press, 1985.

4. Tyler, Parker. *The Hollywood Hallucination.* New York: Creative Age Press, 1944.

5. *Bulfinches' Mythology Online.* 25 Jan. 2000. <http://longman.awl.com/mythology/glossaries/phrase_h.asp>

6. Simon, Bennett. *Mind and Madness in Ancient Greece.* Ithaca: Cornell University Press, 1978.

7. Brièrre de Boismont and Alexandre Jacques Francois. Reprint of 1853 ed. *Dès Hallucinations, ou Historie Raisonnée des Apparitions, des Visions, des Songés, de l'extàce, du maganetisme et du somnambulism.* [Hallucinations, or The Rational History of Apparitions, Visions, Dreams, Ecstacy, Magnetism, and Somnambulism]. New York: Arnot, 1976.

8. Packer, Sharon. Preliminary observations.

9. Alighieri, Dante. *Inferno,* Canto I.

10. *Bulfinches' Mythology Online.* 25 Jan. 2000. <http://longman.awl.com/mythology/glossaries/phrase_h.asp>

11. Bloom, Alan. *The Closing of the American Mind.* New Haven: Yale University Press, 1988.

4

Film and Photography

Until cyberspace arrived, no medium could capture the fleeting, disjointed, visual imagery of dreams nearly as closely as cinema could. Not only did cinema mirror dreams amazingly accurately, but it quickly became one of our most important forms of *mass media*. Cinema did not require literacy, the same way that books or newspapers did, although one had to learn "film language" to understand its full message.[1] Nor did film require (of its audience) the money that professional staged performances demanded, after vaudeville ended. To see a film, one did not need to live near an urban center that was large enough and wealthy enough to support serious theater or opera or ballet companies. One did not have to make do with amateur theater. All but the most impoverished could afford to see the finest quality film.[2]

Cinema became accessible to all strata of society. It could compete with the free performances of passion plays, Ramayana ballets, and liturgical and cantorial music offered in churches, synagogues, mosques, and temples. Since cinema was essentially secular, it could reach out to everyone, without being bound by the sectarianism of religious groups. So cinema became a major venue for conveying modern myth and for creating cultural currents. Culture, in turn, affects dream content.

This mandala-like cycle of dream influencing film and of film then influencing dreams, both in form and in content, continues in a seemingly endless circle. To see how this circle began, we can retrace the steps that led to the invention of film.

FILMS AND PHOTOS

Before there was Film (with a capital "F"), there was photography (which used "film" with a small "f"). When photography was first invented in the 1830s, they called it the "waking dream." Photography could reproduce images placed before the camera with complete clarity. This feat had previously been reserved for sleepers and for the very best "trompe-l'oeil" illusionists. A century after its invention, Salvador Dali paid photography the ultimate compliment, when he compared his surrealist dreamscapes to "hand-painted dream photographs."[3]

While the wealthy could commission perfectly rendered portraits, the common person had never seen an exact reproduction of his or her face before, unless asleep or when looking in the mirror. Photography could change all that. Its ability to capture an image correctly was uncanny. Some religious groups still forbid any photography at all, because they believe that the camera captures their soul and transfers it onto the image.[4]

Photography recreated reality so exactly that it became the medium of choice for the rendition of the ultimate non-reality: the "spirit." "Spirit photos" became spectacularly popular by the 1880s and remain colorful reminders of quaint Victorian sensibility. They were ultimately embarrassing, both for the purchasers and the providers, once word got out that the "spirits" they showed were merely the by-products of deliberate double exposure.

Photography persisted and improved, since its invention in the 1830s. First used for clinical and scientific purposes, it eventually evolved into an elaborate and impressive art form. It overcame objections voiced by angry protesters, who railed against recognizing photography as an art. Its clinical use continued and expanded, so that photography became essential to physicians, botanists, biologists, and criminologists. Even psychiatrists came to appreciate photography, because photographs captured the peculiar poses of the insane.[5]

Technology triumphed, again, when "moving pictures" appeared in 1895. "Movies" quickly replaced the once popular "magic lantern shows" that were the forerunners of films as we now know them. Through movies, photography could be combined with a plot and inserted into the dramatic and distancing passageway of the proscenium theater. The proscenium theater that movies emulated had been an innovation unto itself, because it seated spectators away from the stage, rather than arranging them around it. It draped curtains at each side of the passageway, or proscenium. This produced a physically distinct and psychologically distancing "portal" for viewing, just as dream does.

These "movies" were near miracles in the nineteenth century. We can compare the enthusiasm about movies to the excitement that cyberspace generates in our own era. Movies offered a multitude of benefits, for sure. Among other things, they presented a far fuller view of the dreamspace than ever seen before, not in dance, not in drama, and certainly not in still and static photographs. Movies were a perfect place to perfect dreamlike photographic techniques, such as "jump cuts," "zooms," "layers," "dissolves," "double exposures," and "pans." Movies also allowed editors to improve upon these camera tricks by cutting and pasting and making montages from film clips, just as our minds do when they manufacture dreams.

By the late 1920s, technology improved again. Sound was introduced. Early silent "movies" gave way to "talkies." Until then, sound was limited to musical accompaniments, and directors relied on "psychic acoustics" that came from overly emotive acting or over-the-top "smoke and mirrors" set designs.[6] "Talkies" had three more choices. They could reproduce conversation. They could mimic the narrative of the unconscious, which accompanies the vivid visual imagery of half of our ordinary dreams. They could include intervals of lyric-free music, to allow the spectator to add his or her own internal dialogue to the film experience, as Hitchcock did in *Vertigo* (1953). Thanks to these advances, cinema assumed its role as the signature of the subconscious. It still reigns supreme in that regard, a full century after its invention.

FREUD AND FILM

Coincidentally—or perhaps not so coincidentally—Freud's revolutionary new "depth psychology" came into being shortly after "moving pictures" appeared. Freud coined the term "psychoanalysis" in 1896. A year before, in 1895, the Lumiere Brothers had screened the very first film in France.

In that same year of 1895, Roentgen invented the x-ray. X-rays revealed the skeletal structure beneath the skin. In much the same spirit, psychoanalysis peeled away the superficial aspects of the personality, to display the deeper psychological structure that lurked behind conscious thought and overt action. X-rays became immediately popular with the public, which was still unaware of the devastating side effects and deadly bone cancers that would develop from their overuse. Psychoanalysis took more time to gain acceptance. Cinema was a hit from the start.

The year 1895 would be a good year for seeing beneath the surface, via x-ray analysis or psychoanalysis. It was the perfect time to produce a brand new surface, through cinema. Psychoanalysis and cinema were destined to interconnect over the new century, as they each carved out new niches and refashioned society in the twentieth century. Because they shared a common starting point and evolved out of the same cultural climate, both psychoanalysis and cinema reflected the experiences and expectations of fin de siècle society. Each would concern itself with the human drama, but for different reasons. So both cinema and psychoanalysis often played off one another, complementing one another and competing with one another.

Though one was a technique of treatment and the other was a technique for entertainment, each vied for dominion over dreams. For the most part, psychoanalysis would concern itself with interpreting personal dreams, while film devoted itself to projecting public dreams. But the boundaries often blurred, and there were territorial disputes. Psychoanalysis and cinema sometimes displayed the sort of sibling rivalry that is seen in families. They fought with one another for public attention, as if they were two children who vied for a finite amount of affection from their parents. At other times, psychoanalysis and cinema showed some semblance of filial affection, based on their common turn-of-the-century roots and their sometimes similar subject matter.

Cinema addressed personal conflicts publically, just as myth and religion had done in the past. It would become the "poor man's psychoanalysis," to use the words of the late, great film critic, Parker Tyler.[7] Because cinema frequently depicted psychiatrists and psychiatric themes, it could create quick stereotypes about psychoanalysis and psychiatry and mold public opinion much more rapidly than professional psychiatric practice could.[8] Not everyone could afford to see a psychoanalyst, and not everyone wanted to. Yet almost everyone could pay to peer in as psychoanalysts plied their trade and probed their patients' deepest and darkest secrets, on the screen of the equally dark movie theater.

So "cinema psychiatry" became a distinct entity, which could easily be confused with the real thing, but which rarely bore any real resemblance to hands-on clinical practice. Cinema psychiatry evolved out of a need to depict psychiatric events dramatically, rather than accurately. It catered to the commercial concerns of film studios, who literally banked on entertaining, rather than edifying. Commercial filmmakers knew that a film's financial success depends on its ability to tap into the hopes and fears of viewers. So they cultivated ways to connect with the unconscious attitudes of their audiences and captured such unspoken sentiments on screen.

Around World War II, many European psychoanalysts resettled in Los Angeles, as they fled Hitler's persecution. This expanding psychoanalytic circle contributed to the film industry's increased awareness of psychoanalysis.[9] Actors and actresses and directors and screenwriters now had friends, neighbors, and relatives who either practiced psychoanalysis, or underwent psychoanalysis, or needed analysis.

As the public became aware of psychoanalytic theories, a reciprocal relationship between film and Freudianism developed. Spectators came to expect their favorite cinematic characters to feel and think and act according to psychoanalytic predictions. As audiences aped these psychoanalytically informed screen personalities, they themselves adopted these psychoanalytic attitudes. Self-fulfilling prophesies began.[10]

Dream analysis became a favorite theme of cinema psychiatry, for several reasons. Dreams present perfect opportunities for filmic action and artistry. The idea of a quick success through dream analysis—often achieved in a single scene—is always appealing. Healing through dreams reflected current psychological lore and tapped into cutting edge cultural concepts. Equally importantly, quick dream cures on screen express atavistic and superstitious ideas about the curative potential of dream, which date to the earliest days of humankind. Dream analysis could reveal a character's secret sinister qualities, make for a blacker and bleaker film noir, add depth to that character's motives, and explain his or her sudden insights.

The 1999 comedy *Analyze This*, with Billy Crystal and Robert De Niro, is an excellent example of this approach. *Analyze This* is about a gangster (De Niro) who is obsessed about his bad dream about drinking black milk. He secures the assistance of a reluctant psychiatrist (Crystal). The psychiatrist cures his patient of his "gangsterism," and his guilt over his father's death, and the "negative nurturing" symbolized by the black milk. *Analyze This* is just one of a long line of quick cures that begin with an idealized dream analysis. We can trace the film's origins to a thoroughly noirish film from the forties, called *The Dark Past*, which we will discuss later.

Occasionally, exploitative episodes of dream analysis drive the plot. That is the case with the noirest of noir films, *Nightmare Alley*. *Nightmare Alley*'s female "consulting psychologist" is appropriately named Lilith. As her name suggests, she is preprogrammed to prey upon her unsuspecting analysands as viciously and vigorously as the life-draining mythological demoness of the same name. In the film, this Lilith records her client's darkest dreams. She passes this information to an accomplice, who uses this data to extort the most vulnerable and the most affluent. As *Nightmare Alley* illustrated, cinema psychiatry was ready, willing, and able to pander to the public's fantasies and fears about what occurred on the secretive psychoanalyst's couch. Although sexual liaisons were the most common exploitation theme in screen psychiatry, there was still room for more innovative, *Nightmare Alley*-type dangers. This trend became such a concern for psychiatrists that the Group for Advancement of Psychiatry (GAP) appointed a special committee to monitor portrayals of the profession in cinema.[11]

CINEMA AT THE TURN OF THE CENTURY

By the time Freud's *The Interpretation of Dreams* came off the press in November 1899, film had primed the public for this renewed attention to dream and had set the stage for a brand new approach to dream. Ever since cinema started in 1895, spectators could see dreamlike imagery reproduced before their own eyes, prancing past them, and affirming the importance of this inner imagery. Cinema turned dream scenes into shared, group experiences, just as religion had done in the past. It released dreams from the confines of the private and personal and catapulted dreams into the public imagination.

Although myth and religion had always delved into dreams, there was a vast difference between the dream themes of film and the dream depictions of faith. For one thing, cinematography was a state-of-the-art scientific advance, and science was all-important to turn of the century society. Science was worlds away from faith.

Today, we take the scientific aspect of cinema for granted. The average person might have forgotten about its technological component entirely, were it not for the 1999 technology boom and subsequent stock market convulsions that followed. Until then, most modern moviegoers did not even use the words "cinema" and "science" in the same sentence. The audience approaches cinema as an art form, rather than as an example of applied technology. Film industry people (and investors), on the other hand, are acutely aware of advances with computers and cameras and camcorders and digital film and DVD. Attitudes were different in the nineteenth century. Those men and women who witnessed the birth of film firsthand realized that film represented an unprecedented technological feat. Cinema carried the authority of science, as much as art, for that generation. It was obvious that the basic scientific discovery of cinema laid the groundwork, before film became a blackboard for artists and actors and auteurs and authors.

Freud, too, invoked the authority of science. He began his book *The Interpretation of Dreams* with a chapter on "The Scientific Literature Dealing with the Problems of Dreams." Such a chapter was essential, considering that a Jewish mystical work on *Interpretation of Dreams* already existed and that the occultist *Interpretation of Dreams and Magic* was currently in print. The fact that new "scientific" cinema was simultaneously scientific and artistic may have been fortunate for Freud, who was also attempting to fuse scientific scrutiny with literary analysis through his personal approach to dream interpretation. One can even speculate that cinema's simultaneous success at bridging art and science acted as one of many factors that helped legitimatize Freud's unusual approach to dream interpretation.

Freud coined a new name for the mind's dream-making process; he called it the "dreamwork." Freud was not concerned with the biological basis of dreams (which were not well understood in the pre-PET scan and pre-SPEC scan and pre-EEG and prechemistry age, anyway). Instead, he hypothesized that this dreamwork process translates abstract thoughts into visual images and dramatic narratives. Dreamwork uses techniques such as "displacement," "symbolization," "condensation," "dramatization," and "secondary revision" to produce the enigmatic dream images and ideas that defy time, space, and logical sequence.

During displacement, an emotionally charged person or place or act is displaced onto a less emotionally charged person or place or act. An unimportant person or place substitutes for someone or something of greater psychological import. Symbolization is the process by which one object symbolizes another and conveys a covert meaning. Condensation, according to Freud, is similar to symbolization but allows for several symbols or objects to condense into a single form or idea. Dramatization means exactly that: the incorporation of abstract ideas or feelings into a plot, staged with actors and a set design, to produce a drama. "Secondary revision" refers to the editing process that supposedly takes place under the direction of the "dream censor." Freud (wrongly, according to later research findings) believed that the dream censor preserved sleep, by concealing ideas that are too dangerous or too uncomfortable for the conscious mind to experience directly while awake.

Freud's claims about the psychological or physiological functions of dreamwork may not be completely correct. Yet Freudian language is a remarkably useful descriptive tool. His dream vocabulary directs our attention to specific elements of the dream, helps us organize our fragmentary recollections of dreams, and shows us multiple meanings behind each dream scene. Some scholars say that filmmakers and cinematographers who are familiar with Freudian ideas about dreams are better equipped to craft their own cinematic brand of dreamwork. The most right wing of these Freudocentric theorists claim that filmmakers deliberately turned to the editing rooms and advanced camera shots to duplicate the dream mechanics that Freud identified. While this hypothesis may be correct in some specific cases, there is ample evidence to show that film's discovery of dreams antedated Freud's.

FREUD'S REFLECTIONS ON FILM

What did Freud say about film? Freud wrote an essay called "Screen Memories" in 1899, four years after the first film screening. Borrowing this title from film, he was referring to the cinema screen. Freud's essay described the earliest, preverbal, "flash-photo" memories that children recollect. He compared them to film stills from moving scenes on the screen.

Though he was willing to incorporate the vocabulary of cinema in his fledgling psychoanalytic theory, Freud made it abundantly clear that he was no fan of film. Freud saw only one movie in his lifetime, in 1909. It was a Western, no less, that most American invention, and he saw it while he was visiting America. This cinematic experience represented more of a concession to his curiosity about American culture than to any concern with film, for he never saw a film in his native Austria. Yet many films were screened in Vienna. Freud also refused a lucrative offer to consult for the famous American film studio, Metro-Goldwyn-Mayer.

There were good reasons why Freud would avoid any association with film. Early cinema screenings in Austria were conducted in quarters that were closer to an arcade than a "movie palace." This setting was not appropriate to the social or professional image that Freud wanted to project. In addition, at that time, Hollywood did not have the social cachet that it enjoys today and was still somewhat marginal. Some early film studios had links to the pornography industry. Someone who hoped to establish the sexually explicit psychoanalytic theory as scientifically credible, rather than as strictly sensational, was wise to avoid such shady associations.

Freud specifically resented the crossover between film and dream. When his psychoanalytic disciples Hanns Sachs and Karl Abraham agreed to act as scientific consultants to Pabst's production of the dreamlike 1926 film, *Secrets of a Soul*, Freud saw this as an ominous sign. Rather than being flattered that Hollywood deemed dream interpretation and psychoanalytic treatment as suitable subjects for a feature-length film, Freud objected to the visual representation of the unconscious. He dismissed it as a regression. His arguments were couched in academic terms, but it is conceivable that the class conscious and socially striving Freud resented the possibility that his carefully crafted psychoanalytic theories would be disseminated through this lower-class conduit of cinema.

A flurry of arcane debates about film and dream followed, both from Freud and from his followers. Freud wrote in German, while some of his most ardent commentators—such as Jacques Lacan—have rephrased and reworked Freud's ideas in French. We are left with translations of translations of translations, many of which are quite opaque and difficult to follow.

It was said that film, like dream, is governed by "considerations of representation," rather than by "real meaning." In other words, the visual vocabulary in film—or in dream—is *not* chosen because it is the best way to express an underlying thought or feeling or experience. The images in film or dream are not necessarily essential for advancing the plot or telling the story. It is the *picture* that is primary, in both film and dream. Both film and dream need visual appeal, to be recognized and remembered and appreciated by the audience. It is the *storyboard* (with its comic book–like graphics and captions)—rather than the *story* per se—that propels the action of both film and dream.⌉

For some filmmakers, sound and story are so secondary that they are dispensable. In fact, student filmmakers are taught to replay their films without accompanying sound during production, to be sure that their camera shots make visual sense and tell the story silently. That great master of mystery, Alfred Hitchcock, acquired this technique automatically, when he made his own successful switch from silent to sound films in the late 1920s.[12]

Novelists have long objected to cinema's pictorial translations of their written work. They complain about the way that directors and screenwriters twist and turn their narratives, swallow up the characters' psychological depth, and lose track of the book's intention. However, Freud objected to the "dream screen" for entirely different reasons. For Freud, the pictorial representation of an idea or emotion, through either dream or film, was worth far less than the interpretation of that dream. Freud stated explicitly that he was interested in his patient's selective recollection of the dream and in the associations that the dream evoked. In a nutshell, Freud was not interested in the finished product of the dreamwork. He was interested in the dreamwork process that produced the finished product.

Freud's younger student Jung developed a very different appreciation for dream. Jung refused to listen to free associations about dreams and insisted that his analysands stay focused on the dream content directly. Jung applied the methods of classic drama criticism to decode dreams. He asked for descriptions of (1) the situation (time, location, and players), (2) the exposition (the representation of the problem), (3) the development (plot), (4) the *peripatea* (critical event that happens), and (5) the *lysis* (resolution or solution). This move away from Freud and toward theater terminology has endeared Jung to theatrical people to this day.

FREUD'S FOUNDATIONS

Unlike Jung, whose psychological philosophy was grounded in German romanticism, Freud was an evolution-minded biologist. Literary and psychoanalytic critic Frederic Crews went as far as to call him the "biologist of the mind," after a book that bears the same name.[13] Like many educated people of his time, Freud was strongly influenced by the Darwinian thought that pervaded the nineteenth century and that shook preconceived ideas about creation. Freud was concerned with progressive stages of psychological development, just as Darwin was concerned with progressive stages of evolution. Freud hypothesized about the existence of psychological hierarchies and developmental stages. He spoke about the psychological progression through oral, anal, Oedipal, latency, and genital stages in much the same way that Darwin wrote about monkeys evolving into apes and apes evolving into men. Freud described psychopathology in terms of fixations at lower levels of development. He spoke pejoratively of regressions that occurred after people achieved higher levels of functioning.

Even before Darwin appeared, it was well known that children learn to see and recognize objects by sight before they learn to speak and articulate and describe them through language. That alone implied that seeing was less mature than speaking and that image was less mature than word. Such immaturity was especially intolerable to someone such as Freud, who stressed chronological stages of development. The appreciation of immaturity and childishness was suitable to romantic writers, but Freud was a direct descendent of Enlightenment thought.

Freud had even more reason to dismiss image and immaturity. Even before he began his pioneering (but now contested) psychoanalytic studies, he was a well respected neurologist, who wrote a book on aphasia, the loss of the ability to speak. He knew that damage to specific parts of the brain (during strokes, head injuries, or some diseases) can cause aphasia and rob the patient of speech or even thought. He would have been completely correct to suspect the presence of disease in a patient who substituted symbols for words. As a psychoanalyst, he went one step further than the neurologists: he focused on the psychological as well as physical causes of such symptoms, when he did his studies on "hysteria."

With this background, Freud was primed to place the visual montage of either dream or film lower on the psychological/phylogenetic scale than the verbal associations that followed. Cinematographers and artists and semiologists (who study signs) obviously see things very differently from Freud and stress the symbolic. If they did not, there would be no visual art at all!

Jung had a very different point of view. Freud's onetime favorite student went so far as to write an entire volume on *Word and Image*. Otto Rank was another member of Freud's original psychoanalytic circle who, like Jung, also eventually fell from Freud's grace. Rank, too, had a very positive approach to film, and to art in general, and wrote a book on *Art and Artists*.[14] Rank's book *The Doppelganger (The Double)* began by describing the "double" scene in the film, *The Student of Prague* (1913, 1926, 1935).[15] Rank realized that the trick photographic techniques, such as superimpositions and use of negatives, were capable of conveying the presence of a "double personality" both quickly and effectively, in a way that literature could not.

Freud's first English-language publisher—novelist Virginia Woolf, who owned a publishing house with her husband Leonard—reacted differently. Woolf is best known for writing protofeminist novels such as *A Room of One's Own,* and for committing suicide by walking into the ocean. But she also published influential essays on cinema around the same time that Pabst's psychoanalytically informed *Secrets of the Soul* appeared, shortly after the 1926 release of *The Student of Prague.* She lauded cinema's ability to depict the " 'dream architecture' of our sleep" and to show "some secret language which we feel and see, but never speak."[16]

The arguments about film as a "dream screen" continued. For some filmmakers, cinema is simply "a dream on the screen," in one form or another. Some academicians were so impressed with cinema's success and with some spectators' fixation on film that they devised attenuated arguments to explain this intrigue. One film scholar hypothesized that cinema spectators become entranced by film, because they project their own internalized images of their mothers' breasts onto the cinema screen and recall the images that they imagined on the breast, as they nursed as infants. This theory says that spectators develop a symbiotic relationship with cinema, just as they did with their mothers when they were suckling. That argument was easily shot down by pointing out that not all breasts are as white as the projection screen and that not all babies are breast-fed.[17] Cognitive psychologists could discredit this argument even further by showing that an infant is completely incapable of conceptualization and so could not possibly be thinking on such a lofty level at such an early stage of neurocognitive development.

These academic discussions about film as dream and dream as film eventually simmered down. They might have cooled completely, were it not for the fact that the 100th anniversary of the publication of Freud's *The Interpretation of Dreams* renewed interest in this long-neglected issue. These discussions were suppressed even further, when "object relations theory" and Jacques Lacan's concept of the "Imaginary" eventually supplanted the early twentieth-century academic discussions about dream. By the 1970s, which is when serious university study of film took root, film scholars were captivated by concerns that had little to do with the issues that drove discussions in the first half of the century. For one thing, feminist film theories commandeered attention. Psychoanalytic studies of film dropped in esteem. Debates about the crossover between dream and film were not nearly so pressing as they had been, when *The Interpretation of Dreams* was a completely novel idea.[18]

This shift in the focus of film scholarship did not dampen Steven Spielberg's concern with dreams. Spielberg's film studio—which is one of the most popular film studios of our own time—salutes dreams, through his company's name. He calls his production company *Dreamworks SKG* and thereby alludes to Freud's idea of dreamwork. This name implies that Spielberg's studio rivals the uncanny abilities of the unconscious, and strives to produce cinema with the same magical skill that the mind uses when it manufactures dreams. But there is more than that. Spielberg himself says that his greatest inspirations come from dreams. In making that admission, Spielberg becomes one of a long, long line of filmmakers and other creators who have owed their inspiration to sleep visions.

FILM AS A FOUNDATION FOR FREUD

Freud's *The Interpretation of Dreams* may have been a significant inspiration for Spielberg's specific approach to cinema, but film history suggests that film influenced Freudianism (if not also Freud) before Freud influenced film. After all, film did come first. There are far, far, far more people who see film than there are people who read intricate psychoanalytic theory. There are also specific examples of dream films that predated Freud's landmark book on dreams, which we will discuss following.

That is not to say that Freud and the psychoanalysts who followed him had no impact at all on film. The example of Steven Spielberg's *Dreamworks* is testimony to the contrary. Freud strongly swayed the surrealist cinematographers of the 1920s and 1930s.[19] Freud indirectly influenced some the German Expressionists who worked during those years. Psychoanalytic insights surely shaped many "underground" filmmakers of the 1940s and 1950s and strongly influenced the "mother" of independent film, Maya Deren, whose own beloved father was a psychiatrist who was educated both in his native Russia and at New York City's Columbia University. Freud's influence was particularly prominent in the 1960s and 1970s, when indie giant Stan Brakhage produced a film entitled *Homage to Freud*. The sexually explicit, transgressive themes in Brakhage's oeuvre and in underground film overall can be traced to Freud's emphasis on sexual symbolism and sexual motivation, both in dreams and in every other aspect of human experience.

Kenneth Anger, the most influential of all the independent filmmakers, began the genre of music videos, when he made a film based on the music score from *Dreamlover*. His *Scorpio Rising* is a sexually charged film about a gay motorcycle club. This cult film includes dream-themed music, as it spoofs the blurred boundaries between fantasy and reality and between sexual symbolism and sexual acts. Anger's later work traces his own sexual coming of age, through Freudian-like dream scenes that become more direct and less subtle as his films progress.[20]

FILM FANTASY AND SPECIAL EFFECTS

If we read the biographies of the first filmmakers rather than the hagiographies written by unflinching admirers of psychoanalysts, we find that early filmmakers such as Melies specifically searched for subjects that could showcase the capabilities of their cameras and cutting rooms. They readily recognized that dream, fantasy, and science fiction were well suited to display their newfound "special effects" skills.

Early fantasy filmmakers like Melies and Starewicz specialized in dreamlike imagery. Today, their work looks cute and creative and comical, simultaneously. Science fiction and fantasy were equally high on their priorities. Onetime stage magician Georges Melies' film *A Trip to the Moon* (1902) is the best known of this genre. Although it was only fourteen minutes long, this film used thirty separate tableaus (scenes) and incorporated superimposed images, dissolves, and cuts. In switching from magic tricks to trick photography, Melies created a modern-looking, capsulized rocket ship that blasts off into space, after being shot from a cannon. It then crashes into the eye of the man in the moon. Once on the moon, the voyagers dismount and meet fantastic moon inhabitants, during a whimsical, dreamlike scene in the court of the Moon King.

The titles of Melies' other films echo this enchantment with dreams, special effects, and film magic that was so adorably demonstrated in *A Trip to the Moon*. *The Drunkard's Dream* (1897), *The Dream of an Artist* (1898), *The Dream of a Beggar* (1898), *The Astronomer's Dream (The Man in the Moon)* (1898), *The Christmas Dream* (1900), *The Rajah's Dream* (1900), *Dream of a Hindu Beggar* (1902), *Dream of the Ballet Master* (1903), *The Clockmaker's Dream* (1904), *The Dream of the Poor Fisherman* (1904), and *Dream of An Opium Fiend* (1908) are listed among Melies' credits. The dates of their release, listed after their titles, demonstrate that many of these films were completed before the publication of Freud's *Interpretation of Dreams* or were in production before November of 1899. Rather than being influenced by Freud and psychoanalysis, such films set the stage for Freud's supposedly scientific study, and primed the public to think about dreams, and reflected a preexisting intrigue with dream themes.

Sadly, Melies' films fell into oblivion once the initial enthusiasm for his simplistic special effects died down. As more advanced techniques appeared soon after his initial success, the ingenious magician was left impoverished, banished to selling toys on the street in order to survive. His reputation has been revived in recent years, and his films now attract wider audiences at revival houses, such as Anthology Film Archives,[21] and on college campuses.

Although Melies is now the best remembered of these early fantasy filmmakers, he was not alone in his predilection for dream themes. Edwin S. Porter produced *The Cavalier's Dream* as early as 1898, before earning his reputation and a permanent place in film history for his rendition of *The Great Train Robbery* in 1905. *Dream of a Rarebit Fiend* (1909), which attributed bad dreams to aged cheese, was another of some 200 short silent films on the theme of dream. *Dream of a Rarebit Fiend* was also part of a long tradition that linked bad dreams to rotted food. (Romantic artist Henri Fuseli, who painted *The Nightmare*, also tried to induce nocturnal terror by eating rotted meat, as did Mary Shelley, of *Frankenstein* fame.)

I do not wish to imply that dream and fantasy were the only suitable subjects for "primitive" filmmakers (as they are known in academic circles today). Thousands of silent films were produced in the early years of film, and so these dream themes represent just a fraction of the entire oeuvre. Furthermore, most of the dream-themed silents were fewer than five minutes long and cannot be compared to the hour and one-half or two-hour feature length films that are currently customary.

The question about whether or not Freudian dream theory was really responsible for film's eventual emphasis on "montage" has been raised. To answer it, we can consider the case of Sergei Eisenstein, one of the century's premiere filmmakers and a major voice in early film theory. The Lithuanian-born Eisenstein, who is best known for his *Battleship Potemkin*, touted the director's role in editing, cutting, and splicing. Eisenstein averred that it was this "montage" that made "film" into "a film." Eisenstein and others were opposed by a diametrically different school of film theorists. Headed by Andre Bazin, that other school emphasized the importance of a film's narrative and literary form. They maintained that the *telling* of the story was more important than the *presentation* of the story.

On the surface, it may sound as though Eisenstein owed his montage approach to Freud's description of dream-making mechanics. However, a thorough study of the life and times of Eisenstein show that it was the Marxist dialectic of history that molded his montage technique. For the Marxist, history was a montage of opposite and opposing forces, that were splintered and spliced together to form a progressive whole that continued in time. Marxism won favor in Eastern Europe and was imposed by force. Filmmakers who deviated from its demands would not see their films released and might even face death if they defied Stalin's strict decrees.

For the Marxist, the outer world of materialism and collective experience was more important than the inner, subjective mindset of the individual. This perspective contrasted dramatically with the Western European mentality and with the post-Freudian emphasis on the inner emotive experience, in particular. It is striking that Eisenstein tempts us to apply both Freudian and Marxist interpretations to his montage.

Around the same time that Eisenstein was filming *Potemkin*, filmmakers and film audiences were literally coming to blows in France, because of a debate about the proper role of dream in film. The very early (and underappreciated) experimental filmmaker Germaine Dulac had turned Antonin Artaud's script about *The Seashell and the Clergyman* into cinema. The acclaimed Artaud (who eventually became catatonic and died after spending twelve years in a mental hospital) denounced Dulac. Artaud claimed that she had taken intolerable liberties when adapting his drama for film. Artaud accused her of "feminizing" his script, partly because she made his play into a replica of a dream, when he intended it to be "dreamlike." The audience was just as split about the proper relationship between dream and film as Artaud and Dulac. Bystanders got involved in a fistfight, right there in the theater. Several arrests followed. Such public demonstrations and indiscretions would become standard fare for surrealists.[22]

These concerns about dream may sound petty today, but the surrealists were known for being dogmatic. They were also profoundly concerned with fine distinctions between "dream" and "dreamlike." It was just this sort of debate that would lead to the banishment of Jean Cocteau from their immediate surrealist circle. Cocteau's *Blood of a Poet* is now believed to be one of the most beautiful dreamlike films ever produced. His late-life *A Testament to Orpheus* opens with a line about a dream and asserts that film allows audiences to dream the same dream together. But Cocteau did not comply with strict surrealist sensibility and may also have lost favor among the camaraderie because he violated the heterosexual norms of the surrealists. His contemporary Luis Buñuel embellished films such as *Belle de Jour* and *Un Chien Andalou* with narrative dream scenes that could be confused with reality, and that undermined women and so was preferred by his peers for both counts.[23]

The cinema was destined to become a passionate preoccupation of surrealist artists and writers and photographers and would be central to their broader artistic statements. Surrealists such as Andre Breton and his immediate circle regularly ran from one theater to another, catching glimpses of different films, without watching a film in an orderly and prearranged sequence and without even seeing a single film to its end. The purpose of this pastime was to replicate the dream experience, where logical causality disappears and displacement of time and place are essential elements.

Dream would loom large, as both inspiration and iconography of avant-garde or experimental filmmakers who appeared in ever-increasing numbers over the next several decades. Acclaimed critic Parker Tyler would write a book called *The Hollywood Hallucination*.[24] Dream (as well as drug-induced dreams) played so large a role in underground film that Tyler himself said that the studios of the underground filmmakers had become the equivalent of the sleep laboratories of the research scientists of the sixties and seventies.[25] When a book about *Hollywood: The Dream Factory* appeared, it needed no subtitle, for everyone understood the connection between film and dream. Hollywood's role in projecting public fantasies was already well accepted, although not necessarily admired by all. The book itself has been long out of print, but the concept of film as a dream factory has lived on independently and has penetrated our everyday vocabulary.

Putting aside these philosophical and historical debates for a moment, we can appreciate the many other practical reasons to deploy dreams for film. Besides being ideal showcases for special effects, dreams are convenient framing devices. They set the stage for the start of a story. Dreams provide a metanarrative and a story within a story, as dramatists and novelists knew before film was invented. Dreams can be proleptic and can foretell the future, or they can function as flashbacks. Dreams themselves are excellent as either inspiration or as iconography, for cinema as well as for other art forms. Dream and film are not a suitable subject for everyone, but this combination certainly served auteurs as diverse as Bergman, Tarkowsky, Kurosawa, Hitchcock, Fellini, Buñuel, and Altman.

Dream is a mainstay of several commercial film genres. Horror, science fiction, and fantasy use dream themes, as do occasional film noirs and melodramas and even action-adventures. Dream seeps into comedy and children's classics and surrealist and expressionist film. Dream has a special appeal for underground and independent film, which, by its nature, is far more personal than commercial film and so is more inclined to include personal and subjective experiences such as dream. As Jean Cocteau said in the first sentence of *The Testament of Orpheus*, "It is the unique power of cinema to allow a great many people to dream the same dream together and to present the illusion to us as if it were strict reality. It is, in short, an admirable vehicle for poetry."[26]

NOTES

1. Arnhem, S. I. *Film as Art*. Berkeley: University of California, 1957. As filmmaking advanced and as filmmakers took more artistic liberties, film aficionados found that they could appreciate film even more after they studied "film

grammars" that amplified upon the filmmaker's intentions and that explained the film symbols that came into use.

2. The economics of filmgoing changed in the 1990s, after admission prices increased and refreshment stands increased offerings made movies as family entertainment far less affordable than they had been at midcentury.

3. MacGregor, John M. *The Discovery of the Art of the Insane*. Princeton, NJ: Princeton University Press, 1992.

4. The Druze are a non-Jewish, non-Muslim Semitic people who live in Israel and forbid tourists to photograph them, for fear that their souls will be captured in the cameras. Some ultra-Orthodox and Chasidic Jewish sects also believe that photographic reproductions violate Biblical laws against idolatry and recreating images of the creator.

5. Gilman, Sandor. *Seeing the Insane*. New York: J. Wiley, 1982.

6. Soren, David. *The Rise and Fall of the Horror Film*. Baltimore: Midnight Marquee, 1997.

7. Tyler, Parker. *Underground Film: A Critical History*. New York: Da Capo, 1995.

8. Greenberg, Harvey Roy. *Screen Memories: Hollywood Cinema on the Psychoanalytic Couch*. New York, Columbia University Press, 1993.

9. Torrey, E. Fuller. *Freudian Fraud*. New York: Harper, 1992.

10. Eberwein, Robert. *Film and the Dream Screen*. Princeton, NJ: Princeton University Press, 1983.

11. Gabbard, Glen O., and Krin Gabbard. *Psychiatry and the Cinema*. Washington: American Psychiatric Press, 1999.

12. Tony Pellegrino, film instructor, editor, producer, Digital Asylum Production Company, School of Visual Arts and New School University.

13. Sulloway, Frank. *Freud, Biologist of the Mind: Beyond the Psychoanalytic Legend*. Boston: Harvard University Press, 1992.

14. Rank, Otto. *Art and Artists*. New York: Norton, 1989.

15. Eisner, Lotte. *The Haunted Screen*. Berkeley: University of California Press, 1990.

16. Heath, S. "Cinema and Psychoanalysis: Parallel Histories." *Endless Night*. ed. J. Bergstrom. Berkeley: University of California Press, 1999.

17. Gamwell, Lynn. *Dreams 1900–2000*. Ithaca, NY: Cornell University Press, 2000.

18. Lapsley, Robert and Michael Westlake. *Film Theory*. Glasgow, G.B., Manchester, Eng.: Manchester University Press, 1988.

19. Lacan's early influence on the surrealists was not as a psychoanalytic theorist but as a contributor to surrealist publications. This psychoanalytic influcence in France did not surface undtil decades later.

20. Adams, P. Sitney. *Visionary Cinema*. 2nd ed. Oxford, U.K.: Oxford University Press, 1979; Tyler, Parker. *The Underground Film. A Critical Appraisal*. New York: Da Capo, 1995; Peterson, James. *Dreams of Chaos, Visions of Order*. Detroit: Wayne State University Press, 1994.

21. 11 Sept. 2001. Anthology Film Archives. <http://www.anthology-filmarchives.org>.

22. Flitterman-Lewis, Sandy. "The Image and the Spark: Dulac and Artaud." Ed. Rudolf E. Kuenzli. *Dada and Surrealist Film*. Cambridge, MA: MIT Press, 1996; Rees, A. L. A *History of Experimental Film and Video*. London: BFI, 1999.

23. Kuenzli, Rudolph, ed. *Dada and Surrealist Film*. Cambridge, MA: MIT Press, 1996.

24. Tyler, Parker. *The Hollywood Hallucination*. New York: Creative Press, Inc., 1944.

    25. Tyler, Parker. *Underground Film: A Critical Appraisal*. New York, Da Capo Press, 1995.
    26. *The Testament of Orpheus*, 1960. Dir. Jean Cocteau. [Jean Cocteau's Orphic Trilogy]. Criteron Collection, DVD, 2000.

5

Cinema and Cyberspace

TELEVISION AND VIDEO

Photography and film opened the floodgates for a host of audiovisual (AV) devices. These AV devices would change postindustrial society and the twentieth century in turn. Television (TV) arrived in the late 1940s and turned into a near-necessity household commodity by the mid-1950s. By 1980, 97 percent of American households owned TVs. The newly affordable "tube" was almost as common as refrigerators and stoves. Television changed the fabric of family life, as it assumed its position smack in the center of the living room, and displaced face-to-face family conversation. Sight-and-sound television programs rapidly replaced the sound-only radio shows that left so much more to the individual imagination.

A few decades later, video cameras and video cassette recorders (VCRs) appeared. Originally too expensive for anyone but the affluent or the dedicated film or photography buff, video eventually fell in price and transformed the American media experience all over again. Cheap VCRs soon stood alongside the ubiquitous TV screen. VCRs brought films directly into the home, ready to be viewed on demand, without the interruption of more reality-oriented TV commercials. The home video player was ready to replicate the dreamlike atmosphere of the nocturnal movie theater, more or less.

The situation repeated itself with video cameras or camcorders. These, too, turned into nonessential essentials, purchased by people who had been content with just a camera a few years before and who were rightfully impressed with the videocam's improvement over the cumbersome home movie cameras. Videocams produced videos, that could be popped into VCRs and played back on TV screens immediately, without any intermediary. These impressive inventions invited a new visual vocabulary of video and TV, and video art came into being.

Because of its affordability and accessibility and ease of use, video appealed to independent artists almost instantaneously. Their films tend to be more innovative or idiosyncratic or introspective than commercial films, which must appeal to wide audiences in order to recoup the studio's investment. New generations of academically-trained film artists saw the dream-inspired independent filmmakers of the 1940s, 1950s, 1960s, and 1970s as their role models. Brakhage, Deren, Anger, and others became heros in this small but growing circle. Virtually all film school graduates knew about Jean Cocteau's pioneering *Blood of a Poet*, which inspired the first generation of independents because of its dreamlike fluidity and unusual special effects. Cocteau himself claimed that this classic film would require "Freudian interpretation" to be fully understood.[1]

While many itinerant filmmakers took their cues from the raw film footage produced by the early independents, many more were put off by financial constraints of low-budget film, and the compromise of quality that resulted. More than a few realized that video was a better and easier and cheaper vehicle for expressing their celluloid visions and put their efforts into video art. Few realized that video footage does not hold up to time the way that film does.

The Museum of Modern Art acknowledged the accomplishments of such dream-inspired video art when it hosted a show on *Video and Dream* in 1991. Since that initial show, video editing abilities have expanded severalfold. Once a humdrum update on the home movie camera, the completely-equipped videocamera can now create dreamlike special effects similar to cinema. It can go light years beyond its original capability to capture quick likenesses of the kids to be mailed away to grandma or archived in the cellar. With the price of such technology dropping every day, and with professional level video editing labs cropping up across the country, and with home computer-based editing programs such as "i-movie" being bundled with standard computer software, it is just a matter of time before unsubsidized artists can recreate their dreams on video and edit them expertly, in previously unimaginable ways. Video art may soon substitute for poetry or painting.

There are many more reasons why we can expect a surge in visionary video very soon. Besides the ever-important utilitarian issues of availability and affordability, the mere fact that video art is increasingly recognized by the art establishment will encourage future video artists. In the year 2000, New York's Guggenheim Museum honored the Korean-born video artist Nam June Paik with a retrospective. Bill Viola's videos were the subject of one-person retrospectives at New York's Guggenheim Museum and the Museum of Modern Art. Many of his installations are based on dream inspirations and bear dream-related titles. His more recent art includes mazelike translucent screens, where images are projected and where viewers walk through, as though they were actors navigating through the disconnected scenes of their own dreams. Displayed in darkened rooms, to replicate sleep, these installations intentionally transport the viewer into a state of altered consciousness and confused dimensions, similar to what they experience each night.

As futuristic as Viola's work appears to the uninitiated, his creations often make direct references to art of the past. One of his most memorable works is called *Sleep of Reason* (1988) and refers to Goya's landmark etching and aquatint entitled *The Sleep of Reason Produces Monsters* (1797–1798), which is on display at New York's Metropolitan Museum of Art. In Viola's video installation, a television set sits atop an unimposing 1950s console, flanked by a simple vase with flowers and an austere lamp on the other side. Unpretentious carpeting lines the room, which is the size of a bedroom but without the bed. At periodic intervals, the lights go off, as if it were bedtime. Then a roaring sound starts, and the TV monitor plays a videotape of nightmares and monsters, some of which strongly resemble the owls and bats of Goya's late eighteenth century original.

Even though he uses the name of Goya's work, Bill Viola's purpose contrasts completely with Goya's. Goya dreaded the nightmarish monsters, partly because dreams and the irrational in general were unfashionable during the Age of Reason when he worked. (It was Goya's own art that inadvertently reshaped popular sentiment and ushered in the Romantic Era.) Goya had other reasons to dread night visions. He suffered from a debilitating, lead-induced, neurological disorder that really did produce uncontrollable nightmares and psychotic episodes, along with episodic deafness and partial paralysis.

Viola, on the other hand, was born into the drug generation, which experimented with altered states of consciousness and which was fully informed by both Freudian and Jungian psychology. So he accepts his nightmares as a muse. Nightmares are useful and expected messengers from his unconscious. Rather than depicting these nightmares in an etching or a painting, as Goya had done, Viola presents them to a public in the medium to which they are accustomed: the television screen. Yet when he situates the TV screen in the bedroom and then replicates sleep on the screen, Viola is making a statement about TV and dreams and contemporary American culture. He tells us that personal dreams are more intriguing than TV, which has become a facile substitute for individual fantasy and a way to drive innovation underground.

Viola's soporific TV screen reminds us of some reasons why dream themes never fared nearly so well on TV as they did in film. Beside the fact that TV does not have the budget that film does and so cannot afford the dreamlike special effects of film, the purpose of TV is entirely different from film. TVs are viewed in the home and are often used to lull oneself to sleep. They are the first treatment choice of the insomniac. Successful TV shows provide a clearcut plot that can be followed easily by everyone. They are the exact opposite of enigmatic dream logic, which demands more attention and focus and interpretation.

It would defeat the purposes of TV producers and their advertisers if they replicated sleep and dreams too closely, and sent their audiences into slumber too soon. TV must walk a narrow path if it is to succeed. That may be one of the reasons why *Sleepwalkers*, an otherwise interesting 1997 TV series about sleep researchers who entered the sleep of their patients to solve their problems, was so short-lived. Science fiction shows such as *Twilight Zone, One Step Beyond,* or *The X-Files* were exceptions to this generalization and were most successful in presenting occasional dream themes in an occult context. Shows such as *I Dream of Jeannie*, which played upon the same covert, erotic connotations of dreams, had nothing in common with real dreams other than its title.

Video games have become a popular means of viewing video and recreating dream scenes. In fact, video games were so popular with young people by the end of the twentieth century that the stock prices of traditional toy stores dropped dramatically, in reaction to this shift in sales. Wall Street was telling us something that children knew full well, that neither Barbies nor board games were selling the way they once did, now that children had shifted their attention to video toys such as Sony's *Playstation* and, to a lesser extent, to Sega's *Dreamcast*, which operates on the same principle as the Sony original.

It made perfect sense that these video inventions arrived via Japanese manufacturers. Japan had long been hospitable to video game arcades. Such brightly lit arcades were a common sight in major cities in Japan, where they attracted afterwork crowds of businessmen in suits. They seemed to be a respectable middle-class diversion. It took a little longer before huge video games appeared in upscale malls and state-of-the-art cineplexes in the United States and no longer needed to be restricted to the working class (or nonworking class) confines of Coney Island, prerenovation Times Square, and shabby beach resorts. Video games had arrived, in the United States, just as they had years before in East Asia.

It would be foolish to say that the sole appeal of these now ubiquitous video games is based on the fact that they permit the user to enter a dreamlike world. The technology itself has an overwhelming appeal, as does the novelty of any new invention. Yet there is an incredible allure to entering an artificial world and altering the action of a dream and impacting on the plot. This individual intervention would never be permitted in a real dream that literally paralyzes sleepers, and deprives them of all voluntary motor movement, and casts them in the role of passive spectators, rather than imaginary players in an action-adventure. For children, there is endless appeal to effecting change in a fantasy, and for parents, who watch their children enthralled in video games for hours, there is endless concern that their children prefer to interact with the unreal world of the video game, when they could be preparing for real world encounters.

Curiously, the strongest parental protests against video games are leveled against their violent themes, rather than against their escapist aspect. The best-selling video games are often the most violent and permit their young users to "shoot" monsters, robbers, and would-be assassins and attackers with alacrity. It is no accident that these games hold the greatest intrigue for children of the very same age that is most susceptible to night terrors. In night terrors (as opposed to ordinary nightmares), children between ten and fourteen (as well as some rare adults) wake up screaming, after seeing imaginary monsters that they can barely remember upon awakening. Many popular video games strongly resemble night terrors, but have one very major difference: the video games permit the young user to attack the attacker, and to provide a sense of mastery over imagined fear. They need not remain vulnerable to their visions, as they do during sleep. What reassurance this provides for children!

Nor is it coincidental that these video games—and their computer-based cousins—are so strongly reminiscent of dream scenes. Artists typically create images from their own immediate experiences. For instance, the Hudson River School of artists painted heroic landscapes celebrating the rivers and rocks of the Hudson Valley. Georgia O'Keefe's images of cattle bones and sandy landscapes and intensely colored cactus flowers were produced in New Mexico, where the desert heat dries the bones of dead animals and scatters them along the sand. The fairy-tale-like castles and towers dotting the backgrounds of Dutch Renaissance painters were real-life buildings in Flanders and Holland, many of which still stand.

But the dreamer need not visit sixteenth century Flanders or twentieth century New York to find a suitable backdrop for his or her story. Because dreaming is a universal experience, it is accessible to everyone and produces a perfect palette for every fantasy artist, video artists included. By reaching back into archaic dreams, the futuristic computer game creator creates a sense of continuity between the past and the present and eases society's transition into digital time. A recent (1999) show at New York's School of Visual Arts saluted the potential to turn nightmares into video art and displayed works of students who had done just that for a class exercise.

CINEMA AND CYBERSPACE

These recent developments in video installation art are indeed interesting, but they produce a different problem: installation art requires a large display space and so is not easily accessible to anyone except the museum-going public. Because they are multilayered and three-dimensional, and require walking as much as viewing to appreciate their full effects, these video installations cannot be replicated in books, photos, TV, or even another video. So one wonders just how much impact they will have overall or if their influence will be felt exclusively by an elite museum-attending audience. Artists who wish to create installations are hampered by realistic concerns about showing time-and-space—specific work.

There is another medium that promises to be far more democratic than video installation art, video, or even film. That place is cyberspace. Cyberspace has the potential to level the playing field that installation art eclipsed. Cyberspace offers unlimited opportunities to recreate or edit one's own dreamscapes and to display them to anyone willing to watch.

Dreamlike hypertext poetry on the Internet is already gaining popularity, both because of our society's enchantment with the powers of our home personal computer (PC) and because of the relative ease with which interactive, illuminated manuscript-like effects can be achieved. Through hypertext poetry, visual poets can make dreamlike links between text and image and move from one screen to the next, with a simple point and click. For someone who is enthralled with dreams and cannot wait to describe their strange melange of thought, sensation, and image, web-based hypertext poetry offers the perfect opportunity. Woven from words that suggest rather than state, from lines that appear and disappear as subtly or explosively as the dreamstate, poetry has always attracted dreamers. PCs permit just one more way to a poem.

Cyberspace allows the skilled user to produce a dreamlike website, replete with moving images that morph, exactly as images do in one's own dreams. All this can be accomplished on a bare-bones budget from a desktop computer. The best-selling software used to achieve these effects is named, conveniently enough, *Dreamweaver*.

The filmmaker is constrained by the cost of film production and by the profitmaking potential of the film. The cyberdreamer has no limits on himself or herself whatsoever, except, perhaps, for his or her personal skill in manipulating the computer screen. Little wonder that many people who are intrigued by the "virtual reality" of cyberspace are also intrigued by the virtual reality of the screen or stage.

But there is a big difference between the interactive environment of virtual reality, be it in *Dreamweaver* software, hypertext poetry, or any of the many computer games, and either dream or film. It has to do with the interactivity itself. Film critics are quick to point out that film viewing is essentially passive, and that the spectator adopts someone else's point of view. It is the filmmaker or the cameraperson who guides the viewer's gaze, by pointing the camera at different objects to control the amount of information available.

Unlike the audience in a theater or ballet, who are autonomous agents, free to shift their eyes as they wish, to see as much or as little of the stage as they choose, from whichever angle they like, the film audience has no such option. Filmgoers are no different from automatons or puppets or perhaps actors, who are also made to feel, see, and think through the eyes and emotions of a character. The only other place where the spectator experiences such immobility and such lack of free will is in dream. In dreams, scenes also shift, without any conscious input from the dreamer whatsoever. Because video game users, or hypertext poetry readers, or web surfers in general all have the option to decide for themselves what they will read, the magic and mesmerizing spell is broken, and the experience becomes very different from a dream.

There are other reasons why it is doubtful that the desktop computer screen will ever eclipse the hypnotic effect of the big screen. Sitting in a darkened movie theater can transport the viewer to the world of night, where dreams take on a larger-than-life importance and where the silver screen substitutes for the "dream screen." Assuming that viewers do not get up for popcorn and are completely undistracted by their partners or other viewers (which is a big assumption), there is the potential to enter into a semihypnotic, symbiotic relationship with the screen, as though in a dream. The viewer retains a different element of control, though, by knowing that he or she can leave the cinema at will and that he or she has (relatively) free choice of which film/dream to view. The viewer also knows for sure that the dream will end after the screening, whereas there is never such a feeling of assurance during the real dream or nightmare.

There was a time, not too long ago, when videos and VCRs first appeared and threatened to make moviegoing obsolete. Many feared that the convenience of watching a video on a home TV screen would substitute for sitting in a movie theater. Before that, it had been thought that TV would replace film entirely. Time has shown that not to be true, at least not in America. (Hong Kong, however, has not fared so well, so far, and the Hong Kong film industry has sunken since the introduction of video.) But in the United States, vast cineplexes are being built with ever-increasing speed, and more and more screens are being added to local movie theaters to accommodate expanding demand. The regal movie palaces of film's early decades may be gone for good, but movies themselves seem to be here to stay, because of the merit of the multi-modality art form and also because the feature film mirrors a basic biological process: the dream.

The fact that film allows the auteur to improve upon nature, by editing and selecting the specific dream, is all the more appealing. Having said that, let us take a look at just a few of the hundreds of excellent examples of dreams and film, in the next section, on film favorites.

FILM FAVORITES

Many favorite childhood films revolve around a dream theme. Classics such as *Alice in Wonderland, Peter Pan, A Christmas Carol,* and *The Wizard of Oz*—which are often just as adored by adults as they are by children—are perfect examples of dream themes. These dream themes appear so often in contemporary children's films and books that many of us erroneously conclude that young children really do dream as much as their cinematic counterparts. It may seem as though young children's dreams drive the market for Disneyesque, dream-themed cinema, when, in fact, just the opposite is true: dream-themed films ignite children's imaginations and can be confused with "real" dreams.[2]

It is worth reflecting on the enormous influence of *Alice in Wonderland* and other fantastic films. While there are dozens of film versions of the original stories that "Lewis Carroll" ("Reverend" Dodgson) wrote for a little girl named Alice Liddell, most Americans know the Disney version best. After dropping down a rabbit hole, Alice enters a dreamlike state of confused consciousness. There, she encounters improbable characters that include the Ugly Duchess, the Mad Hatter, the Talking Cards, the White Rabbit, the Grin without a Cat, and the hookah-smoking Caterpillar, who sits on a mushroom holding his hallucinogenic pipe in hand.

The distorted reality of *Alice in Wonderland* inspired many psychedelic renditions of the original story, including the classic "acid rock" music of Jefferson Airplane's *White Rabbit*. Film director David Fincher plays upon this same theme in a much later, more sinister, filmic adaptation of *White Rabbit* music for his 1997 film, *The Game*. (Fincher also directed *Aliens 3, Seven,* and *Fight Club,* which we shall discuss shortly.) The darkest, most un-Disneyesque version of *Alice* was created by Czech surrealist, Jan Svankmajer, who mastered the tedious art of puppet animation to achieve an even more unreal effect than even the Carroll original. Still another film, *Dreamchild,* portrays the hypothetical story of the grown-up little girl who inspired Dodgson to write the Victorian-era *Wonderland* stories.

This same *Alice in Wonderland* theme reappears in the acclaimed cyber-sci-fi thriller, *The Matrix*. There, the lead character (Keanu Reeves) is a doubled-identitied, corporate programmer/computer criminal nicknamed "Neo." Neo receives a spontaneous, computer-generated message to "follow the white rabbit," just after admitting that it is difficult to tell whether he is living his life or existing in a dream. Moments later, he sees a woman whose shoulder is tattooed with a white rabbit. After a series of daring adventures, Neo (Reeves) is asked to choose between a blue pill and a red one, in much the same way as *White Rabbit's* musical Alice could choose between "one pill that makes you smaller, one pill makes you large."

By picking the blue pill, Neo's virtual state dissolves, and he reenters the physical realm of existence, only to find that it is unpleasant, and incredibly squalid, and occupied by humanoid machines that have overpowered society. The "virtual reality" of cyberspace disappears, which could also represent the disembodied consciousness of a psyche-delic state or just a dreamstate. This metamorphosis leads Neo to a middle-aged man known as Morpheus, who bears the same name as the Greek god of dreams. Morpheus (Laurence Fishburne) will help Neo and the rest of the crew navigate through the Wonderland-like maze of virtual reality and will inspire Neo to save the world from the domina-tion of humanoid machines. Morpheus' role is played by an African-American actor who has "morphed" into a new, nondescript, neutral race, thanks to pale stage makeup and a billiard-bald head. Morpheus will introduce the messianic Neo to an ordinary-appearing, older African-American woman known as the "Oracle." The Oracle foretells the future, just as the belladonna-dosed priestesses at Delphi did two thousand years earlier. Only *The Matrix's* Oracle accomplishes this feat in clear consciousness, while cooking in her neat but bland kitchen and smoking nothing more potent than a standard-brand cigarette.

While navigating through the action-oriented plot, the trio of Morpheus, Neo, and Trinity—the leather-clad female lead (Carrie-Anne Moss)—add a philosophical subtext to the hyper-high-tech production. Their symbolic names tacitly alert the audience to the crossovers be-tween *Alice in Wonderland*, cyberspace, psychedelia, drug-assisted an-cient oracles, religious revelations, and nightly dreamstates. The winner of several Academy Awards, *The Matrix* may not be for children, but it is destined to be a classic, because of the completeness with which it addresses contemporary philosophical concerns about dream and identity, physical reality and virtual reality, and the clash between human and machine, as of 1999.

Compared to *The Matrix*, with its state-of-the art computer-generated imagery (CGI), MGM's technicolored *The Wizard of Oz* looks positively retro, but that is part of its charm. Like *The Matrix*, *The Wizard of Oz* contains several different dream (and drug) themes. Based on a book that Frank Baum published in the same year that Freud published *Interpretation of Dreams*, the 1938 MGM masterpiece begins with Dorothy's dreamlike, postconcussion confusion. Dorothy, played by the pigtailed, pubescent Judy Garland, is rendered unconscious after tornado winds shoot through her Kansas farmhouse and blow her bedroom window straight out of its frame, hitting her on the head and knocking her off her feet.

From that point on (and until Dorothy returns to Kansas), the black-and-white film footage turns technicolor, to dramatize the difference between waking and dreaming reality. (Such a sudden switch from black-and-white to color film, or vice versa, or a switch to slow motion or negative stock, is a typical cinematic signal for the start of a dream scene.)

Dorothy directs our attention to dreams, once again, when she sings her classic song about "Over the rainbow" and praises the place "where dreams come true." She and two of her newfound friends—the Scarecrow and the Cowardly Lion (but not the Tin Man)—experience the most intense dreamstate of all, after they all fall asleep in a poppy field while walking to meet the Wizard. The poppy primes their perceptions, before they set foot in the fabled and flamboyantly dreamlike Emerald City. There are pharmacological references galore in the Emerald City, but there were ample political implications to the 1938 film, which were not relevant when Baum first penned his novels. The plain Kansas farm setting of the film recollected the plight of the farmers in Depression-era Kansas, and the illusory Emerald City echoed the era's enchantment with populism's utopian promises.

It has been said that *The Wizard of Oz* is the ultimate American myth, because it chronicles the journey that allows Dorothy, the Scarecrow, the Tin Man, and the Cowardly Lion to reach their goals on their own. They need not rely on an illusory external authority, represented here by the befuddled carnival barker who conned Oz's citizens into believing that he was the omniscient Wizard. Dorothy and her companions demonstrate the American ideal of self-reliance and self-actualization and overpower even the most awesome aspects of imagination with that same old frontier spirit. As testimony to its centrality in American folklore, *The Wizard of Oz* is rebroadcast on TV each Thanksgiving, on the one holiday that distinguishes America from all other countries. The Thanksgiving story has other parallels with Dorothy's. Both celebrate the fortitude of the Pilgrims who set sail to the New World in search of personal freedom, just as Dorothy embarked on her perilous journey along the Yellow Brick Road. Watching *The Wizard of Oz* at home, each Thanksgiving, implies that the living rooms of ordinary, middle America, rather than the mythical Oz, are the place where "dreams really do come true."

By the end of the film, after Dorothy returns to Kansas, we collectively applaud all-American values and feel that we have exercised our imaginations (even though we have simply shared the visions of the cinema). We have also come to realize how dreams (and psychotic states) transform images from ordinary waking reality into extraordinary-appearing symbols. Once we are back in Kansas, so to speak, and are able to see reality much more easily, now that it is literally in black and white, we quickly see that the wonderful wizard is the very same street huckster whom Dorothy passed that morning. The Wicked Witch of the North is identical to the nasty lady who threatened Dorothy and her little terrier Toto earlier in the day. We see that the phantasmagorical Scarecrow, Tin Man, and Cowardly Lion possess the faces of the familiar farm hands, who were standing outside minutes before Dorothy passed out in her farmhouse. Even Dorothy's kind but plain Aunt Em had turned into the beautiful and protective Good Witch.

Most of Dorothy's adventures in Oz turn out to be the day residue of a dream, to use Freud's term, where both significant and insignificant events of the preceding day are described and disguised during the dream. Jungians who think in terms of universal archetypes have an equally easy time explaining the symbolism of the Wicked Witch and the Good Witch, as do those Kleinians (followers of Melanie Klein) who focus on the "good mother" versus the "bad mother." The midget Munchkins represent all children, everywhere, who labor under the unfair laws of their capricious parents. But, most of all, *The Wizard of Oz* is an excellent illustration of the Freudian concept of dreamwork and of the way that dreams turn the familiar into the unfamiliar and then back again, as we free-associate about the symbols and recognize their origins in our own experiences.

These straightforward psychological dimensions make *The Wizard of Oz* eternally appealing and help us think beyond its more circumscribed social significance of the post-Depression era. It is this archetypal psychological appeal that goads us into appreciating the fading technicolor of the film, and that makes us adore the campiness of this classic, even when recent advances in CGI reach way beyond the cinematography of 1938. Because viewers identify with Dorothy on so many of these different levels, America was all the more heartbroken when the real-life Dorothy—Judy Garland—grew up very differently from her film persona. Sadly, child star Judy Garland broke with her triumphant film role and never returned to safe territory, in the way that she did after her imaginary excursion in Oz. She ultimately committed suicide, after enduring a lifetime of psychiatric disorders and prescription pill addictions.

Although there are some slightly scary scenes in *The Wizard of Oz*, when the Wicked Witch reigns and when the flying monkeys appear, and although some of Dorothy's adventures were nightmarish, next to no one would ever consider *The Wizard of Oz* to be a classic horror film. However, the same Depression years that begot *The Wizard of Oz* produced some of the best-known horror films, even though that era is typically associated with escapist themes, such as Busby Berkeley musicals and fantastic Fred Astaire-Ginger Rogers dance scenes. *Dracula, Frankenstein, The Mummy*, and their many sequels all began during the Depression. Blood-sucking vampires became an easy metaphor for "blood-sucking capitalists," who were blamed for the economic disaster.[3]

Horror films have been continuously popular since the start of cinema, with the notable exception of the World War II years, when the realistic horrors of war turned daily life into a nightmare, so that no one needed any extra fantasy outlets for fear. Such films have an enduring appeal for many people, regardless of the economic climate. Dracula portrays the archetypical villain whom we have encountered in our own lives, as well as in our dreams. Witnessing his rise and fall allows us a sense of mastery over the impending doom he represents. There is an erotic, sadomasochistic component to horror films, and they (usually) function as safe releases for otherwise dangerous tendencies involving pleasure and pain and control or passivity. They also allow us to rehearse fears about death, mortality, and resurrection.

Horror films have the greatest appeal for adolescents, whose bodies are changing just like the monsters and whose acne-attacked skin often shows strange similarities to the dermatological destruction endured by film monsters. Penetration by vampire fangs parallels sexual penetration and plays upon adolescent concerns about intercourse. The fact that vampires live by night opens up comparisons with other nocturnal activities, such as dreams and sex.

There are important crossovers between horror films and dream states or, more correctly, with nightmares. Some theoreticians refer to nightmares as "nocturnal panic attacks," because they produce the same sort of intense panic that grips panic attack sufferers or post-traumatic stress victims during the daytime.[4] Horror films allow us to relive and rehearse those nightmares. They lend a sense of mastery and catharsis, simply because we know that the panic will end when the film ends and that we will be none the worse. We also know that we can walk out of a horror film or any other film for that matter, which is a luxury that we do not have in either real life or dream life. Knowing that we can leave at will creates a strong sense of control and provides an equally strong contrast to the realities faced by a child, who knows that he or she cannot simply get up and walk away from diabolical parents or adverse social surroundings. Some horror films reflect contemporary social problems, while others recreate a more universal nightmare. While the early horror classics were typically set in remote or exotic locales, such as ancient Egypt (*The Mummy*) or remote and inaccessible mountainous regions of nineteenth century Transylvania (*Dracula*), the most successful nightmare/horror film of recent times was startlingly current. The slasher film *Nightmare on Elm Street* was deliberately situated on that anonymous street that appears in any American hometown. It was so commercially successful that it spawned several direct spin-offs, as well as dozens of lesser imitators.

Nightmare on Elm Street, directed by Wes Craven, chronicles a nightmare that could happen to anyone, anywhere, but this particular nightmare just happens to concern a very contemporary and highly publicized social problem: child sexual abuse. Unlike real child sexual predators, whose identities often elude the authorities until dozens of children are victimized, the child abuse of *Nightmare on Elm Street* is perpetrated by a single man, that most villainous villain, Freddy Kruger. Freddy was the sexually abusive school janitor. He was officially acquitted by criminal court but was burnt alive by vindictive parents, who extracted retribution for his unspeakable crimes against their children. Only now, in *Nightmare on Elm Street*, Freddy reappears after having been left for dead. With a fire-scarred face that is more frightening than any mask and with phalliclike knives extending his burnt-off hands, he haunts children's dreams and terrorizes them in their minds, even more mercilessly than before.[5]

Nightmare on Elm Street has none of the subtlety of the early *Dracula* films, where fangs stood for phalluses and where Dracula drank blood that subtly symbolized the blood shed during defloration. *Nightmare on Elm Street* incorporates the same symbolic castration seen in *The Mummy*, where the sexually transgressive Egyptian priest's tongue is severed, after he is wrapped and bound and rendered impotent and unable to penetrate the princess he once violated. But *Nightmare on Elm Street* substitutes knives for hands and makes its villain even more menacing than before. *Nightmare on Elm Street* was part of a whole new genre, known as the slasher genre, which was popular in the 1980s and where sex and blood and gore and crime and unabashed retribution attracted adolescents as much as such films repulsed their parents. In slasher films, waking reality intertwined with nightmarish horror in an uncomfortably realistic way.

Nightmares were fodder for many other horror films, although no recent examples were anywhere near as successful as the *Nightmare on Elm Street* series. Films such as *In Dreams* appeared in 1999, and played upon the familiar theme of dreams, insane asylums, and flagrantly confused reality. In *In Dreams*, a psychotic male inmate murders a nurse, dons her dress, and reappears in the dreams of newer asylum inmates in a way that is too cliched to deserve further comment.

Ken Russell's *Gothic*, which used Henri Fuseli's Romantic painting of *The Nightmare* as its advertising poster, was hardly horrific. This film was the standard, slightly humorous, never subdued, irreverent Russell fare, this time documenting the nightmarish hallucinations experienced by drugged-out authors and poets who bedecked the Romantic literary landscape. The colorful film chronicles Mary Shelley and her husband Percy Shelley, cavorting with Lord Byron and their compliant physician, on the lightning-struck night when she entered a drug-induced dream state (or a dreamlike drugged state) and conceived of her famed *Frankenstein* novel.

There are several films which refer to nightmares in their titles, but which are anything but. The unique *Nightmare Before Christmas*, conceived by Tim Burton, is exactly the opposite of *Nightmare on Elm Street*. With its silly but sweet stop-motion animation, *Nightmare Before Christmas* is perfectly suited for children and grown-up children and is nightmarish in name only. As this film demonstrates, film titles are deceptive, and neither the word "dream" nor "nightmare" in the title guarantees that such a subject will be central to the film. In fact, the worst nightmares of all typically appear in films that never directly alert the audience about what is in store. Alternatively, nightmares can lead the way to salvation, because they alert the characters to deeper and deceptive reality, as we will see in the next section.

NOTES

1. Cocteau, Jean. *The Art of Cinema*. Trans. Robin Buss. London: Marion Boyars, 1992.

2. Foulkes, David. *Children Dreaming and the Development of Consciousness*. Boston: Harvard University Press, 1999.

3. Soren, David. *The Rise and Fall of the Horror Film*. Baltimore: Midnight Marquee, 1997.

4. Shneerson, John. *Handbook of Sleep Medicine*. Oxford, U.K.: Blackwell Science, 2000.

5. Bulkeley, Kelly. *Visions of the Night*. Albany: State University of New York Press, 1999.

6

Sleep and Social Control

THE CABINET OF DR. CALIGARI

We can start our discussion of "Sleep and Social Control" by referring to one of the most famous films of all, *The Cabinet of Dr. Caligari*. This silent classic from 1919 is so well known that it is often erroneously assumed to be *the* first great film ever made, or *the* foremost example of German Expressionism, or *the* earliest horror film, or *the* original depiction of an evil psychiatrist, or something else that was equally illustrious.[1]

None of these old adages is quite true, but that does not detract from *Caligari*'s stature. There were great films made before Robert Weine created *Caligari*, and there were evil cinematic psychiatrists galore prior to 1919. There were many excellent examples of German Expressionism, and the horror genre was well established prior to *Caligari*. Plus, sleep and dreams and hypnotism and insanity were well-established themes in cinema long before 1919.[2] However, the mere fact that *Caligari* came so close to achieving all these various honors, and so many more, makes it so memorable and worthy of first mention. Even people who never saw *Caligari* know about it and react to it; the imagery and style of *Caligari* inspired director Tim Burton's black comedy *Beetlejuice*, even though he had never seen a screening of the silent film itself and had only stills on which to base his impression.[3]

Caligari's crooked streets and jarring angles and mismatched roofs, originally inspired by German Expressionism and the art of Edvard Munch and Alfred Kubin and the theater of Max Reinhardt, have endured in contemporary set design and illustrated children's books. Anyone who has ever seen a Dr. Seuss book has already seen evidence of *Caligari*'s visual inspiration. Anyone who was fortunate enough to watch Seuss' comical and kaleidoscopically colorful *5,000 Fingers of Dr.*

T can appreciate how easily *Caligari*'s silent, black-and-white, over-the-top imagery and character study could quickly be translated into a campy kiddie classic.

Caligari was so important to future film that it also inspired several books about its legacy. *Caligari's Children* is a wonderful read, both about *Caligari* and its influences and the horror genre in general. Film historian and theorist Siegfried Kracauer produced a much more controversial chronicle of authoritarian, hypnotic protagonists in pre–World War II German film in a provocatively titled volume, *From Caligari to Hitler*.[4] That book, however disputed it was by many critics, played a tremendous role in immortalizing *Caligari* and in establishing its significance, not just as cinema, but also as social theory and political philosophy and perhaps even as prophecy. By linking the charismatic but ultimately crazy, carnival performer-turned-killer Caligari to history's archvillain, Adolf Hitler, Kracauer linked the whimsical and improbable and obviously imaginary stage sets of *Caligari* to the most real and revolting episode in the twentieth century.

With all of these important ramifications, it seems to be a disservice to confine our discussion of this great film to the circumscribed theme of dream. In doing so, we risk implying that this is the only level on which this film should be appreciated. Clearly, it is not. With that caveat in mind, we can look at the implications of hypnosis, dreams, and social control in *Caligari* by starting with a summary of its story.

Directed by Robert Weine and written by Carl Mayer and Alfred Janowitz, the convoluted story of *Caligari* is recounted by two gentlemen talking in a garden. Caligari is an asylum director turned carnival hypnotist. As hypnotist, he takes complete control of his somnambulist Cesare (played by Conrad Veidt, who went on to play the Nazi commander in *Casablanca*). But it is only near the end of the film that we learn the complex origin of Caligari the carnival performer.

For now, all we know is that Caligari keeps the somnambulistic Cesare in a coffin, when Cesare is not assisting in side-show-like performances of trance states. Caligari secretly commands Cesare to kill. He starts with a city clerk who humiliated Caligari when he applied for a permit to perform. The second victim was the storyteller's friend Alain. At Caligari's instigation, Cesare finally attempts to take the life of the heroine Jane herself. He threatens her with a knife but cannot carry out Caligari's deadly command, because he has fallen in love with her. She faints, and he swings her body over his shoulder to kidnap her and presumably save her from Caligari's evil intentions. Cesare himself eventually collapses, and drops Jane, and then drops dead himself (according to the storyteller). She escapes, whereas Cesare lies dead in a field. Then the "real" truth is discovered . . . in several more steps.

By this point, Jane's male companion Francis had grown suspicious of Caligari and was secretly tracing his footsteps. Francis followed Caligari into a nearby insane asylum and learned that Caligari is not just an ordinary carnival performer but that the hypnotist is also the head of the asylum. What is more, Caligari the carnivalist had been emulating the experiments of a mountbank named Caligari, who lived in 1703 and who hypnotized his subjects into committing murder.

It turned out that Cesare had been admitted to Dr. Caligari's asylum and was conveniently chosen as the subject of Caligari's evil experiments. The staff at the institution discover that Caligari is himself insane and that he must be stopped. By the end of the story, Caligari is handcuffed by his own asylum staff and stuffed into a cell.

Just as all the loose ends are about to be wrapped up, the film returns to its original framing device, where Francis the storyteller and another man are sitting in the garden. Francis is finishing the retelling of this story. It is only then that we the viewers learn that our storyteller, Francis—who portrayed himself as an important protagonist in the story—is also an inmate at an asylum. This unexpected revelation makes us, the audience, uncertain as to whether this story ever took place anywhere other than in Francis' deluded imagination.

As imaginative as the plot of *Caligari* appears to be on the surface, it was actually a fairly close rendition of a certain reality. One of the authors, the Czech Janowitz, had a very good reason to portray the psychiatrist-hypnotist as the ultimate embodiment of evil. Janowitz received a dishonorable discharge from the military in World War I on psychiatric grounds. He became hostile toward all psychiatrists as a result and was ready to blame them for disrupting his own dreams and for turning other soldiers into killing machines.

Carl Mayer, his collaborator, had a more prosaic reason to recount this tale. Mayer had been walking through the park in Munich one day and saw a child disappear into the thicket. The next day, he read that a little girl had been murdered in the bushes by a madman, maybe in the same spot where he had walked. Maybe this was the same child he had seen the day before! This real life experience fired his imagination and added some extra details to Janowitz's original idea.

By writing *Caligari* in collaboration with Mayer, Janowitz not only vented his vendetta against psychiatrists, but he also created one of cinema's greatest classics. He carved out a screenwriting career that was far more formidable than any career he could have achieved as a soldier. He certainly attained far more lasting fame than the psychiatrist who ousted him from the service. But Janowitz was greatly disappointed when his original script was deliberately defused by the studio, which decided to soften the story by presenting it as the recollection of two asylum inmates, rather than as a direct statement of fact. This framing device made the truth of the tale more ambiguous, and avoided any direct condemnation of psychiatry, and definitely disguised Janowitz's original intentions.

As interesting as all this is, what does it have to do with our theme of dream? First, let us say that hypnotism was viewed as a way to produce artificial sleep. It was seen as an opportunity for the hypnotist to insert dreams into the subject. Even though hypnotism is not the same as sleep, hypnotism was specifically named for Hypnos, the Greek god of Sleep. Subjects in hypnotic trances were known as "somnambulists," which is the same word that is currently used to describe sleepwalkers. Because of the intense societal as well as scientific interest in the cross-over between hypnotism, dreams, and sleep, many scientific studies about dream control through hypnosis were conducted in both the nineteenth and twentieth centuries.[5] Several nineteenth century novels described hypothetical crimes committed by somnambulists. A few criminal cases concerning crimes allegedly committed by sleepwalkers came to the attention of the courts, and some of the accused were actually exonerated because the judge and jury believed that they acted without volition while asleep.[6]

There are broader social implications of hypnotism to consider, to see how these concerns translate into cinematic themes. Although hypnosis makes its subjects appear to be asleep, so that they could be presumed to be dreaming, hypnosis is actually the ideological opposite of the democratic dreamstate. In the dreamstate (or at least in the post–Romantic Era dreamstate, which emphasizes the input of the individual), the individual synthesizes his or her own special dreams and produces a unique and personalized product through each dream experience.

Hypnosis, on the other hand, induces a sleeplike state where someone other than the dreamer controls the content of the sleep state. Hypnosis is the ultimate expression of authoritarianism and totalitarianism. It reeks of social control that overrides individual autonomy. At best, it is a holdover from the days of magicians and sorcerers, who could cast spells over their chosen victims and send them into unending but uneventful sleep, of the sort experienced by that famous fairy-tale character, *Sleeping Beauty*. At worst, hypnosis allows the hypnotizer to insert his or her most evil impulses into his unwitting victim, as per *Caligari*. Hypnosis is potentially more dangerous than supernatural ideas about deities actively inducing dreams in passive dreamers because hypnosis permits a single irresponsible individual to seize control, whereas supernatural ideas about dreams are culturally sanctioned and so are subject to the approval of a broader segment of society.

The Cabinet of Dr. Caligari dramatizes the conflict between the public (or social) control of dreams and the personal (or psychological) control of dreams. This issue became a great concern in the twentieth century. Conceived just after World War I, *Caligari* mirrored the modernist spirit that shook Western Europe after the Great War. Modernism advocated the autonomy of the individual in a way that was not possible under the old regime and in a way that was not even necessary before the disastrous first world war ruptured citizens' faith in the state and nurtured a "lost generation."

It is easy to see how Kracauer could compare Dr. Caligari to Hitler. Hitler, too, could entrance followers to follow him blindly to murder millions of innocent people, just as Caligari extracted the unbending obedience of his somnambulist Cesare (until Cesare's love for Jane interfered). Caligari was the prototype of the authoritarian and fascist ruler, who was himself insane and who forced others to commit equally insane acts. *The Cabinet of Dr. Caligari* was, indeed, eerily reminiscent of the events that would take place in Nazi Germany. But Kracauer's arguments about the crossover between the German mindset and cinematic themes became all the more compelling after he pointed out that Caligari was just one of a long line of such characters featured in pre–World War II German film.

The wider social dimensions of hypnosis become even more interesting when we consider that hypnosis represented a pivot point in Freud's career. Freud's gradual shift from standard neurology to his more innovative and idiosyncratic psychoanalytic style began when he studied hypnotism with Charcot and then Bernheim in France. His early attempts to treat hysteria, which he deemed to be a disease of the mind rather than the body, were based on hypnotism. It was only after considerable experience with both hypnosis and hysterics that he substituted dream interpretation, free association, and the "talking cure." Freud made this history-making transition at the turn of the century, presumably because he found the talking cure to be more effective.

However, this paradigm shift that Freud made famous paralleled the broader cultural shift at the cusp of the twentieth century, when emphasis on external control (as represented by hypnosis) gave way to internal control (as represented by the dream). It is intriguing to think that Freud's methodology may have been potentiated by this cultural current, and it is equally intriguing to think about the ways that Freud's methodology reciprocally influenced the broader culture.

Either way, director Robert Weine was inadvertently indicting the old psychiatric regime only, when he portrayed the evil psychiatrist in *Caligari* as a hypnotist. By acting on Fritz Lang's suggestion to add a framing devise to the film, Weine was actually opening up the possibility that the new psychiatric regime inaugurated by Freudian free association and dream interpretation would be less evil than the old.

Clearly, this did not sit well with Janowitz, who had other motivations besides the story.

We must ask ourselves why *The Cabinet of Dr. Caligari*, the silent film, is still so compelling to so many of us today, in spite of its antiquated style and lack of speech and its ponderous plot and painfully slow pace. *Caligari* still shows at art cinemas, and was recently rereleased, with a new musical accompaniment. *Caligari*'s continuing success suggests that people are still perturbed by the possibility of losing control during dream and sleep, and that people share a near universal fear of committing criminal acts while unconscious, and that people harbor a lingering fear of archvillain authority figures who impose themselves on others. Essentially, this 1919 classic is still capable of tapping into our deepest concerns about social control and personal responsibility.

We can turn to several Hollywood films, which deal with this theme of social control and dream, to see how this irrepressible idea is updated. *The Manchurian Candidate* and *Total Recall* are two excellent examples of films that portray both paranoia about social control as well as testimony to the truth-telling potential of personal dreams. George Orwell's acclaimed novel *Nineteen Eighty-Four*, which also addresses this subject, was turned into two films, one British and one American, each of which pales next to the novel but each of which deserves our attention, simply because of the stature of the novel. But we shall start with the greatest of these film feats, *The Manchurian Candidate*.

THE MANCHURIAN CANDIDATE

On the surface, the sleek black-and-white design of *The Manchurian Candidate*, together with its serious political concerns with the Korean War and McCarthyism, seems light years away from the lighter-weight, special effects–heavy, futuristic science fiction of *Total Recall*. With an all-star cast of Frank Sinatra, Angela Lansbury, Laurence Harvey, Janet Leigh, and Tony Curtis, *The Manchurian Candidate* seems even further removed from *Total Recall*'s action-oriented, sex symbol stars, Arnold Schwarznegger and Sharon Stone. *The Manchurian Candidate*'s perfectly polished cinematographic style is equally distinct from a film like *Nineteen Eighty-Four*, which is intended to evoke the verbal style of its namesake novel, without exploring new visual dimensions. However, these films share a certain similarity; each depicts personal dreams as revelatory events, which help break the spell of evil, exploitative, double-dealing political powers. Each offers the protagonist the opportunity to dream at night and to see the light, so to speak, during the dark. That is a power of which *Caligari*'s Cesare was woefully deprived.

John Frankenheimer's *The Manchurian Candidate*, adapted from Richard Condon's book of the same name, was first released in 1962. It begins with a title, "Korea 1952." This title will serve as a cue card, to remind the audience of the astoundingly successful and highly publicized brainwashing experiments carried out by the Koreans during the Korean War. Audiences of 1962 were well aware that the communist North Koreans had captured several patriotic American sailors, along with their submarine, and subjected them to sleep deprivation and "reeducation" to the point that the Americans publically denounced American policy and advocated on behalf of the Korean communists. Viewers in 1962 were equally familiar with the fanatically anticommunist McCarthy campaigns of the early 1950s, which were waged by Americans against Americans. The public was still trying to make sense of the impassioned trials that were televised the decade before and so was a captive audience, so to speak, for such subject matter.

In the first scene, we meet Frank Sinatra as Captain Bennet Marco and Laurence Harvey, as Sergeant Raymond Shaw. The younger Sergeant Shaw is returning home from Korea. The son of one of the most intensely evil mothers to be seen on the screen (Angela Lansbury) and the stepson of an aspiring, self-serving, and slimy vice presidential candidate (James Gregory), Shaw is ready to receive the coveted Congressional Medal of Honor—for an act of heroism that he does not really remember.

Shaw's commanding officer, Captain Marco (Frank Sinatra), as well as the nine surviving members of his patrol, describe the heroism Shaw demonstrated when he saved the lives of his platoonmates, after their capture by Manchurians. Shaw is pinned by no less than the President of the United States, at an event that was publically staged by his publicity-seeking stepfather. Afterward, unpleasantries are exchanged between the youthful Shaw and his parents, which are important to the plot but less important to our concern with dreams.

The scene shifts to Major Marco, who has been reassigned to a cushy post in Army Intelligence in Washington, D.C. In spite of his pleasant surroundings, Marco is distressed because he is suffering from serious nightmares, which recur with astounding regularity and clarity, and which the camera captures in one of the most famous dream scenes in cinema.

In the dream, Marco and his men are sitting together at a ladies' auxiliary meeting. The scene swiftly shifts to another scene, the "brainwashing" scene in Manchuria. Seeing that Marco is still asleep, our first instinct is to think that the quick, disjointed scene shifts are nothing more than the jump cuts that take place during dreams. We soon realize that these juxtapositions are telling a truth that is not accessible anywhere else. The camera returns to the garden meeting, where an elderly white woman is speaking to her two dozen, horticulture-happy associates about "Fun with Hydrangeas," as the soldiers look on from the sidelines. The camera shifts back, to show that an East Asian communist doctor has replaced the garden lady in center stage. The captured Americans sit behind posters of Joseph Stalin and Mao Tse-tung, while two dozen uniformed Chinese, Korean, and Soviet soldiers look on.

The doctor proceeds to explain that he plans to demonstrate the powers of hypnotism to his communist cohorts. In Sinatra's dream, the doctor points to the American soldiers and states specifically that "I have conditioned them—or brainwashed them, which I understand is the new American word. They believe that they are waiting out a storm in the lobby of a small hotel in New Jersey where a meeting of the ladies' garden club is in progress."

The dream scene shifts again, this time back to the garden, where Raymond Shaw (Laurence Harvey) is simulating a game of solitaire. He goes through the hand motions of dealing himself nonexistent cards. When Shaw is asked if he has ever killed anyone, he replies that he has not. The evil Asian doctor/politico calmly disagrees and plans to demonstrate Raymond's ability to kill. He asks Raymond to choose the one member of his platoon whom he dislikes the least. When Raymond chooses Captain Marco, the doctor objects, stating, "That won't do, Raymond. We need the Captain to get you your medal." So Raymond names a second choice, Ed Mavole (Richard LePore). Obediently, Raymond strangles Mavole with a white scarf, while Captain Marco yawns and as the rest of the platoon sit by bored and unreactive. Mavole then dies in the dream.

At that point, Captain Marco awakens abruptly from his nightmare. Distraught by these dreams, Marco consults an army psychiatrist, who, incidentally, is African-American, at a time before the Civil Rights Act of 1964 was passed and at a time when blacks were still so disenfranchised from the American "establishment" that they could readily represent an alternative establishment, if not necessarily an "antiestablishment." Marco tells the "good" American doctor about his dream and about the fact that Shaw was honored for saving the lives of all but two of the men in the platoon. The two he did not save were presumed missing. One of those presumed missing was Mavole, the very same man who was murdered in the dream. Marco then repeats a phrase which will be important to deciphering the secret of the plot. He says, "Raymond Shaw is the kindest, bravest, warmest, most wonderful human being I've ever known in my life."

As a reward for this revelation, Captain Marco is reassigned to a less stressful post. The plot thickens when another young member of the platoon experiences strikingly similar dreams about his wartime experiences in the prison camp. Only this time the dreamer, Corporal Al Melvin (James Edwards), is black. When he dreams of the garden party, he dreams of an African-American garden club, where equally boring, elderly black ladies are dressed in their Sunday best. In Corporal Melvin's dream, he sees Captain Marco stating that his first duty upon return will be to recommend Raymond Shaw for the Congressional Medal of Honor for saving the lives of their platoon and for taking out a complete company of Chinese infantry. Then, in the dream, Corporal Melvin sees Raymond kill Mavole, just as Marco did in his dream. Upon seeing Mavole's blood splatter on Stalin's portrait, Melvin awakens, screaming and awakening his wife. When his wife attempts to reassure him, Melvin repeats the exact same line that Marco said: "Raymond Shaw is the kindest, bravest, warmest, most wonderful human being I've ever known in my life."

Corporal Melvin is just as disturbed by his dreams as Captain Marco, but he drafts a letter to Raymond to describe his dreams and unburden his fears of going crazy. Raymond reads the letter but soon shifts into playing solitaire, just as he did in the dream.

To contemporary psychiatrists, these recurring nightmares would be consistent with the disturbing dreams and disrupted sleep of "post-traumatic stress disorder" that veterans often describe. But, fortunately for the plot, this film was made in 1962, before such a diagnosis was added to DSM-IV (and before DSM-I, II, III, or IV existed). Fortunately for Marco, he starts to suspect that something is up, and heads for New York, to call upon Raymond Shaw, who has been busy dealing with Chinese agents in his Manhattan apartment. After a furious fight scene between Marco and Shaw's Chinese employee, Shaw reveals to Marco that he has been having the same recurring dream that Corporal Melvin described in his letter.

From that point on, the plot gets more complicated, and *The Manchurian Candidate* develops even more twists and turns than *The Cabinet of Dr. Caligari*. Now that both Captain Marco and the audience know the truth through the dream scenes, they are free to find out that the wartime memories were engineered with the help of the evil Russian Pavlov Institute, which reprogrammed the entire platoon into believing that Shaw was a hero, when he was really a killer, however unwitting. Moreover, Shaw could be commanded to kill again, at their will, whenever he saw a certain playing card which would cause him to re-enter that twilight state of hypersuggestibility. The "killer" card that clouds his consciousness is a Red Queen. (Although nothing else in this film is *Alice-in-Wonderland*-like, the audience itself is already preprogrammed to believe in the irrationality of playing cards, thanks to Alice's adventures in Wonderland and her own experiences with the irrational deck of cards.)

It turns out that it is not the communists who commit the ultimate evil; it is Shaw's own mother (Angela Lansbury), who is a secret communist operative and another sort of "Red Queen." She and her communist cronies are plotting to kill the presidential candidate so that her husband can win his vice presidential campaign, ascend to the presidency, and then take over the country and hand it over to the communists. But even the evil mother, who has been cooperating with the communists all along, is shocked to learn that the all-controlling communists have chosen her own son to complete the final killing essential for the communist takeover.

In the meantime, Marco has been struggling to unravel the mystery. He wants to test out his theories about Raymond Shaw and to rid Raymond of his irresistible control that he feels, whenever he sees the Red Queen in the deck of cards. Sadly, an irrevocable act occurs before Marco can intervene: Shaw enters another "altered state," engineered by his evil mother, and kills his fiance and her father and thus destroys the only positive part of his life. The grand finale occurs at the political convention, where Shaw, now painfully aware that he is irrepressibly programmed to kill on command, aims his rifle at the stage. Unable to rid himself of either the communist or the parental control and unable to accept his killings in his own conscience, Shaw the sharpshooter shoots each of his parents to put a permanent end to this episode. With nothing more to live for, he turns the weapon on himself. (This final scene is a homage to Hitchcock, who showcased a similar twist in *The Man Who Knew Too Much*.)

The enduring appeal of *The Manchurian Candidate* is manifold. Many people think that it was a wonderful way to showcase singer Frank Sinatra's talents as an actor. Frank's most fanatical fans would be happy enough to see and hear him in anything. Stardom's allure aside, *Candidate* provides sophisticated political commentary. It addressed America's brush with McCarthyism, current concerns with brainwashing and America's involvement with the Korean War, the emergence of African Americans in proto-civil rights' society, and maybe even the evolving role of women in 1960s society and the potential evil that may befall society and their sons should they be empowered.

Above all, *Candidate* details a distorted and destructive Oepidal relationship between an unassuming son and a ruthless, self-involved, narcissistic mother, who will stop at nothing—not even the sacrifice of her own son—so that she can achieve her own ends and so that she can promote her second husband, again at the expense of her natural son. For all its commentary about current events, *The Manchurian Candidate* functions as just another fairy tale, Cinderella-style, this time about the evil stepfather and the victim son and the complicit natural parent.

One could reasonably argue that the dream theme in *The Manchurian Candidate* is not really about dreams at all and that dream it is simply a way of unfolding the drama and revealing the plots and subplots, the narratives and metanarratives. Yet the director's use of a dream is deliberate and highly successful. By choosing a dream to demonstrate the duplicity and double-dealing that reverberates throughout the plot, the director is also reminding us of the double reality that each person experiences during night and day. He implicitly compares this duality of ordinary human experience to the extraordinary experience of *The Manchurian Candidate*. At the same time, the film tells us a tremendous amount about the American concept of dreams and about the dream's alleged ability to override even the most intense communist brainwashing efforts, that arrive via Russia's renowned Pavlov Institute. For Americans, it is the individualizing experience of the dream that triumphs over the homogenizing efforts of communist conditioning.

Curiously, *The Manchurian Candidate* was even more appealing to audiences when it was rereleased for public viewing in 1987, after having been pulled from theaters when the string of political assassinations that shook the 1960s made it impolitic to continue screening this assassination story. It is this complexity of plot and subplot, achieved largely through the introduction of dream, that gave *Candidate* an endless life, long after it ceased to speak to contemporary social concerns, and long after the greatest glory days of its all-star cast.

After watching *The Manchurian Candidate*, we fully understand why George Orwell began his famous futuristic novel, *Nineteen Eighty-Four*, with a dream sequence. For Orwell, as well as for director John Frankenheimer, the last place left to evade political control and thought police is the dream.

NINETEEN EIGHTY-FOUR

Nineteen Eighty-Four, the novel, endured far better than either of the two films that were based on the book. *Nineteen Eighty-Four* was first published in 1949 in London, where the author Orwell lived. Penguin Books published the first paperback edition in 1954 and reprinted it twenty-six times since then.[7] The American film remake of *Nineteen Eighty-Four* was released, appropriately enough, in 1984. It was directed by Michael Radford and starred John Hurt, Richard Burton, and Suzanna Hamilton. There had been a British version, nearly two decades earlier, from 1956.

Neither of these two films did justice to Orwell's literary original, but not because of any fault of the filmmakers. There is an inherent difficulty in translating a work like *Nineteen Eighty-Four* into film, and that difficulty arises from the fact that cinema depends upon visual imagery as well as action to make a story interesting on screen. However, Orwell's work derives its power from concepts and words, rather than from story or scenery. (The scenery that it does describe is grim and gruesome enough to disengage viewers without drawing them further into the story.)

It is the language of *Nineteen Eighty-Four* that had its most powerful impact and that captured the imagination of several generations. Terms that remain a part of everyday vocabulary—such as "Big Brother," "Doublethink," "New Speak," "Thought Police," and especially the aphorism "Big Brother is Watching You"—were coined by Orwell in *Nineteen Eighty-Four*.

The film depicts a future, state-run society controlled by "Big Brother," where the economy is dependent upon war. The cinema version emphasizes the fact that love is outlawed in such a state and presents the point of view of state employee Winston Smith (named for Winston Churchill and played by John Hurt). Winston falls in love with Julia. The two try to escape Big Brother's ubiquitous listening and viewing devices, which monitor citizens' words and deeds everywhere. They eventually succeed in having sex and then join the underground dedicated to the party's overthrow. But because nobody can really escape in this society, the two are caught and then tortured and brainwashed for their crime.

The personal love story that drives the plot fared well in the "free love" generation that thrived in the 1960s and 1970s, even though this romance paled in importance compared to Orwell's loftier political message. The relationship between Winston and Julia was a way to introduce far broader concerns about social control, the relationship of the individual to the state, the utility and purpose of war, the duplicity of government, the futility of underground movements in overthrowing all-powerful government agendas, and, secondarily, the potential subversiveness of sex and the individuality and humanity inherent in dream.

When first published in 1949 Britain, Big Brother was a powerful metaphor for World War II fascists such as Hitler, Stalin, and Franco. The book's preoccupation with social control and double-dealing, self-serving government became equally important over the next several decades in the United States, where McCarthyism, the Watergate break-in, and, above all, the Vietnam War lent *Nineteen Eighty-Four* a whole new life. Its importance to coming-of-age college students persists, because their personal conflicts about personal autonomy and parental control can find easy metaphors in *Nineteen Eighty-Four*, even though the real year 1984 has long since passed.

Nineteen Eighty-Four, the film, begins in 1984, sometime after the end of the "Atomic War." There is a never-ceasing war off the Malabar Coast on the southwestern shore of India. This war does not really exist, but self-interested government bureaucrats want citizens to believe that the world is still at war, in order to ensure their own positions. The world has been divided into three states: Oceania, Eurasia, and Eastasia. London is the capital of Oceania. Its economy is dependent upon war against the other states. It is ruled by a party that has gained total control over its citizens. The party itself is headed by Big Brother.

Big Brother monitors everyone, everywhere, through the use of telescreens and through employees known as the Thought Police. Telescreens broadcast party propaganda and are connected to videocameras that record citizens' activities for review by the Thought Police.

The party controls reality itself, because it can alter the past and dupe people into believing in a completely reconstructed history. It hires people such as Winston Smith (John Hurt) to rewrite the past. They use the principles of "doublethink" to brainwash citizens into believing slogans that say: "War Is Peace," "Slavery Is Freedom," and "Ignorance Is Strength." Winston has some reservations about his role in this society but does not have the freedom to express his distress. It is in a dream where he first begins to doubt. In this state-run society, dreams alone are free from the control of the Thought Police.

Winston has several dreams during the course of the novel, which take him back to the past, the real past, rather than the rewritten past presented by Big Brother. His dreams also transport him to a future, where his own wishes prevail over the plan of the party. In his dreams, Winston also maintains a conscience, which is a personal luxury that is not permitted to members of the party. He also has sexual desires in his dreams and need not confine sex to the sole purpose of procreation, as the party has determined. These dreams begin the process of individuation, which distinguishes Winston from the collective identity that has been imposed upon him by the party. This process leads to his subversive activities and his attempts to overthrow the party.

Winston begins by dreaming about his mother and sister, who starved to death in the war because he was self-centered enough to eat all of the family's ration of white chocolate by himself, even though he knew that his sister was already wasting away from lack of food. Such pangs of conscience could compromise Winston's complicity with Big Brother's program, where "War is Peace" is a favorite motto, and where war is perpetuated, because it ensures the status of the governing party and ensures continuation of the economy.

What really begins to destabilize Winston is not so much his mind as his body. He dreams of having sex with a woman worker, Julia, whom he saw during the state-sponsored "Two Minute Hate." It is this dream that will begin his undoing. Winston's dreams open up an opportunity to reflect upon alternatives that are not permitted during the waking world. Images of the underground leader of the Inner Party, dedicated to the overthrow of Big Brother, appear to Winston, both in dreams and while awake. Dreams, for Winston, become as important as the telescreens that monitor his daily activities; they are screens from which he cannot escape and which reflect his ideas, without any conscious control of his own. When Winston finally does succeed in escaping the monitors long enough to have sex with Julia, he does this in a place that he has already seen in a dream. It is only the images of dreamlife that are able to override the "newspeak" and "doublethink" that Big Brother imposed on the ordinary language of daily life.

Orwell's view of the dream as a route to personal freedom is a very twentieth century idea and had actually been expressed in a strangely similar Russian novel of 1920. This concept had already been embraced by the surrealists, who arose in the aftermath of World War I, and who deified personal dream partly (but not solely) because dream was the opposite of the destructive governments that led the world into the Great War and because dream countered the totalitarian governments that assumed power in the 1930s.

Freud himself hypothesized that the dream and the free associations that dream inspired during the waking state could free an individual from the bonds of the past, which he deemed to be responsible for repetitive, self-destructive behavior. Thus, the dream, according to Orwell, has political and as well as psychological potential. This point has been confirmed many times over by political scientists and can be a fascinating point of departure for those interested in this unexpected association. We will return to this important point when we discuss the political repercussions of the Reverend Dr. Martin Luther King's "I have a dream" speech, but, for now, we shall continue with our discussion of science fiction and sleep, to see how *Total Recall* fits into this paradigm.

NOTES

1. Prawer, S. S. *Caligari's Children*. Oxford, U.K.: Oxford University Press, 1980; Robinson, David. *Das Cabinet des Dr. Caligari*. London: BFI, 1997.
2. Soren, David. *The Rise and Fall of the Horror Film*. Baltimore: Midnight Marquee, 1997; Eisner, Lottie. *The Haunted Screen: Expressionism in German Cinema*. Berkeley: University of California Press, 1969.
3. Salisbury, Mark. *Burton on Burton*. New York: Faber, 1995.
4. Kracauer, Siegfried. *From Caligari to Hitler*. Princeton, NJ: Princeton University Press, 1947.
5. Woods, Ralph L. *The World of Dreams*. New York: Random House, 1947.
6. Ellenberger, Henri. *The Discovery of the Unconscious*. New York: Basic, 1970.
7. 2 Mar. 2000 http://www.saltdal.vgs.no/engelsk/orwell/1984.htm.

Science Fiction and Sleep

TOTAL RECALL

Paul Verhoeven's *Total Recall* is easy to follow, when compared to the convoluted plot of *The Manchurian Candidate*. It translates into film far better than the bleaker black-and-white visions of *Nineteen Eighty-Four*. Based on a story by science fiction giant Philip K. Dick ("We Can Remember It For You Wholesale"), *Total Recall* captures the paranoid futuristic fantasies for which the amphetamine-addicted Dick was famous and turns them into an action-adventure thriller tailored to the taste of the space-age-crazed American public. Director Verhoeven (who also directed the spectacularly successful *Robocop)* says that "it's an action-adventure sci-fi movie about a mind." Set in 2075, written by Dick in 1975, *Total Recall* is far more corporeal than the more cerebral *The Cabinet of Dr. Caligari* or *The Manchurian Candidate*.

The protagonist, Douglas Quaid, is played by the archbodybuilder Arnold Schwarzenegger. Quaid (Schwarzenegger) is not subject to the comparatively simple psychological control of hypnotism or Pavlovian conditioning or reeducation that we witness in *Caligari* and *Candidate*, respectively. Rather, Quaid receives a real physical implant that interacts with his dreams and waking memories. A "memory bolus" will be implanted in his brain, through a surgical instrument that is inserted up his nose. This procedure is performed in exactly the same way as some neurosurgical procedures are done today, although it should be noted that ancient Egyptians also entered corpses' brains through the nose to extract the brain before mummification.

As soon as we see the film's stars, Schwarzenegger and Stone, who are both known for their physical presence rather than their psychological subtlety, we, the audience, are prepared for this bias toward the physicality of subjective experience. If we know that the film is based on a 1975 story (which, incidentally, remained in development for fourteen years), we can deduce that the plot was a product of the tail end of the drug culture. In those years, it was common knowledge that external, biological sources produced dreamlike experiences just as easily as the internal, psychological sources that Freud or Jung emphasized. Furthermore, any awareness we have of Philip K. Dick's life history, and his own struggles with amphetamine habituation, and the paranoia it produced helps us appreciate this emphasis on materialism and de-emphasis of idealism even more.

Before the dramatic "memory bolus" scene takes place, Quaid's dreams foreshadow the ever-present evil that is about to be revealed. Each night, Schwarzenegger's character Quaid is awakened abruptly by the same dream about a voyage to Mars. His lovely and loving wife, Sharon Stone, lulls him back to sleep with falsely reassuring words. Because Schwarzenegger as Quaid is a workaday construction worker who leads a simple and straightforward life, it would be out of character for him to self-reflect about this dream, as a more psychologically astute person would have done in 1975. Besides, this is the future, and who knows what even educated and insightful people will do to decipher their dreams one hundred years hence?

To learn more about this troubling nocturnal memory, Quaid buys a vacation package at a company called "Rekall, Inc.," although he neglects to mention this to his wife. Rekall (as in *Total Recall*) sells implanted memories of perfect vacations, which are far better than the real thing because nothing ever goes wrong. Airplanes are never delayed, hotels are never oversold, rain never obstructs the sun, and no one gets a cold.

But something goes seriously wrong during the procedure. Quaid goes berserk and starts tearing the place apart. It turns out that he already has a "memory bolus" implanted, of which he had been unaware. This second surgery interferes with the first and causes a serious interaction. Quaid suddenly starts to recall that he really was on Mars, where he was a secret agent who fought the evil Mars administrator, Coohagen. But he is still not sure of the accuracy of this new perception and will have to navigate through this dreamlike world of dual identity for the rest of the film.

Quaid might have been content to write all this off to dream and delusion were it not for the fact that government agents appear out of nowhere, and try to subdue him, and then kill him. In the meantime, we see his loving wife being chastised by her government employers, because she lost control of her husband after being entrusted with ensuring that Quaid continue to live his simple existence without questioning his identity or recalling his past. From this interchange between Stone and the enforcers, we learn that Stone herself is just another government agent, posing as Quaid's wife. From there, the real action starts.

Quaid travels to Mars to test the truth of his dream memories, and to find the secret of his past existence. Of course, he has to battle many evil people along the way, like a true action hero. He (and we) will witness spectacular special effects scenery during his journey, both on Mars in general and in a vaudevillelike "Venusville," where lowlifes and mutants live together, crowded into the colorful squalor of a futuristic red-light district. In Venusville, Quaid meets his true helpmate, a kind-hearted, dark-skinned street walker. The streetwalker will help him combat his duplicitous blond wife and her control-happy government cronies, as they try to kill him in order to suppress the "truth": that Mars' greedy governor, Coohagen, has pillaged Mars' natural resources, polluted the environment, enslaved its citizens, and reduced the planet to poverty.

In the end, Quaid recaptures his true identity, sutures the split between his dream identity and his real life ideal, and saves Mars and all its inhabitants from destruction. The action-adventure ends with the audience convinced that dream-reality and waking-reality can indeed become confused, in much the same way that "reel life" and "real life" become blurred in a successful action-adventure.

As futuristic as this film is, it offers viewers some very ancient wisdom, along with seemingly mindless entertainment and standard-brand sex and violence. Even though it is set in the late twenty-first century, *Total Recall*'s message is very twentieth century: listen to your dreams and to your dreams only, for they alone tell the truth. Dreams can set you free, free of inhibitions that govern waking life and free of equally corrosive government control. Dreams, for postpsychoanalytic man, are the voice of autonomy, rather than authority. Whereas ancient man's dreams were populated by deities, who sent messages through dreams, modern man's dreams are portrayed as being impervious to the most invasive assault and are bulwarks against even the "memory bolus."

Science fiction has such a wonderful way of repackaging myths and methods recycled through many millennia to make them seem new and innovative, even though the essential ideas are really as retro as can be. Schwarzenegger's Quaid has discovered the same secrets known to Joseph of the Bible, and to the Egyptians and Assyrians who came before him, and, implicitly, to all those who will come after him. It is reassuring to know that dreams of the past will help us navigate through the future, even if that future includes double-dealing wives and state-sanctioned assassins, perilous space travel, imaginary landscapes, and currently unimaginable medical treatments. Rather than expecting a magic amulet, or a silver sword, or a yellow brick road, to show us the "way," *Total Recall* viewers come away agreeing with turn-of-the-twentieth-century psychoanalysts, who also thought that personal dreams could illuminate the darkest days.

FIGHT CLUB

It is a bit of a stretch to compare the dream theme in *Fight Club* to *Total Recall*, especially since the sleep/dream connection in *Fight Club* is so subtle, whereas *Total Recall* presents an unabashed and unambiguous dream theme. Both films involve gratuitous violence, and both focus on personal versus political control. Both depict dreamlike double identities, and both begin with disturbed sleep as both foreshadowing and framing device. Like the protagonists in *The Cabinet of Dr. Caligari* or *The Manchurian Candidate*, who are victimized by unscrupulous others while they sleep and victimize innocent others as a result, *Fight Club*'s hapless antihero also becomes a victimizer nonvolitionally, as a result of his loss of sleep and dreams. He is also a victim of his own irrepressible urges, which would have been confined to fantasy and nocturnal reverie had he not suffered from insomnia.

But the similarities end there. *Fight Club* is not about a society that imposes external control on the individual and interferes with individual dream. *Fight Club* is about an internal locus of control that has gone out of control. It concerns an individual who wreaks havoc on society, rather than the other way around. *Fight Club* depicts the ultimate endpoint of dream, the point where raw and unrepressed libidinal desires that are ordinarily expressed in dream eventually invade waking life, simply because the protagonist is deprived of sleep and is denied the ordinary dream outlet.

However, very few viewers see the controversial film *Fight Club* as a statement, however subtle, about dreams and dreamers, about ego and id, about dream censors and dreamworks that operate during sleep, about the Freudian concept of the dream as an unfulfilled wish, or the Jungian concept of the "coniunctio" that occurs when the "self" meets the "other" in dream. In *Fight Club,* the violence that follows the opening scenes is so intense that the audience often forgets how the film started and has to go back for a second viewing, to see exactly how Ed Norton (unnamed) and Brad Pitt (Tyler Durden) got their goals and identities confused.

Fight Club begins shortly after a sleepless accident investigator played by Ed Norton consults a doctor about his insomnia. The nameless narrator (for convenience I will call him Norton) and ultimate office drone tells us that "with insomnia, you're never really asleep; you're never really awake." But his unsympathetic physician refuses to treat the nondescript Norton and irritatedly insists that no one ever died from lack of sleep. "If you want to see pain," his doctor says, "go over to the hospital on Tuesday night, to see testicular cancer patients."

Norton, who lives in a neat, Ikea-furnished condo, heeds his doctor's advice. He begins to frequent patient support groups, feigning whatever illness is involved, and crying and commiserating with real cancer victims. He laps up every ounce of sympathy and camaraderie offered. He starts with testicular cancer, as per his physician's suggestion, and finds that he is finally able to sleep, after crying his heart out in the arms of a big-breasted "Big Ed," played by Meatloaf. Big Ed is a onetime professional bodybuilder who has now developed "bitch tits" as well as testicular cancer from illegal anabolic steroids. Hooked on the hospital support groups and especially on the alternate identity adopted at "Being Men Together," Norton joins other support sessions as well, each time shifting his name and identifying data and disease. His schedule includes brain cancer, lung cancer, intestinal parasites, and other improbable but incurable diseases.

All is going well for Norton, until he spots Marla Singer (Helena Bonham Carter) frequenting his support groups. She is easily identifiable at "Being Men Together," and her constant cigarette smoking is almost as out of place among the lung cancer survivors. After the testicular cancer meeting, Norton confronts the half-crazed, chain-smoking, pill-popping Singer in the street, denouncing her as a "tourist" and demanding that they split their support group schedule between them. He impatiently explains that he cannot cry in the presence of another faker but cannot risk losing out on his sleep, which will surely happen if he is deprived of this emotional outlet. She eventually consents to this arrangement but not until after insisting that she has more right to visit "Being Men Together" than he, because "he still has balls, whereas she doesn't."

For the first half of the film, the dark humor is hilarious, and Norton's deadpan first-person narration is a load of laughs. We are not prepared for the vicious shift that takes place later, when Norton switches identities with Tyler Durden (Brad Pitt), in a scene that lies somewhere between *Jekyll & Hyde* and *The Student of Prague*. Most of us first meet Tyler Durden on a plane, sitting next to the ever-despondent Norton, who is en route to investigate an auto accident for his insurance adjuster employer. (A truly astute observer might have seen Durden standing behind Norton, for a flash, as the two crossed in opposite directions at the airport.)

Durden is pleasant and affable, but bizarrely dressed and slightly unkempt. He explains that he sells soap and tells the buttoned-down Norton how to make explosives from simple household chemicals. The lonely Norton welcomes his company, proclaiming Durden to be his "best single-serving friend" in his lonely world of single-serving airplane portions. Before we grasp the hidden implications behind Norton's praise for his newfound companion, the plane goes through some sort of gyration. Their conversation is interrupted, and there is a temporary rupture in time, which we see on the screen. There is also a rupture in something else, in Norton's sense of self, which we realize only in retrospect. Right then, all we see is that the plane regains its path, the flight ends safely, and the two part company . . . but just for a while.

When Norton attempts to exit the airport's baggage claim section, he is stopped by airport security, because someone suspects that his vibrating suitcase contains either a bomb or a battery-operated dildo. The incident seems like comic relief at the time and assumes importance only when we reflect upon it later. Then, when the paleface, plain-talking Norton returns to his Ikea-equipped condo, he finds that his condo has been bombed. The rest of the building is still standing, undisturbed. Without anywhere else to go, Norton calls Durden, whose card he collected on the plane. He then proceeds to a very dismal part of town, where Durden lives in a neglected building, that is completely unlike Norton's neatly manicured apartment. Now the action starts.

Norton learns that Durden works as a film projectionist, but only at night. During the day, he sells overpriced soap, handmade from cellulite that plastic surgeons suck out of rich women by day and that he steals from garbage bins by evening. Durden also works as a waiter at upscale catering events, where he secretly urinates in the food. By night, Durden grows even more transgressive; he splices shots of penises into ordinary film to startle and shock audiences.

Most significantly, Durden wants Norton to hit him and to learn to fight. With the two of them tumbling and rumbling together outside near an abandoned building, they attract a crowd of other men, who are just as eager to learn to fight. "Fight Club" has unofficially started.

With Durden as its inspiration and instigator and Norton as its more compliant, corporate-type organizer, Fight Club grows and grows and grows. It assumes a dark dimension that is totally different from the funny first part of the film. Men of all sorts attend Fight Club, huddled together in a basement before expanding so much that they overtake Durden and Norton's house (and symbolically inhabit every aspect of his existence). Some wear suits, some are young and handsome, some are black, some are brown, some are yellow, and some are blond. Most are service personnel or working class. All enjoy being pummeled and pummeling, to regain their masculine identities that they allegedly lost in a world run by women. In other words, pure id breaks loose in Fight Club, and unrestrained violence follows, in the absence of tempering feminine influence. Except for a few bedroom scenes with Marla Singer,

Fight Club is a world of men, for men, and by men. It is also a world of night.

Norton eventually leaves his "day job," but only after extorting a full salary and a supply of airplane tickets, because he hit himself in his boss' office to make it appear as though his boss had assaulted him. Now that Fight Club has acquired "corporate sponsorship," Norton is free to devote himself completely to Fight Club.

The club expands to other cities. It expands it scope, as well, and splinters off into "Project Mayhem," which stages random acts of violence throughout town. Project Mayhem becomes such a threat to society that the police chief organizes a meeting to stop its ascent. The police chief's efforts are thwarted when Fight Club members kidnap him, pin him down on the ground in a hotel bathroom, and threaten him with castration.

Throughout all this, Norton remains completely convinced that he personally is just a passive participant and that Tyler Durden is the brains beyond the secret society—until Fight Club members in other cities salute Norton as their leader. Norton finally grows suspicious and starts to retrace his tracks by traveling to those seedling Fight Club cities and asking Fight Club followers who he is. All insist that it is he who started Fight Club and that it was he who flew to other cities to start new chapters.

Eventually, Norton realizes that Tyler Durden does not really exist but is not completely convinced until he sees that Durden is not hit by a bullet from a gun he fires. To be extra sure, he quizzes Marla about their relationship, knowing full well that she was once Tyler Durden's abused lover but that she had no physical contact with the nerdy Norton. Slowly but surely, he and the audience become aware that Norton and Durden are one and the same and that Norton became Tyler Durden on those nights when he should have been sleeping. It appears that it was none other than Norton who projected pornographic images during night cinema screenings, when he should have been dreaming.

The truth is now known to Norton, but it is too late. He, and he alone, is the leader and founder of Fight Club. But Project Mayhem has become independent of Fight Club and is completely out of control. Perfectly orchestrated plans to blow up buildings throughout the city are in place.

Norton tries to stop the destruction, but his own men stop him. They hold him down and try to castrate him, informing him that he himself instructed them to do just that, if ever he tried to interfere with the functioning of Fight Club. Fearing that he will harm Marla because she is the only real link between him and his alter ego as Tyler Durden, he sends her away on a bus.

Alone, Norton ascends the top of a tall building, but Tyler Durden appears (in pseudo-Superman style). Desperate to destroy Tyler, whom Norton now recognizes as a splinter of himself, Norton puts a gun in his mouth to kill himself. He pulls the trigger but does not succeed in suicide. He only manages to blow a hole through his jaw. But Tyler disappears.

Marla reappears at this moment, struggling and confused and angry as she is carried in, horizontal, by Norton's men. In the final scene, Marla and Norton stand together, side by side, and gaze into the glowing sky, as buildings are bombed and as explosives light up the night. This last scene is a strange substitute for the romantic sunset and serves as a wonderful counterpoint to the cliched close.

Again, the theme of dream is nothing more than a minor theme in *Fight Club*, which has a much greater emphasis on issues of identity, masculinity, and castration anxiety than on sleep and dream per se. *Fight Club* presents castration as the ultimate act of emasculation, and contrasts it with uncontrolled animalistic aggression—the ultimate statement of masculinity—but shows no world in between. *Fight Club* also comments on the vacuousness of material comfort in an affluent society and on the need to express raw emotion and animal-like existence in the face of advanced civilization and serious consumerism.

On a psychological level, *Fight Club* has much in common with the famous silent film *The Student of Prague*, where the protagonist battled an imaginary double (doppelganger), who appeared in the mirror and assumed a real-life existence. Like *Lord of the Flies*, it documents the ease with which ordinary humans regress to a state of primitivism and animalism. Like *Jekyll and Hyde*, it depicts the dark side of human nature, which was no new concept whatsoever, considering that this dark side was well-documented in centuries past but was attributed to the Devil before these same attributes assumed psychological proportions. It also appears throughout the Bible in brothers Cain and Abel, twins Jacob and Esau, and others.

How do sleep and dreams fit into this formula? Do we even need to consider the impact of Norton's initial insomnia, given all that has gone on? For those of us living in post-Freudian society, we do indeed need to see the statement that *Fight Club* makes about dreams. For *Fight Club*, dreams are synonymous with "wish fulfillment," just as they were for Freud. Dreams offer us an opportunity to indulge in acts which the censorious superego would not permit during ordinary waking consciousness. Dreams provide an imaginary outlet for primitive, regressive desires, and what could be more regressive than the savage and uncivilized state that Fight Club members seek? Fight Club offers an arena for action and actualization of these impulses, whereas sleep literally produces physical paralysis. The dreams that accompany sleep translate these innate urges into images and render then innocuous.

For most people in the Western world, dreams and fantasies are acceptable channels for unacceptable desires and are easily distinguished from everyday reality. (However, there are many nonindustrialized tribes which regard dream activity as essentially the same as waking activity and punish dream perpetrators as much for their sleep visions as for their daily deeds.)[1] But we shall judge *Fight Club* by our own standards. Fight Club founder, "Norton," never expressed any desire to divest himself of his dreams. On the contrary, Norton desperately sought sleep, enough to consult a doctor, an uncaring one at that, and enough to trek off to those strange support groups for solace. It was only after Norton lost sleep, night after night, and was involuntarily deprived of the opportunity to dream that he lost the safety valve available through sleep. If we mentally play the film in reverse, we see that *Fight Club* would never have happened had Norton been able to sleep.

This is a rather remarkable message about the evolutionary purpose of sleep and dreams, which is all the more distinct when compared to the supernatural sheen that dreams have acquired during the New Age. The author of *Fight Club* is no romantic or neoromantic. Unlike Jean-Jacques Rousseau, who glorified the virtues of "natural man" and lamented that "man is born free, but everywhere he is in chains," *Fight Club*'s creator Chuck Paluhkian sees only dark days ahead for those who set themselves completely free of society.

Unfortunately, this message was diluted, if not lost altogether, because a few intensely violent scenes diverted the audience's attention away from more significant philosophical and psychological issues, which were written into the novel by the same name. Rather than realizing that the film is warning us about the dangers of unrestrained id, what we see is a bloody and brutal mess. I suspect that the edited British edition of *Fight Club*, which eliminated some of the more gruesome fight scenes from the second half of the film, may make its point better. For *Fight Club*, in many ways, is simply a restatement of statements already made in *Civilization and Its Discontents*, where Freud said, specifically, that civilization cannot exist unless some instincts are suppressed, so that they can be sublimated into loftier levels of expression.

Fight Club also begs for Jungian interpretation, because it demonstrates Jung's concept of "coniunctio" so perfectly. The coniunctio supposedly occurs when the self meets the other, usually in a dream sequence. During the coniunctio (derived from the Latin word for "conjugation"), the two opposites unite and merge into a single, seamless whole. Jung placed great weight on the other or the "shadow self" in his broader philosophy. He also accorded these secondary selves equal value, rather than relegating them to the second-class status that Freud did. Jung aspired to reunite and to incorporate these opposing selves, rather than to repress or overpower them. Jung posited his gentler goal of coniunctio, to replace Freud's critical and often quoted credo, "where id was, ego shall reign."

The fact that *Fight Club*'s action took place in a substitute dream state and that Tyler Durden was indeed "Norton's" repressed other makes us wonder if the story's author, Chuck Paluhkian, was versed in Jungian psychology as well as Freudian. However, there is a caveat to this Jungian interpretation: according to Jungian theory, this meeting with the other during dream should result in a rapproachement of the two opposing selves or in the coniunctio or tying together of these opposing personality elements. But Tyler Durden and "Norton's" final scene together does not result in the reunion of the two distinct personalities. Just the opposite occurs: Norton has to shoot himself in an attempted suicide, so that he can divest himself of the destructive impulses embodied in Tyler Durden.

Miraculously, Norton survives the self-inflicted gunshot, not as a unified and integrated and "individuated" person (to use another Jungian term), but simply as someone with a gaping hole in his face. Norton's physical presence now mirrors his inner emptiness and his deficient sense of self. The coniunctio has failed, in the end, but perhaps only because Norton aspired to destroy his other self completely, rather than to integrate it, as Jungian ideals advocated.

A hard-cord Freudian would say that Norton's wounded face goes one step beyond castration to create an open orifice, which symbolizes more extreme emasculation and further feminization. However, a diehard Jungian would say that the curative coniunctio could have occurred and that Norton and Durden's opposing powers could have fused had Norton had the chance to sleep and dream, and to work out his conflicts during the appropriate nocturnal reverie (and with the aid of a qualified Jungian analyst). Maybe that is so, maybe not. We have no way of knowing.

What is certain, though, is that *Fight Club* presents a most pessimistic view of postmodern man. Having identified that, let us turn back in time to the romantic era of the late eighteenth century to see a very different approach to dream.

NOTE

1. Tedlock, Barbara. *Dreaming*. New York: Cambridge University Press, 1987; Frazer, Sir James. *The New Golden Bough* (abridged). New York: Criterion, 1956.

8

Deities and Demons

SUPERNATURAL SLEEP

At the turn of the twenty-first century, most people attribute dreams to internal, individual inspirations.[1] When asked directly, the majority say that dreams come from the unconscious. This belief is so common that it is woven into the fabric of contemporary culture, to the point that it has become part of our "collective consciousness."[2]

Not all cultures believe that dreams arise from something inside the individual. Some contemporary cultures and many more ancient cultures think that dreams are imposed by a force that resides outside the individual. The belief in the internal, individual origin of dreams did not gain widespread acceptance until the Romantic Era of the nineteenth century.[3] Psychoanalysis codified this idea around the turn of the twentieth century. By the mid-twentieth century, the concept of the unconscious origin of dreams was thoroughly intertwined with Euro-American thought.

Yet for most of humankind's history, sleep states were closely connected to supernatural states.[4] It makes sense that ancient peoples concerned themselves with the supernatural sources of dreams, considering that they also focused on the supernatural sources of grains, or grapes, or weather, or cattle, or children. It is ironic that concerns about the supernatural or "spiritual" sources of dreams resurfaced near the end of the twentieth century and that such concerns are often expressed in the psycho-spiritual language of Jungian psychology, which combines twentieth century depth psychology with arcane occult ideas.

For societies that believed that dreams were governed by deities and demons, rather than by individual dreamers, it was critical to determine whether the dream came from a divine or a demonic source. Making such a determination was a complicated job that was best left to specialists. A profession dedicated to interpreting dreams and identifying their sources developed. Practitioners were known as "oneiromancers." Freud and Jung were oneiromancers of sorts, although it sounds strange to put twentieth century psychoanalysts in the same category as first century necromancers (who conjured the dead) or soothsayers (who told fortunes) or augurers (who found supernatural secrets in, say, the intestinal folds of dead animals).

Dreams induced by drug or drink were not necessarily dismissed, as they might be today. Nor were they necessarily categorized as natural, although they followed an obvious and identifiable physical stimulus. On the contrary, because they catalyzed contact with the supernatural and accessed supernatural sources more quickly and reliably than otherwise possible, these psychoactive sacraments were presumed to possess supernatural properties of their own.

In contrast, the Old Testament and the Jewish Talmud made a point of condemning the drug-induced dreams of idolaters. That was one way to separate Hebrew prophecies from competing pagan prophecies and to promote the Hebrews' unique visions and revelations. This opinion was unpopular at the time and went against the grain of the ancient world. These Old Testament ideas are a cornerstone—and a counterpoint—for many of our current ideas about dreams in general and about dreams and drugs in particular. So, they deserve our immediate attention.

SLEEP IN THE ANCIENT NEAR EAST

The oldest of the Old Testament stories occur against the backdrop of the ancient Near East. Before the Hebrew tribes arrived in Canaan, this region was inhabited by Sumerians, Assyrians, and Babylonians, in that order. These people were the polytheistic idol worshipers who were described by and despised by Old Testament prophets. They are the people who left huge stone statues in what is now Iraq, some of which are now on display in the British Museum and at the Metropolitan Museum of Art.

Archaeologists who unearthed the remains of their cities and their libraries added to our awareness of these complex pre-Biblical civilizations. Professor Leo Oppenheim made especially impressive contributions to our knowledge of dreams and ancient Mesopotamia when he reviewed the cuneiform dream books found in the library of King Ashurbanipal and compared them to Biblical accounts.[5] Those cuneiform books dated to the seventh century B.C.E., around the same time that the Old Testament book of Deuteronomy was "rediscovered." Oppenheim was already well established as a scholar of pre-Israelite civilizations when he coauthored a book, *The Interpretation of Dreams in the Ancient Near East*, with Freud. This collaboration lent academic and anthropological support to Freud's daring ideas about dreams and was another factor that helped anchor Freudian theory in the broader intellectual framework of the twentieth century.

Professor Oppenheim found references to three types of dreams: (1) the message dream (which revealed divine messages to kings and important political figures), (2) the "symptomatic" dream (which concerned the physical or spiritual health of the dreamer), and (3) the "mantic" or prophetic dream (which stressed apocalyptic themes of world destruction). Dismally depressive "prophetic" dreams about the end of the world were common and were very much in keeping with the generally morose mentality of Ancient Assyria.[6]

These destructive dreams would repeat themselves in the Old Testament Book of Daniel. The Book of Daniel, in turn, foreshadowed the cosmic catastrophes described in the New Testament visions of Revelations. These end-of-days dreams were worlds apart from the Hebrew prophet Isaiah's idyllic dream of world peace and pastoral landscapes. Isaiah envisioned an earthly kingdom where the "lion would lie down with the lamb" and "nations would beat their swords into sickles." Even the Old Testament Prophet Ezekiel's visions of the "valley of dry bones" was more optimistic than these other dreams, because Ezekiel's death imagery referred to an era when the dead will rise from their graves and live again.

In the Sumerian literature, a dream foretold of a coming flood. This Sumerian flood story is strikingly similar to the flood that Noah escaped in his ark, in the book of Genesis.[7] But the Hebrew version has a happy ending and tells of the world being repopulated, through Noah's efforts and, of course, through divine intervention. The *Epic of Gilgamesh*—the literary and mythological masterpiece of the Sumerians—tells of an even more dismal dream, where Gilgamesh's friend Enkidu found himself alone in the universe. Then the death deity appeared to him and dragged him off to the underworld.

Given the way that Sumerian dreams typically foretold impending doom, it is not surprising that they attributed dreams to demons and other malevolent deities who dwelled in the underworld. These catastrophic cuneiform dreams were similar in tone to the end-of-days dreams reported by LSD users and by some schizophrenics. They are reminiscent of records from "psycholytic therapy" conducted when LSD was still legal and the source of legitimate scientific study.[8] Such doomsday dreams can signal the onset of spontaneously occurring schizophrenic episodes.

Such dreams of world destruction are nearly universal and are not confined to the ancient Near East, or any place else. They recur in the

myths of completely unrelated peoples who have no cultural or biological connection to one another. Some theorists, such as Jung, claimed
that these concepts are biologically based and are inherited through a
hypothetical "collective unconscious" or "racial unconscious." Yet it
seems more reasonable to think that the human mind can perceive
ordinary climatic events, such as heavy rainstorms and thundershow-
ers and lightning bolts, and transmute this imagery into nocturnal
visions. The mind amplifies these events into monumental significance
and translates them into the language of dreams and delusions. These
dreams, in turn, become encoded as myth and enshrined as universal
truth.[9]

In the ancient Near East, dreams were associated with the all-important practice of prophecy. As a result, dreams acquired a special social
and supernatural significance. Someone could stamp a message with
an extra seal of authority and authenticity, by claiming that his or her
message arrived via dream. Similarly, someone who reported an accurate or predictive dream could be seen as a prophet or a seer. The
ancients' belief in the authority of dream is the polar opposite of
contemporary culture, which dismisses false or flighty ideas as "just a
dream."

The ancient Near East did not accept all messages that arrived
through dream as sacred. Deciding which dream messages represented
true prophecy, as opposed to false prophecy, was a difficult endeavor
that stimulated lengthy Talmudic debates. Different societies devised
different rules and regulations governing dreams and prophecies.
Many societies found it easier to identify special persons (such as
priestesses or prophets) as their designated dreamers, or special circumstances (such as sacred sites or sacred times) could be set aside, for
receiving sacred dreams. The ancient Hebrews showed striking ambiv-
alence in their approach to these matters and often adopted the very
attitudes and practices that their prophets despised.

The Hebrews strived to carve out a unique culture and religion in
Canaan. Yet they absorbed many customs and concerns of neighboring
pagan peoples. They also carried Egyptian ideas about dreams with
them, even before they arrived in Canaan. The wandering Israelite
tribes had come into contact with Egyptian beliefs during the hundreds of years that they spent enslaved in Egypt, before Moses led
them through their historic nomadic sojourns in the desert. They
fused those residual Egyptian ideas with newer Semitic concepts
acquired from the "idol-worshipping" inhabitants of Canaan. The
prophets tried their best to dissuade the people from adopting these
practices, but they were not particularly successful. Much Biblical
literature documents the cultural and philosophical and religious
tug-of-war that followed.

Though the Biblical book of Deuteronomy specifically invokes the death penalty against the witches and sorcerers who foretell the future through dreams, several sources state that the Israelite nation practiced these perennially popular dream divination techniques. The book of Samuel, one of the older books of the Old Testament, says that "the Lord did not answer [Saul, the first king of Israel], either by dreams or by lots or by prophets" (1 Samuel 28.6). Biblical commentators read into this passage that it shows that the Hebrews attributed dreams to divine sources, at a time when their pagan counterparts ascribed dreams to "demons of the night."

The Hebrew tribes borrowed another colorful belief from the surrounding Assyro-Babylonian culture, this time concerning the female night demoness named "Lilith." Lilith is mentioned twice in the Old Testament and enjoys a prominent place in the Midrashic explanations of the creation story. It was said that these Liliths attacked men in their sleep, and enticed them into involuntary copulation, and caused seemingly spontaneous nocturnal emissions. Lilith played another important role in Biblical lore. The rabbinical Biblical commentators theorized that the first human was an hermaphrodite, with one side woman and one side man. The female half was named Lilith, but she flew away, after she was cleaved from Adam and learned that her male half expected her to lie under him. According to this legend, the more compliant Eve was created from Adam's rib after Lilith's departure.

Some twentieth century feminists glorified these legendary Liliths. A Jewish feminist magazine bears the name *Lilith*. In *Nightmare Alley*, which is one of the finest examples of 1940s "film noir," the female lead is a demonic "consulting psychologist" named Lilith. Like her ancient Near Eastern counterparts, this filmic Lilith preys upon sleeping victims. Rather than having intercourse with them, as the ancient Liliths did, this twentieth century Lilith extracts damning details about her patients' pasts, by listening to their dreams during Freudian-like psychoanalytic sessions. She proceeds to extort these trusting and troubled dreamers, through the help of a male accomplice, whom she also destroys in the end.[10]

These nocturnal demons and demonesses of ancient Assyria and Israel resurfaced as succuba and incubi in the European Middle Ages. Their presence was dreaded, because persons who consorted with succuba were suspected of consorting with the Devil and could be doomed to the death penalty. These succuba and incubi star in the art of Henri Fuseli's illustration *The Nightmare*. A copy of this famous romantic-era painting hung on the wall of Freud's apartment in Vienna. It also appears in Jung's last book, *Man and His Symbols*. A black-and-white print appropriately appeared on the bookplate of Ernest Jones' book *On The Nightmare*. In this book, Jones amplified Freudian dream theory and proved that these beliefs about nocturnal sexual activity are nearly universal, and are not confined to a single culture.[11] The same plate metamorphosized again as a movie poster for *Gothic,* Ken Russell's tongue-in-cheek film about the writing of Mary Shelley's *Frankenstein.*[12]

OLD TESTAMENT AND THE ANCIENT ISRAELITES

The Old Testament can be even more interesting than the cuneiform clay tablets discussed previously, because it collates information about several cultures in the same place. While it focuses on the "sacred history" of the Children of Israel, it also alludes to the Canaanites, Egyptians, Babylonians, Sumerians, Assyrians, Greeks, Philistines, Persians, Medes, and many more "nations" who interacted with the Twelve Israelite Tribes. As a written document handed down dutifully through the ages, the Old Testament is a more complete source than broken bits of clay or incompletely preserved papyri. The Old Testament is also the threshold to the New Testament, at times foreshadowing the New Testament and at other times standing as a counterpoint to the New Testament.

The New Testament has many, many references to dreams, as does the Old Testament. These dream tales reaffirm the supernatural significance of dreams, over and over again. The cultural, literary, artistic, and even scientific impact of the Old Testament is too immense to require further comment here. We could fill an entire book with descriptions of dreams from the Old Testament and nothing but; but we will restrict ourselves to just a few selections, starting with the dreams of Joseph.

Joseph's dreams are the favorites of young children and so tend to remain in our memories indefinitely. Unlike some other Old Testament dreams, Joseph's dreams are straightforward enough for young minds to grasp. They have a narrative and a plot and translate well into a play. So well, in fact, that they inspired the musical *Joseph and His Amazing Technicolor Dream Coat.* Because Joseph's dreams revolve around his conflicts with his brothers, these chapters speak directly to children, who struggle with related conflicts with their siblings.

As the title of the Broadway hit implies, Joseph's saga revolves around his dreams. Had Hitchcock been a Biblical commentator, he would have said that Joseph's dreams are the "MacGuffin" that drive the plot. Dreams are both his undoing, near the beginning of his story, and dreams are instrumental to Joseph's triumph in the end.

The book of Genesis tells us that Joseph's attention-starved brothers sold him into slavery. They were jealous of his status as the favorite son of their father's favorite wife. Jacob had just given Joseph the "technicolored coat" that would gain both Biblical and Broadway fame. Joseph would make his way from the proverbial rags to riches, several times over. He would rise to high rank, after arriving in Egypt and working in the pharaoh's household. He would be also thrown into prison, after his rejection of the pharaoh's wife's sexual solicitations resulted in false accusations of sexual harassment. Joseph would regain his freedom and rise to even higher rank, by virtue of his dream-deciphering ability.

Long before Joseph arrived in Egypt, he was already an active dreamer and was dismissed by his brothers as a "Baal chalomoth," which, in Hebrew, means "dreamer." He told his brothers that he dreamed that the sun and moon and stars bowed down before him. Upon hearing these thinly-veiled dreams of grandeur, Joseph's siblings perceived that Joseph was telling them that they, like the stars, would bow down to him, as though he were the moon. Rather than winning their respect, as he expected, Joseph found himself wallowing at the bottom of a pit after his unrepentant brothers literally "dumped him in a ditch." Then they sold him to a passing caravan that was on its way to Egypt.

Because Joseph was literally blessed with an ability to interpret other peoples' dreams, he correctly interpreted the dreams of a butler and baker who shared his prison confines. He gained the attention of the pharaoh as a result, who asked for Joseph's help with his personal dreams. Joseph forecast seven years of famine after seven years of plenty for the land of Egypt, after identifying specific symbols in the pharaoh's dreams. Luckily for him, Joseph turned out to be right.

The Bible does not entertain the idea that Joseph used standard economic indicators to predict the future. Nor does it suggest that Joseph accumulated useful clues about the meaning of the dream content by observing the dreamers' demeanors, as they retold their tales. Yet it is entirely possible that Joseph noticed that the grass was green, that the tides were high, or saw other signals that suggested that drought was not yet approaching, and then deduced that feast would be first and that famine could follow. Joseph never suspected that his early dreams of the sun and the moon and the sheaves of grain bowing down before him in the field reflected his own desire to get more respect from his brothers. Only the post-Freudian reader is prepared to see Joseph's dreams as classic examples of the wish fulfillment dreams that Freud described.

Instead, all symbols in Joseph's dreams are seen as supernatural. The number symbolism in these dreams is especially significant. Joseph ascribes his ability to interpret dreams to his God, Jahweh, rather than claiming credit himself or, even worse, leaving himself open to suspicions of sorcery. Some Biblical interpreters say that the Bible was acutely aware that Joseph could be confused with heathen demons whose names begin with the epithet "Baal," because he was described as a "*Baal* chalomot," which literally means "master of dreams." But "Baal" was also the name of the primary pagan deity and a symbol of idolatry. So Genesis assures us that Joseph sought divine, rather than demonic, intervention to aid him in his dream interpretation.

Some 3,000 years later, Freud, in *The Interpretation of Dreams*, referred to the Joseph story. But Freud credited psychoanalytic theory, rather than divine inspiration, for his dream interpretations. Freud was concerned with distinguishing psychoanalysis from superstition, in much the same way that the Old Testament was preoccupied with distinguishing the divine from the demonic. When Freud emphasized the part played by his own intellectual ingenuity and scientific observations, he was as immodest as Joseph was modest.

Genesis presents another intriguing dream tale and another supreme example of sibling rivalry in its account of the Jacob and Esau struggle. Jacob (later the father of Joseph, who presented Joseph with the "dream coat") had betrayed his older brother Esau in a much earlier episode. Jacob had placed sheepskins over his smooth arms to trick his blind and dying father Isaac into believing that he was his hirsute warrior brother Esau, who was the firstborn and who was entitled to inherit his father's possessions.

Feeling his son's hairy forearms but unable to see him and the sheepskins directly, Isaac unwittingly gave Jacob the blessing that rightfully belonged to his brother Esau. Jacob received this birthright as planned, but he came to fear the wrath that would arise in Esau, when he learned that he had been swindled out of the family fortune. So Jacob fled his father's home and set up camp at Bethel, in Canaan. Jacob did not know that his random campsite was located on sacred ground.

Jacob fell asleep there and dreamed a dream, which confirmed his destiny. In his dream, "there was a ladder set up on the earth, and the top of it reached to heaven; and behold, the angels of God were ascending and descending on it! And behold, the Lord stood above it and said, 'I am the Lord, the God of Abraham your father, and the God of Isaac; the land on which you lie I will give to you and to your descendants; and your descendants shall be like the dust of the earth. . .' Then Jacob awoke from his sleep and said, 'Surely the Lord is in this place; and I did not know it.' And he was afraid, and said, 'How awesome is this place. This is none other than the house of God, and this is the gate of heaven.' " (Genesis 28)

Jacob's dream demonstrates the belief in sacred dreams that occur at sacred sites. Egyptian and Grecian "incubation" rites, performed in sacred temples, are variations on this theme. Similar practices occurred in the Indus Valley and continue in parts of rural India to this day.[13] Several Islamic cultures and Islamic-influenced cultures, also venerate these sacred sleep sites, as will be described in the section on Islam that follows. In fact, the belief that the gods send healing dreams to those who sleep in sacred sites is common enough to suggest that this myth results from universal human deduction, as well as direct cultural transmission.[14] Interestingly, dreams associated with the secular sacred site of the psychoanalytic session are also believed to have magical properties, curative properties that go above and beyond the ordinary dreams or daydreams experienced on an ordinary bed or sofa.

Over the years, the visionary imagery of Jacob's ladder attracted the attention of psychologists and mythographers and Biblical scholars and true believers. It also inspired poetic and cinematic and artistic adaptations. Visionary artists, including William Blake, produced profound "visual poetry" about these enigmatic Biblical verses. Unlike Joseph's more linear narrative, where dream sequences are integrated into a strong story line, Jacob's dream is too amorphous and ambiguous to permit easy retelling. That ambiguity makes it ideal for visual artists to add their own interpretations to the murky text.

An unusual film named *Jacob's Ladder* appeared in 1990. The screenplay was written by Bruce Joel Rubin, a Jewish-born playwright who spent four months in a Tibetan Buddhist monastery. The film successfully meshes two seemingly divergent traditions, as it chronicles the struggles of the "soul" between the time of death and the moment of "rebirth." It compares the "betwixt and between" state described in the Hebrew Bible with the Tibetan "intermediary" state of the "bardo." Because the action starts after the lead character smokes a "cigarette," *Jacob's Ladder* draws also comparisons between established religious concepts and illicit drug effects.

The plot centers around the nightmarish existence of a young man, eking out a living in a post office. He drives through garbage-laden streets of Brooklyn, where cars zoom past him carrying people who peer out at him, their faces menacingly distorted. Eventually, the film's Jacob is wounded and whisked down a hospital corridor, apparently near death. Although the astute observer notices clues earlier on, most viewers must wait until the end of the film to learn that the protagonist was technically dead before the action began. Jacob had been shot while serving in Vietnam. Like the Patriarch Jacob, the film's protagonist, played by Tim Robbins, was living in a netherworld, experiencing a dreamlike alternative reality during the time that he spent passing from earthly life to celestial life. It is completely unclear how much plant chemicals in his last cigarette contributed to his condition.

We are reminded of the many points of convergence and divergence between Old Testament approaches to dream and Tibetan Buddhist parallels. Unlike the Western tradition that the Old Testament ignited, Buddhism does not distinguish between dreaming and waking states, and does not summarily dismiss ideas imparted during dream, and does not disregard chemically-inspired insights. Rather, Tibetan Buddhism looks to dreams for both spiritual guidance and for medical diagnosis. Like the Hindu Ayurvedic healers who set the foundation for Tibetan medicine many centuries earlier, Tibetan pulse doctors identify diseases of internal organs through dream symbols of the sick patient.[15] This method of medical diagnosis clearly contradicts Western empirical science and was one of many reasons why Chinese authorities refused to grant Tibetan traditional medicine the same status as Chinese herbalism or acupuncture.

On the other hand, the hallucinatory dreamworld described in *The Tibetan Book of the Dead* assumed special significance to the drug culture of the 1960s. Harvard psychologist-turned-LSD guru Timothy Leary rewrote the sacred Tibetan text for American audiences and pointed out the parallels between the hallucinatory state of death, the hallucinatory state of LSD, and the hallucinatory state of dream. Carl Jung's introductory essay on *The Tibetan Book of the Dead* called further attention to this eastern text.[16] Given the amount of attention they have received in the past few decades, it is conceivable that these Western approaches to Eastern thought will be assimilated into mainstream Western tradition at some point in the near future.

ANCIENT EGYPT AND MODERN ISLAM

When we think of Egypt, we think of pyramids and the mummies buried within them. We think of hieroglyphics and papyri, of Nefertiti and pharaohs, and the Sphinx. In short, we think of archaeological remains and a material culture devoted to the elaborate Egyptian death cult and the desert tombs.

Yet the Egyptians were also concerned about dreams, dream interpretation, and "dream incubation." Their ideas about dreams were integrated into their death cult, because they believed that sleep prepares people for death. They thought that both the sleeping soul and the dead soul wander through the same paradises and purgatories. Dreams had important political, as well as metaphysical, implications for the ancient Egyptians. The Great Sphinx itself bears an inscription of a pharaoh's dream on a stele, nestled between its paws. The stele states that the pharaoh Thothmes IV received instructions from the Sun God Ra, who appeared to him during a dream in the form of "Horus on the Horizon." Horus informed the prince that the deities planned to give him the Kingdom of Egypt. This same dream messenger told Thothmes to salvage the Sphinx from its current state of neglect. When the prince ascended the throne of Egypt, he freed the Sphinx from its premature burial beneath the desert sand and restored the monument to its original magnificence. He proceeded to inscribe the details of his dream onto pink granite.

Thothmes' dream was typical of political dreams of the ancient world. He stamped his self-serving message with the authority of the supernatural when he said that it arrived through the medium of dream. The ancient Hebrews parroted this Egyptian practice of invoking authority and authenticity through dream. Moses also received word of his divine mission during a dreamlike vision. It made sense that Moses turned to this Egyptian custom, given that he was reared in the pharaoh's household since infancy and became acculturated into Egyptian tradition.

Other ancient Egyptian documents offer even more details about dreams. Papyrus Chester Beatty III records a dream interpretation tradition from the Middle Kingdom period (2000–1785 B.C.E.). This papyrus ascribes meanings to different dream symbols. For instance, a snake means prosperity, whereas a dead ox foretells the death of one's enemies. This papyrus made it clear that oneiromancy was an already established profession.

The Egyptian approach to dreams has special significance to psychoanalysis, because Freud was fascinated with Egyptology and called psychoanalysis the "archaeology of the mind." He filled his house with Egyptian artifacts, and devoted half his antiquities collection to Egyptian items. These artifacts remain on full view at the Freud Museum, housed in Freud's second home in North London. In their own way, these small-size mementos rival the mammoth-size assemblage of Egyptology that is on display at the British Museum in central London.[17]

Today, Egypt is largely Islamic, populated by people who are ethnically and religiously distinct from the ancient Egyptian pyramid-builders described by the Bible. The Islamic religion practiced by Egypt's modern citizens has no relationship to the religious systems of the pharaohs. Yet Islam has its own fascinating relationship to dreams and to other altered states of consciousness. Mohammed, the founder and prophet of Islam, was said to be an epileptic, who received divine messages during his seizure-induced twilight states. As a result, Islam has shown special reverence for epileptics and others who enter unusual mental states.[18] Dreams, as the prototype of unusual mental states, receive special attention in Islamic lore.

Yet dreams are not always benevolent. In many Islamic countries to this day, people believe that dreamers can be possessed by a seductive spirit or *jinn*, who engages in intercourse with sleepers. This act can cause the dreamer to awaken in a psychotic state, with prominent sexual preoccupations. Some Islamic and North African folklore says that illnesses such as impotence can be contracted during dream. To cure these conditions, the healer must persuade the invading spirit to leave the body.

Such cures often require a pilgrimage to a healing shrine of a saint, where curative dreams can undo the damage done by the demonic *jinn* who entered during earlier dreams. This practice has been well documented among Moroccan Muslims. Moroccan Jews observe the same rites, even after they leave Morocco and relocate to Israel. Like their Islamic compatriots and like much earlier inhabitants of North Africa and Asia and the Greek Isles, distressed Moroccan Jews make lengthy and costly pilgrimages to religious shrines located at the gravesites of Sephardic Jewish saints.

In the West, we are very much aware of these ancient Islamic *jinn*, even if we do not immediately recognize them by their original name. American *jinn* have been filtered through the distorting lens of American pop culture. The television sitcom *I Dream of Jeannie*, of 1965, played upon the concept of the sexually provocative *jinn* who appears to men as they sleep. Yet the family-oriented television producers turned the temptress into an attractive but innocuous woman named "Jeannie" (Barbara Eden), who mysteriously appeared in modified and modest harem garb, whenever her master summoned her from her otherworldly abode.

Disney Studios did much more to perpetuate the Muslim concept of the *jinn*, through its blockbuster animated version of *Aladdin*. In *Aladdin* and in most other Western adaptations of "Oriental" lore, the destructive and demonic *jinn* becomes the servile and docile "genie," whom children adore, but who offends many Arabs and Arab Americans. Literary critics such as Edward Said elaborated on this point in the 1970s. His heirs in film criticism, who wrote about *Visions of the East*, claim that this tamed *jinn* serves as a metaphor for the taming of the Near Eastern-Islamic world by Western colonialists and imperialists.[19] According to this theory, these potentially destructive Islamic demons were rendered harmless, because they fell victim to Western domination. Critics, who are more psychologically than sociologically minded, might differ with Said and say that the transformations of threatening *jinn* to harmless genie assuages children's fears of sleep and dreams and convinces them that the demonic visions of "night terrors" are not as harmful as they seem on the surface.

Such Islamic dream cures persist in "Inani medicine." Inani is an unusual folk medicine that blends bygone Islamic and Greek medicine. It is based on the Greek system of the "humours." It has been preserved in Islamic parts of Pakistan, Persia (Iran), and Northwest India, having arrived there through Arabic-speaking physicians who translated Greek medical documents into Arabic many centuries earlier. The Islamic Indian healers are known as "pirs." These pirs continue to delve into their patients' dreams for clues to the diagnosis of both somatic and psychological disorders.

Needless to say, these dream-based diagnostic techniques are completely dissimilar to Western medical diagnostics, but some say that the practice serves a purpose. The pirs' approach to dreams is similar enough to psychoanalysis to merit mention in Sudhir Kakar's study of *Shamans, Mystics, and Doctors*. According to Kakar, a Delhi-born psychoanalyst who is not a physician, pirs operate in very humble conditions and provide bare-bones medical and spiritual care for people who cannot afford other outside intervention. It is a practice for the poor, by the poor, and might be dismissed outright were it not for the fact that it carries on a medical tradition that was once well-regarded, but which has since been replaced by more modern methods. It remains to be seen if medically-trained physicians agree that these dream-based diagnostics are valid spiritual supplements, as Kakar contends, or if they are outdated obstacles to more modern care.

ANCIENT GREEK CIVILIZATION

Greek civilization was amazingly complex, far too complex to cover in a small section on supernaturalism and superstition. Greek thought evolved over time, from its origins in the classical age of Homer, to the dawn of philosophy during Hellenic times, to the Greco-Roman period that coincided with the birth of Christianity. Greek civilization provided the foundation of the Western intellectual tradition.

Philosophy began in Greece, and philosophy was based upon reason, rather than superstition or presumption. E. R. Dodds' often-quoted volume, *The Greeks and the Irrational,* came as a surprise to many scholars, who thought that Greek thought headed toward the rational and left superstitious ideas behind. However, Dodds' eccentric-sounding theories have gained support since he first proposed them in 1951. Evidence suggests that Greek popular traditions that esteemed the irrational and the supernatural existed side by side with protoscientific and philosophical approaches to dreams. Interest in supernatural explanations of natural phenomena surged in direct response to the humiliating public defeat suffered during the Peloponnesian Wars.

This increased interest in supernaturalism revitalized interest in the Greek dream cult and in "dream incubation." Greek dream incubation had been practiced since ancient times and was similar to, if not the same as, Egyptian dream incubation. The purposes of dream incubation

changed over time. By the time Christianity arrived, the Greek dream
healing cult focused on dream cures for physical and psychological
ailments. The seeds of these theories appear in writings attributed to
"Hippocrates." Archaeological remnants of this dream cult are scattered throughout Greece and Sicily to this day.

It was believed that the deity Apollo healed through dreams,
through his agent Aesclepius (also known as Aesculapius). Sick people
journeyed to any of Aesclepius' 300 temples and slept there, hoping
that the deity would appear in a dream and heal them. They were
so eager for a cure that they were willing to believe that any figure
in their dreams was a messenger of the deity.[20] A Greek statesman
named Aristedes left elaborate letters about his own dream cure.
These letters have been incorporated in histories of medicine and
public health. Aristedes followed dream directions that told him to
purge, fast, and even amputate part of his finger to rid himself of
his somatic and psychic distress.

Though the special, sacred, "incubated" dream received complete
credit for the pilgrim-patient's cure, it appears that much more happened at the temple than simple incubation. This pilgrimage to the
Aesculapian temple was often a form of family therapy, because it
brought the patient together with the family and made the patient the
center of attention. Because the temple stay was so costly and time-consuming, the pilgrimage demanded that the family sacrifice for the sake
of the sick person, rather than scapegoat or ostracize him or her as might
otherwise happen. Staying in the temple was also a way for humble
people to spend time in an opulent environment that was not otherwise
available to them. Like the milieu therapy practiced in psychiatric
hospitals today, this temple stay was an opportunity to share experiences with strangers and get psychological support in the process.
Insightful or inspiring dreams probably did occur during this time,
since dreams often reflect the events that occur during the day. Such
dreams could conceivably change the attitudes of the dreamer.

The Greeks' belief in the healing powers of dreams anticipates psychoanalysis. A reference to the Aesculapian rites appears in Freud's *The
Interpretation of Dreams.* However, the Aesculapian rites credit the deity,
while psychoanalytic theory credits the psychoanalyst and the psychoanalytic process. Just the same, note that the psychoanalyst also assumes a godlike importance to the patient, through a difficult-to-
describe process known as "transference."

It is no coincidence that both Freud and Jung were thoroughly con-
versant with classical culture, as were other educated people of their
time. Both punctuated their writings and their conversations with
Greek and Latin quotes and gained additional authority by linking their

innovative ideas to a culture that enjoyed such a high status in the nineteenth and early twentieth century.

In *The Interpretation of Dreams,* Freud discussed yet another aspect of Greek dream lore: Artemidorus' book on dream symbols from the second century C.E. While he disparaged Artemidorus' dream symbology, Freud praised Artemidorus' personalized approach to dream interpretation and his willingness to ask questions about the dreamer's character, mood, and life situation before interpreting the dream.[21] Artemidorus' dream books remained in print over the centuries and are still consulted by many modern-day Greeks and Greek-speaking Greek Americans.[22] Artemidorus' symbolic approach is echoed by many New Age dream books, to the point that one wonders if this ancient text continues to influence American pop culture nearly two millennia later. Perhaps this interest in dream symbology is simply a reflection of a basic human tendency to manufacture meaning and does not need to be seeded by outside influences. It is equally possible that some New Age authors and audiences first learned about Artemidorus by reading Freud's arguments against him and then, in a fit of rage against Freud and all that he represents, returned to very same techniques that Freud criticized.

Greek and Greco-Roman culture also had a clear-cut influence on nascent Christianity, which was born from its midst. E. R. Dodds, who wrote *The Greeks and the Irrational,* researched the interrelationship between the cult of Christian saints and the earlier Greek incubation rites. Dodds theorized that the Christians retained earlier pagan dream practices but substituted their own saints for Aesclepius. The Eastern Orthodox Church perpetuated dream incubation in Cyprus and Constantinople, while the Roman Catholic Church incorporated dream incubation cures at Saint-Martin de Tours and at Saint-Julien de Brioude in France.[23]

CHRISTIANITY AND THE NEW TESTAMENT

By New Testament times, the authority of dreams was well established. The New Testament could draw upon dreams already described in the dream-laced Old Testament, and it could add new dreams to counter Old Testament accounts. The New Testament also reflected the surrounding Greco-Roman culture. Another curious influence on the New Testament dream texts were the "apocrypha" and "pseudiepigrapha."

The books of the apocrypha appeared during the so-called intertestamental period. The Old Testament was already codified, but the New Testament writings had not yet appeared. The validity of these apocryphal writings was hotly contested, to the point that the English word *apocryphal* became synonymous with the word *false*. The apocryphal books are excluded from official versions of both the Hebrew and the Protestant Bibles but are included in the Roman Catholic and the Greek Orthodox Bibles. The Jewish Talmud outlaws these books outright.

The bans against the apocrypha did not affect their popular appeal. Their dreamlike accounts are stylistically similar to the visionary episodes of the Old Testament's Daniel and Ezekiel. They foreshadow the New Testament's Book of Revelation. The Book of Enoch, the best known of these books, comes complete with elaborate descriptions of Enoch's walks with angels. Its flowery language appeals to people with strict religious sensibilities and to those with strictly secular artistic and literary mindsets.

The canonized version of the New Testament also contains many references to dreams. In the New Testament, as in the Old Testament, God communicates His will to humans through dreams. For instance, Joseph, the husband of Mary, was told to marry the pregnant Mary in a dream (Matthew 1:20). It is through a series of dreams that the Wise Men and Joseph learn that they must flee the evil King Herod, together with the infant Jesus and his mother Mary (Matthew 2). The Book of Acts tells us that Peter received a dream, advising him to accept the Gentile Cornelius as a convert (Acts 10:9). Paul's dream directed him to preach the Gospel in Macedonia (Acts 26:9).

A dream was responsible for the turning point in Church history and in Western history by default. The emperor Constantine decided to convert to Christianity because of directions received in a dream. Constantine's conversion legitimized Christianity and transformed it from a marginal cult to a statewide religion. From that time forward, Christianity became the dominant religious, cultural, and legal force in the West, if not also the world. World history would have been decisively different, were it not for this dream.

Dream induction eventually became just as important to Christianity as dream interpretation and dream incubation had been in the past. St. Joachim, the father of the Virgin Mary, deliberately induced a dream by going out to the desert and fasting for forty days and nights. This act mirrored the foodless forty days and forty nights that Moses spent on Mount Sinai, preparing to receive his message from Jahweh. These pre-Christian dream-induction techniques can be compared with the dream-induction techniques of the American Plains Indians and many other peoples.

Over the next several centuries, the "desert fathers" of Christianity emulated Joachim's isolation, asceticism, and dream induction. St. Anthony was the first of these desert fathers. Anthony's dreams became a favorite subject of artists, both because of their spiritual significance and because of their visual intensity. Matthias Grunwald's Isenheim Altarpiece, which is now found in a museum in Colmar, France, contains magnificent illustrations of the demons that tempted Anthony during his dreams.[24] The great fifteenth century fantasist Hieronymous Bosch left an equally wonderful rendition of St. Anthony's demonic dreams, as did surrealist artists such as Max Ernst.

Like their pagan Greek and Roman compatriots, the early Christians were preoccupied by the distinction between the body and the soul. Their debates about dreams reflect their concerns about the "mind-body problem." In E. R. Dodds' comparison of *Pagan and Christian in an Age of Anxiety*, he quotes the Christian thinker and theologian Maximus (d. 370 C.E.). Maximus recommended that one suppress the physical senses to perceive deeper truths sent from God directly. Dreams that result from the body or the senses drown out God's voice, according to Maximus and other early Christian colleagues.[25] Maximus recommended that one "strip away the outer garments, abolish in thought the preoccupation of the eyes, and in what remains [one] will see the true objects of your longing."

Maximus' repudiation of the senses in general and of sexual sensation in particular provide a colorful contrast to Freudian thought. Freud's theories called attention to the same sexual and sensual sources that repulsed early Christian thinkers such as Maximus. Rather than attempting to abolish his patients' sexual perceptions to make way for the "purer" or "truer" ideas sought by Christian theologians, Freud insisted that sexual instincts seeded higher ideas and were sublimated into other forms to disguise the true instinctual origins. Freud decoded dreams in order to unlock the sexual secrets that the Christian's ascetics strived to suppress.

This distinction between these two approaches to dreams—the Freudian psychoanalytic and the classic Christian—is profound. It is remarkable that Freud's ideas did not meet with even stronger opposition by devout Christians than they did. This difference in attitudes toward the senses and toward sex makes it even more understandable why Freud's early psychoanalytic circle was exclusively Jewish, at a time when the Austrian population was predominately Catholic. It is equally interesting that Carl Jung, who was the first non-Jew to enter the tightly-knit psychoanalytic circle, clashed with Freud on the influence of sex and the importance of religion. The son of a Protestant minister, Jung eventually decided that Freud's emphasis on sexuality was excessive and developed his own approach to psychoanalysis. Jungian analytical psychology depended heavily on dreams and stressed the significance of universal religious, occult, and mythological dream symbols instead. The next section on sorcerers and shamans will explore these issues in greater depth.

NOTES

1. This inference is based on a sample of 300 persons interviewed in college courses on dreams.

2. The term "collective consciousness" contrasts with Jung's concept of the "collective unconscious" and describes an idea that is culturally ingrained into most of society's members.

3. When Shakespeare suggested that there was a continuum between individual identity and personal dreams in the seventeenth century, when he said that "we are such stuff as dreams are made on," he foreshadowed psychoanalytic ideas.

4. There are many exceptions to this generalization. See Jacob Zimmel. *Magicians, Theologians, and Doctors*. New York: Aronson, 1997; Henry Sigerest. *A History of Medicine: Primitive and Archaic Medicine*. New York: Oxford University Press, 1951; Henry Sigerest. *A History of Medicine: Early Greek, Hindu and Persian Medicine*. New York: Oxford University Press, 1961; Jacob Neusner, Ernest Frerichs, and Paul Virgil McCracken Flesher. *Religion, Science and Magic*. New York: Oxford University Press, 1989.

5. Oppenheim, H. Leo. *The Interpretation of Dreams in the Ancient Near East*. Reprint. AMS Press, June 1958.

6. Eliade, Mircea, ed. *Encyclopedia of Religion*. New York: Macmillan, 1987.

7. Campbell, Joseph, ed. *Primitive Mythology*. Harmondsworth, U.K.: Penguin, 1976; Graves, Robert, and Raphael Patai. *Hebrew Myths*. New York: Greenwich, 1983; Gordon, Cyrus H. *The Ancient Near East*. New York: Norton, 1953; Hooke, S. H. *Middle Eastern Mythology*. Harmondsworth, U.K.: Penguin, 1963.

8. Grof, Stanislav. *Birth, Death, and Transcendence in Psychotherapy*. New York: State University of New York Press, 1986; Frazer, James G. *Folklore in the Old Testament*. New York: Macmillan, 1923.

9. Eliade, Mircea. *Myth, Dreams, and Mysteries*. New York: Harper, 1957.

10. Bergstrom, Janet, ed. *Endless Night. Cinema and Psychoanalysis: Parallel Histories*. Berkeley: University of California Press, 1999, 25–56.

11. Jones, Ernst. *On The Nightmare*. New York: Liveright, 1951. Jones, who achieved more fame from his biography of Freud than from his study of nightmares, devoted an entire volume to the cross-cultural study of succuba and incubi and found that myths about demonic dreams and nocturnal sexual activity are nearly universal and are not confined to the ancient Near East or the Middle Ages.

12. See chapter 10 on Reason and Romance for more information on Fuseli and dreams.

13. Kakar, Sudhir. *Shamans, Mystics, and Doctors: A Psychological Inquiry into India and Its Healing Traditions*. Chicago: University of Chicago Press, 1982.

14. This belief seems to be as common as the belief in sleep demons that Ernst Jones described in his book *On The Nightmare*, but deserves more study for final confirmation.

15. Sigerest, Henry. *A History of Medicine, Vol. I: Primitive and Archaic Medicine*. New York: Oxford University Press, 1951; *A History of Medicine, Vol. II: Early Greek, Hindu and Persian Medicine*. New York: Oxford University Press, 1961.

16. Evens-Wentz, W. Y. *The Tibetan Book of the Dead*, 3rd ed. London: Oxford University Press, 1960; Jung, C. G. Foreword: "A Psychological Commentary to the Tibetan Book of the Dead." *The Tibetan Book of the Dead*. 3rd ed. W. Y. Evens-Wentz, ed. London: Oxford University Press, 1960; Metzner, Ralph, Gordon Alpert, Karma Glin-Pa Bar do, and Timothy Leary. *The Psychedelic Experience. A Manual Based on the Tibetan Book of the Dead*. New York: Citadel, 1995.

17. Gay, Peter. *A Godless Jew: Freud, Atheism and the Making of Psychoanalysis.* New Haven, CT: Yale University Press, 1989; Gamwell, Lynn, and Richard Wells, eds. *Sigmund Freud and Art: His Personal Collection of Antiquities.* London: Thames and Hudson, 1989.

18. Pincus, Jonathan H., and Gary J. Tucker: *Behavioral Neurology.* 3rd ed. New York: Oxford University Press, 1985; Mora, George. "Historical and Theoretical Trends in Psychiatry." Harold I. Kaplan, Alfred M. Freedman, Benjamin Sadock, ed. *Comprehensive Textbook of Psychiatry.* 3 vols. Baltimore: Williams and Wilkins, 1980, 4–98; Alexander, Franz, and S. T. Selesnick. *The History of Psychiatry.* New York: Harper, 1966; Zilboorg, Gregory. *A History of Medical Psychology.* New York: Norton, 1941.

19. Nadel, Alan. "A Whole New (Disney) World Order: *Aladdin,* Atomic Power, and the Muslim Middle East." Matthew Bernstein and Gaylyn Studlar, eds. *Visions of the East: Orientalism in Film.* New Brunswick: Rutgers University Press, 1997, 184–206.

20. Rosen, George. *Madness and Society.* Chicago: University of Chicago Press, 1968.

21. Freud, Sigmund. Introduction. *The Interpretation of Dreams.* Trans. J. Strachey. New York: Norton, 1965.

22. Spanos, Dr. Stephanie, Greek Alliance for the Mentally Ill.

23. Coxhead, David, and Susan Heller. *Dreams.* New York: Thames and Hudson, 1976.

24. Packer, Sharon. "Jewish Mystical Movements and the European Ergot Epidemics." *Israel Journal of Psychiatry.* 35:3 (1998): 227–239; Packer, Sharon, and Warren Dotz. "Epidemic Ergotism, St. Anthony's Fire and Jewish Mysticism." *Dermatopathology: Practical and Conceptual.* 4:3 (July–Sept. 1998): 259–267; Hayum, Andree. *The Ishenheim Altarpiece: Gods' Medicine and the Painter's Vision.* Princeton, NJ: Princeton University Press, 1989; Mellinkoff, Ruth. *The Devil at Isenheim: Reflections of Popular Belief in Grunewald's Altarpiece.* Berkeley: University of California Press, 1988.

25. Kilbourne, Benjamin. "Dreams." *Encyclopedia of Religion.* Mircea Eliade, ed. New York: Macmillan and Free Press, 1987, 483–492.

9

Shamans and Sorcerers

MEDIEVALISM AND MODERNISM

In the twenty-first century, we labor over the distinctions between "mind" and "brain." We wonder if biological forces determine dream content, or if psychological influences play a role, or if there is a cultural contribution. Mostly, we debate about the chemicals, or electrical impulses, or physical forces that alter the dream.

Our contemporary philosophical concerns are the by-products of scientific discoveries of the late twentieth century.[1] The medieval world had an entirely different set of concerns, and the concerns of the Christian world were not necessarily the same as the concerns of their Islamic or Jewish contemporaries. The concerns of the medieval Christian revolved around the supernatural. Dreams could come from divine inspiration or demonic influence. It was up to the Church to decide the source and to determine if the dreamer was a saint or a sinner. Saints could enjoy the elaborate benefits of paradise, but often not until after they were martyred. Sinners faced the death sentence and often died in most unpleasant ways, particularly after the invention of the proverbial medieval torture chamber. Admitting that one dreamed invited the risk of scandal and execution and terrible trials. Just facing trial to decide whether someone was demonically "possessed" was a daunting and often deadly endeavor. As a result, most medieval people denied that they dreamed at all.

Ironically, many schisms and heresies began during this time, often because their founders had personal dreams that they presented as prophetic.[2] Millennial sects that preached about the end of days were particularly common during medieval times and often sprang from doomsday dreams. Sometimes, dreams led to a mainstream religious career. St. Francis of Assisi, whose selfless actions inspired the

Franciscan friars, cast off his possessions and lived in nature, in response to instructions he received during a dream. Other dreamers, such as Joan of Arc, did not fare as well as Francis. Joan's visions led to accusations of sorcery and eventual execution, though her dream-inspired military tactics sent her beloved France to victory. Joan would not be exonerated or beatified until after they burned her at the stake.

Medieval mystics routinely ascribed supernatural significance to perceptions that most modern people would identify as dreams or visions or maybe even migraine. Their writings do not distinguish between dream, vision, hallucination, or divine message. In modern medicine, in contrast, differentiating the nighttime dreams of ordinary people from the daytime hallucinations of schizophrenics is critical. It is even more necessary to distinguish the perceptual distortions produced by life-threatening medical conditions from more benign conditions such as migraine.

Like many of their predecessors, medieval people were indifferent to the distinction between drug-induced dream states and spontaneous dream states and focused on the divine/demonic distinction instead. In contrast, contemporary practitioners are acutely concerned with identifying withdrawal states and with preventing their potentially devastating consequences. For the medieval mind, it did not matter that witches and warlocks used plants and potions to induce artificially altered states. What mattered was their *intent* to conjure demonic powers. Anthropologist Michael Harner noted that the perception-altering henbane, wolfbane, and other herbs of medieval and Renaissance-era witches were pharmacologically similar to the plant hallucinogens used by Central American shamans. Yet medieval and Renaissance Europe marginalized its witches and condemned them to death. South and Central American shamans won admiration and respect in their respective cultures and earned high social status, even if they did live on the fringes of society.[3]

In spite of the dangers posed by dreaming during the European Middle Ages, there was widespread interest in dreams. Many dream books circulated during those times. Dreams may have been more common and more intense during medieval times, because ergot epidemics rocked parts of Western Europe repeatedly, between the tenth century and the eighteenth century. Ergot poisoning starts with strange dream states. Eventually, dreamlike visions occur during the waking state. Psychosis, strokes, or seizures may follow, if ingestion of the food-borne poison continues. These epidemics of ergotism primarily attacked poor people, because they consumed poor quality rye bread and grain-based beers infested with the same ergot-secreting bread mold used to manufacture LSD. These outbreaks were most intense in

France and Germany near the Rhineland but spread to many other regions. They persisted in Russia and Eastern Europe for centuries after they had been eliminated elsewhere.

Christian, Islamic, and Jewish mystical movements mushroomed at the same times and places when ergotism was most intense in Europe. During these mystical outbreaks, many individuals experienced ecstasies and visions, along with mystical or macabre dreams.[4] Members of different religious sects, who were segregated from one another, reported remarkably similar experiences, suggesting the presence of a biological or psychological rather than a cultural or philosophical source.

During those years, the Jewish mystical system known as Cabala became important. Cabala came complete with secret meanings and number mysticism and dream decoders. Cabalistic study suddenly spread to the masses during the Middle Ages, after having been confined to secluded groups of Jewish scholars in the past. Cabala even attracted the attention of mystically-inclined Christians, including the physician and alchemist Paracelsus, whom Jung discussed at length in his book about alchemy and psychology.

There is no doubt that Jung incorporated alchemical ideas about dreams directly. He wrote an entire chapter on alchemy and dreams. Jung never denied the crossover between his own theories and occultism. On the contrary, he cultivated the occult and looked for occult insights into the spiritual problems of modern man and the human condition overall. He specifically invited scholars of mysticism, such as Gershom Scholem and Erich Neumann, to his annual Eranos conferences in Switzerland.[5] He even wrote about Cabalistic passages and referred to the Cabalistic cum alchemical concept of the "Unio conunctionus" (union of opposites).

Freud's relationship to these medieval Jewish mystical ideas is more complex and less clear-cut than Jung's. Some overly enthusiastic theorists claim that Freud adapted his ideas about dreams and about sexual instincts from Cabalistic traditions. The evidence for these claims is still tangential at best, but there is no doubt that Cabalism claims that sexual urges galvanize both human and divine personality traits.[6] The parallels between Freud's approach to dreams and traditional Talmudic approaches to dreams are so profound that they will be discussed at length in a later chapter.

Freud himself never said that Jewish mysticism inspired his theories. Yet the fact remains that the writings of the Jewish mystical writer Schlomo Almoli circulated among the Hasidic people of Galicia, where Freud's relatives lived. It is not known if Freud came across a copy of Almoli's *The Interpretation of Dreams and Magic*, but it is known that he visited this region while on vacation when he was young.

DEMONS AND DREAMS

Freud was intrigued by these antiquated demonological explanations of dreams, as was his onetime mentor and teacher, the neurologist Jean-Martin Charcot. Once an artist himself, before pursuing medicine and neurology as a career, Charcot compiled illustrations of "demoni-acs" from the art of the past and published them in a book by this name.[7] Charcot diagnosed these "demoniacs" as hysterics or as end-stage syphilitics. Freud took a different direction but in 1923 wrote an equally interesting (but glaringly inaccurate) essay on a "demoniac" artist of the seventeenth century. This artist, Christoph Haitzmann, had seen a one-breasted devil during a series of dreams. Severely depressed and unable to work in his profession, he sought relief at Mariazel, a popular healing shrine near Vienna. Mariazel was sometimes known as the Lourdes of Middle Europe, on account of its famed miracle cures. It was customary for recovered patients to stay on at the monastery as brothers and to help heal others as they had been healed themselves.

Church officials dutifully recorded Haitzmann's ordeals and his treatment plan and left these manuscripts for posterity. Haitzmann was whipped by the brothers, who tried to drive away the demons that they held responsible for the artist's demonic visions. He eventually became partially paralyzed and died of a seizure, during the last of three episodes. As an artist, Haitzmann was able to draw his visions as well as he could describe them. Freud evaluated those drawings, along with other monks' manuscripts, three centuries later.

Interestingly, Haitzmann specified that his dreamy states of demonic possession occurred whenever he suddenly stopped drinking, after a temporary episode of "overindulgence." Note that "alcoholic hallucinosis" occurs on the day after cessation of prolonged alcohol consumption. Delirium tremens (d.t.'s) start on the second or third day. Vivid visions occur during either alcohol hallucinosis or d.t.'s, but d.t.'s can cause fatal seizures in 10 to 15 percent of untreated people.

Haitzmann also mentioned that he subsisted on a diet of grain-based dumplings, at a time when bread-spread ergot epidemics ravaged his native Bavaria. Ergot toxicity causes strange mental states, seizures, strokes, and waxing and waning paralysis and possible death, just as the artist suffered. Ergotism occurs earlier and more intensely in alcoholics, perhaps because of preexisting liver damage or an interaction between alcohol and ergot. We now know that undiagnosed ergotism was commonly "cured" when afflicted pilgrims visited shrines and ate where better quality, unblighted bread was donated to the clergy.[8]

Rather than searching for still-undiscovered scientific explanations for Haitzmann's symptoms, the Church masters who treated Haitzmann concerned themselves only with the supernatural source of

Haitzmann's demons. They did not consider that natural causes could be responsible for Haitzmann's afflictions and apparently believed that these dreamlike visions were real, rather than imagined. They were understandably unaware of the association between hallucinations and alcohol withdrawal, or between grain consumption and ergotism.

Somewhat more surprisingly, Freud's retrospective analysis also overlooked the chemical causes of Haitzmann's condition, although he did report that his subject suffered from intermittent paralysis and that he died of seizures that followed his delirious dreams. Freud focused instead on the patient's troubled relationship with his father, his remorse over his father's death, and his unexpressed sexual yearning for his father. As the founder of psychoanalysis, Freud confined his study to the reason behind the patient's dreams and delusions and showed no concern with their naturalistic cause. He analyzed the content of Haitzmann's visions according to psychoanalytic principles.

In his essay, Freud emphasized the distinction between his own explanation and the explanations offered by the Church masters. He contrasted his modern and scientific psychoanalytic and psychosexual approach to dreams with the Church's outdated supernatural approach. Ironically, Freud's strictly psychoanalytic interpretation of Haitzmann's dreams sounds as dated to us today as the supernaturalistic explanations sounded to him. In our era, most people are impressed by the fact that Haitzmann developed permanent partial paralysis, and ultimately died of a seizure, when he clearly had a potentially treatable poisoning or withdrawal syndrome.

ASSUMPTIONS ABOUT AUSTRALIAN ABORIGINALS

"Dreamtime" is a prominent theme in Australian Aboriginal lore. Aboriginal myth claims that the cosmos came into being during Dreamtime. As charming as this concept sounds on the surface, it turns out that the Aboriginal creation story does not revolve around dreams directly. Rather, "Dreamtime" is an inexact translation of an idea that defies translation. This dreamtime refers to a parallel place and time. The Aboriginals chose this term because no better English word was available.[9]

An Australian film attempts to clarify this idea or perhaps to exploit it. In *The Last Wave*, an idealistic young non-Aboriginal attorney (Richard Chamberlain) must defend several young urban Aboriginals who are accused of murder. The court expects some Aboriginal witnesses to testify against the true killer. Yet each of the accused denies knowledge that the deadly barroom brawl took place, though many people present saw them at the crime scene. The attorney attempts an innovative defense. He proposes that the innocent men were in Dreamtime when the crime was committed, and so cannot remember the events in question, and cannot be expected to identify the man who delivered the deadly blow.

The court is not convinced, because the prosecutor argues that urban Aboriginals are too out of contact with tribal belief to enter this Dreamtime. Richard Chamberlain becomes a believer in Dreamtime himself, after he chances upon a remote Aboriginal burial ground and becomes confused and disoriented in this timeless place. This burial ground comes complete with ancient totems that make for an ideal stage design. Chamberlain's psychological state spoke to the film's late 1970s audience, which was still familiar with the lore of the drug culture and with the concept of higher states of consciousness. The film ends with Chamberlain successfully defending his clients. He also wins back the respect of his family, who had come to doubt his legal abilities, his paternal commitment, and, above all, his sanity.

Though the authentic Aboriginal Dreamtime is not as dreamy as its name implies, there are other reasons why Aboriginals have a special relationship to dream. Certain tribes require their male members to live alone and apart from society, from the ages of fifteen through twenty-five. During these years of isolation in the desert, the young men develop a lifelong appreciation for the spirit world that surrounds them, because they have direct contact with unseen supernatural forces.

Since we know that isolation and sensory deprivation invite hallucinations and dreamlike visions, we can be confident that these tribesmen truly do experience protracted daytime dreams. Admiral Byrd's crew had similar experiences during their journey to the North Pole. After seeing nothing but glaciers for months on end, they saw visions and heard voices. Similarly, desert travelers who see only sand for protracted periods also see mirages of fountains and gardens. Considering that contemporary psychiatric research suggests that psychotic states are more persistent, if allowed to continue unchecked, it is feasible that prolonged daytime dreams may very well change a person's perceptions permanently.

The nineteenth century witnessed much interest in Aboriginal culture for several reasons. Freud's book *Totem and Taboo*, where he theorized about Aboriginal tribal rites, was one of a long line of scholarly works on this subject. Freud's work was strongly influenced by the writings of ethnologist Sir James Frazer (*The Golden Bough*). Frazer, in turn, was influenced by the nineteenth century anthropologist and Oxford anthropology chair, Sir Edward Tylor. Tylor felt that human dreams, rather than divine revelation, inspired unfounded beliefs in the soul, the spirit, and the supernatural. Later generations of anthropologists and historians of religion criticized Tylor's theories about dreams and the origins of religion. Still, Tylor's theories deserve study, because they reflect the nineteenth century fascination with the nodal point between the psychotic state, primitive religion, and the most common psychotic condition of all, the dream.[10]

SHAMANS AND SEERS

The subject of shamans and their mental states never fails to generate controversy. It is known that some shamanistic cultures recruit epileptics or schizophrenics as their shamans and that others identify shamans through initiatory dreams. As a result, many people equate shamanism with schizophrenia or epilepsy, and dismiss it as a manifestation of undiagnosed psychopathology, and refuse to recognize its spiritual or cultural significance. Other scholars take an opposite view and insist that someone who functions as a shaman cannot possibly be psychotic or epileptic, even if that shaman has the same altered perceptions as schizophrenics.[11]

We can put these polemics aside by confining our discussion to the initiatory dream of the Siberian shaman. Although Siberia is hardly the only culture that revolves around shamanism, Siberian shamanism is probably the best known and best studied and most debated of the many types of shamanism. The prolific historian of religion Mircea Eliade did field research in Siberia and expanded upon the records left by an eighteenth century Swedish military officer, who was imprisoned in Siberia for twelve years. Eliade meshed his firsthand observations with his vast knowledge of the history of religion and published all this information in *Shamanism: Archaic Rites of Ecstacy*.[12]

This 1974 book arrived at the right time, because Siberian shamanism had already attracted wide popular attention since the 1960s, once word got out that these shamans induced their shamanic dreams with the hallucinogenic Amanita mushroom. It was even more intriguing to learn that even ordinary villagers participated in this ritual by collecting the shaman's urine and drinking it, in order to imbibe some psychoactive chemicals that are excreted unchanged. The drug culture celebrated these acts of shamanic devotion as much as it venerated the chemicals contained in the mushrooms. These shamanic rites were spectacles that were worthy of the attention of the generation that invented rock concerts, happenings, be-ins, and other forms of audacity.

Eliade's topics appealed to the counterculture, but his staid, spiritually-oriented theories did not. Although he never denied that Siberian shamans used ceremonial plant drugs, Eliade felt that the shamanic vision occurred on a different spiritual plane. He was equally adamant in denying that shamans are schizophrenic or epileptic. As a true spiritual seeker himself, who had lived in various devotional communities after leaving his home in Romania, Eliade insisted that these shamans possessed spiritual powers that extended far beyond the psychedelic or the physical or the psychological stimuli that preceded their visions.[13]

The details of the "initiatory dreams" of these Siberian shamans cause less contention than the meaning of shamanism itself. In both Siberia and the Arctic, protoshamans are awakened to their callings by dreams that have fairly circumscribed themes. These dreams often concern dismemberment, followed by replacement of their internal organs and viscera. Eliade himself wrote about a shaman who dreamed that his limbs were removed and disjointed with iron hooks, his bones cleansed, his body fluids discarded, and his eyes torn from their sockets. These body parts were gathered up again and refastened with iron to produce this resynthesized shaman. Some shamans dream of being cooked alive. Dialogues with supernatural beings or spirits and souls of dead ancestors are prominent themes in these shamanic dreams. These shamans typically awaken believing that they received secret or special knowledge while they slept.

Not everyone who experiences such dreams decides to become a shaman, and not all persons who say they are shamans are accepted as shamans by their respective societies. Those who do rise to their shamanic callings after their initiatory dreams will be asked to invoke these visionary skills in the future, when their clansmen consult them about personal or political problems. Some of those who rejected their shamanic calling after their first dream eventually accept their role as shamans, in hopes of relieving the mental and physical distress that followed the initiatory dream.

Many popular sources claim that shamans are distinct from schizophrenics or epileptics, because shamans can induce these dreams at will and welcome these dreams, whereas true schizophrenics do not have such voluntary control over their mental states. Yet the evidence says otherwise. Even those people who go on to become full-fledged shamans find themselves at the mercy of these dreams and endure overwhelming anxiety throughout each dream. The main difference is that shamans' culture concurs with the supernatural significance that they ascribe to these dreams.

Note that many schizophrenics claim that their psychotic states started during a dream. This schizophrenic dream simply never ends, as sleep dreams do. The French, who use a different psychiatric classification system from the Americans, still speak of oneroid schizophrenia, which literally means dreamstate schizophrenia, as does the World

Health Organization's classification of diseases. Furthermore, not all true schizophrenics deteriorate. At least one-third to two-thirds of people who experience a schizophreniform episode have symptom-free remissions, when they are perfectly capable of functioning as shamans or of living peacefully in a simple society.

It is equally interesting that some temporal lobe epileptics experience a dreamy state during their brief, motion-free seizures. These "complex partial seizures" of temporal lobe epilepsy bear no outward resemblance to the dramatic movements of "grand mal" seizures. Many temporal lobe epileptics have schizophrenic-like or manic-depressive–like mental changes after their seizures, and some rare people who have unusually severe seizure disorders remain in these dreamy states between seizures. Some people with temporal lobe epilepsy also suffer from major motor seizures and so have attacks of uncontrolled movements and uncontrollable moods at different times. As subtle as it is, temporal lobe epilepsy is more common than its better known and more obvious cousin.

While distinguishing "true" shamanic states from "true" schizophreniform or epileptiform states is not easy, it is easy to see that some societies value shamanism and provide socially meaningful roles for people who experience such disruptive dreams and altered mental states. In contrast, contemporary American culture does not offer a comparable social role for such people. This country casts such people into the role of psychiatric patients and sets their status far lower than the status of their peers and far, far lower than the status of shamans in shamanistic societies.

There are some exceptions to these generalizations. Rare performers or artists self-describe themselves as shamans and earn popular support in the process. Jim Morrison was one of those. The lead singer of *The Doors*, Morrison became intrigued with Amerindian shamanism during his childhood in the American Southwest. He sincerely believed that his emotionally evocative rock gave him shamanic powers and enabled him to see "the other side" about which he sang. Jim Morrison met with the other side sooner than most, when he died a premature death from drugs and alcohol at the age of 26. One might say that the lasting appeal of Morrison's music has proven that he did indeed cast some sort of spell, though not necessarily a supernatural spell. Morrison's mentor, the turn-of-the-century poet Rimbaud, also saw himself as a seer. Like Morrison, Rimbaud advocated a disordering of the senses through drug and drink.

Following in the footsteps of Morrison and Rimbaud, some young Americans try to induce shamanic dreams with hallucinogenic drugs.[14] These self-described urban shamans assume a different social role from either schizophrenics or shamans. As users of illicit plants, they exist on the margins of society (as of the year 2000) and become outlaws by their own choosing. This outsider, outlaw status is the polar opposite to the essential social role that shamans play in societies that venerate shamans and ritualize shamanic behavior.

However, not all self-described American shamans use chemicals or skirt the law. Drug-free "shaman workshops" that rely upon drumming and chanting became popular in the 1990s. These workshops were started by a prominent anthropologist who previously published books on *Shamanism and Hallucinogens*.[15] They train people to tap into their "shamanic potential." A small subculture of American shamanism resulted, and one workshop gave birth to another. Understanding the appeal of such an approach was easy: dreamlike, dissociative states that are pathologized by professional circles are given the status and meaning of "shamanic." People who might otherwise be marginalized become part of an accepting and approving community of like-minded shamanic aspirants. Yet this produces an all-shaman community, which is quite different from a shamanic society, where the indigenous shaman is the designated dreamer for his or her respective society.

Contemporary American attitudes toward shamanism may change, as happened with the 1960s and 1970s youth culture and the counterculture. Until then, this new breed of urban shaman is doomed to pursue a personal rather than a social quest and so is diametrically different from Siberian shamans who function within their society. It may be that American shamans are destined to pursue such individualistic courses, because they retain some values of American society and so become heirs to the distinctively American belief in individualism.

DREAM IDEAS OF AMERICAN INDIANS

The dream quests, shamanic dreams, and induced dreams of American Indians (Native Americans) have a special relevance to American culture. Native Americana remains part of the cultural consciousness of the entire nation, regardless of whether or not one has Native American origins. Though American Indians have been marginalized and missionized and brutalized by mainstream American society since the Americas were settled by Europeans, their spiritual practices were not summarily dismissed by everyone. Long before the New Age developed an interest in Native American dream rituals and long before the drug culture turned an attentive ear to the Peyote Cult, colonists expressed interest in Native Americana. Folk wisdom held that Native Americans possessed superior healing abilities and herbal knowledge. White settlers sought out native healers.

At the turn of the millennium, more and more Americans seek to emulate Native American dream quests and coming-of-age practices, as the New Age interest in spirituality awakens interest in this uniquely American heritage. The counterculture of the 1960s and 1970s laid the foundations for this interest, when it applauded almost anything Native American and cheered for underdogs everywhere. Drug-induced dream quests of Amerindian tribes earned prime time during the heyday of the drug culture, but it was the 1951 publication of Weston La Barre's Ph.D. dissertation that perked public interest in peyote.[16] The Baby Boom generation reared on spaghetti Westerns and incessant Bonanza reruns and even Disney's animated and romanticized version of the Pocahantas story was primed to identify with Indians, rather than with Caucasian cowboys, because Indians were portrayed as childlike, like real children.

Another important link was the psychologist and author, Erik Erikson, author of *Childhood and Society*.[17] Erikson lived with two North American Indian tribes, and observed their coming-of-age rituals, adolescent maturation, stages of life, and dream quests, and applied this information to his classic study of childhood maturation. Erikson's works were required reading in psychology courses of the 1960s and 1970s. A bastardized and thoroughly transgressive approach to Native American vision quests is found in the "Modern Primitives" movement. This "movement," if indeed it can be called a movement, adopts the outward markings of Indian rites, such as tattooing and piercing, without demanding acceptance of the underlying spiritual or psychic significance of these coming-of-age quests.[18] Dream quests and other ethereal rites decline in importance in this sensation-seeking, self-indulgent arena.

Native Americans themselves have been reexploring dream rites in the last few decades. Many people who lost contact with these practices, either because of acculturation or discrimination, have returned to these religious rituals. Some are motivated by a desire to reconnect with their culture and to find meaning in once-abandoned rituals, whereas some seek an effective alternative to the more Americanized Alcoholics Anonymous. Healing circles and dream quests and sweat lodges that aim to abolish alcohol and drug abuse among Indians enjoyed extra attention, as the Recovery Movement swept across America.[19] The Native American Church's efforts to legalize the use of ritual peyote once garnered a great deal of publicity and popular support. However, most turn-of-the-millennium efforts to revitalize Native American dream quests are motivated by the desire to avoid further drug use or to compartmentalize it into a manageable ritual, rather than to promote drug use per se. Unlike the counterculture of the 1960s, the dreams— rather than the drugs—are most important.

There are complete books devoted to American Indian ideas about dreams, attesting to the complexity of these concepts.[20] Each Indian tribe has unique lore and customs that have little or nothing to do with the rites of other tribes. Each deserves its own separate study. The Ojibwa approaches to dreams are particularly appealing to contemporary American culture, as we will see.

Before becoming a fully-functioning member of adult Ojibwa society, the Ojibwa adolescent male undertakes a dream fast and undergoes prolonged social isolation and food deprivation. During these dreams, the young man gets powers from a supernatural guardian spirit in exchange for promises to do or not to do certain acts in the future. The boy must be sexually pure and physically clean before starting his sacred fast. He must avoid contact with the earth during the fast, and so he climbs into a tree and perches in a nest specifically built for this purpose. The dreams that occur during this ordeal are the most important experiences of the young man's life and are said to determine the course of the rest of his life.

We can compare these Ojibwa initiation dreams with psychoanalytic dreams. Though Freudian psychoanalysis flatly denies that dreams divine the future, many analysands hope for a life-changing dream while they undergo psychoanalysis. American psychoanalysis—as opposed to European psychoanalysis—was especially conducive to this belief. American psychoanalytic institutes emphasized the importance of recollected memories, while the Europeans focused on the curative powers of the transference that result from the relationship between the analyst and the analysand. The persistent American folk belief in life-changing dreams makes itself manifest in innumerable films from many different eras, including *Spellbound* or *The Dark Past* or *Analyze This.* One wonders if America's Indian heritage, with its elaborate dream rituals, in some small way encouraged this specifically American approach to therapy.

Jung's approach to dreams is particularly compatible with these American Indian ideas. It is no accident that both Jungian depth psychology and Amerindian lore find themselves intertwined in New Age ideas about dreams. As someone who treated mostly middle-aged patients, Jung sincerely believed that the mature adults could make major life changes. For Jung, dreams opened awareness of new paths for the future. Jung emphasized the process of "individuation," through which the analysand integrates disjointed and superficially contradictory parts of his personality to achieve a sense of wholeness and a reconciliation with the past.

The Jungian dreamer initially sets out on a solitary dream quest that is reminiscent of the Protestant emphasis on individual experience and that is consistent with Jung's own Protestant upbringing. However, the true Jungian dreamer is trained to seek out symbols of the "collective unconscious" in his or her dreams to reunite with humanity as a whole and with history. Jungian dreamers can also search for evidence of Jung's hypothetical and controversial "racial unconscious," to find a sense of ethnic or national or "racial" belonging through their dreams. Though Jung's emphasis on the individual superficially contrasts with the Native American's tribal ideals, his theories about connecting with a collective unconscious or a racial unconscious are remarkably reminiscent of the Indian's quest for union with a larger group. It is no wonder that the New Age mentality venerates both Jungianism and Native Americana.

CARLOS CASTANEDA

The baby boomers' infatuation with Native American dream quests was seeded, in part, by the controversial anthropologist Carlos Castaneda and his series of books about dreams, drugs, shamanism, consciousness, culture, and, above all, imagination. His books became bestsellers, after he abandoned customary academic restraint and began to write with uncensored abandon. Though many of Castaneda's claims proved to be fraudulent, his writings were a formative influence on the counterculture of the 1960s and 1970s. Castaneda ranked a close second to Timothy Leary in his unwavering advocacy of drug-induced dream quests and in his ability to add the stamp of academic authenticity to countercultural pursuits.

Castaneda claimed that he based his *Conversations with Don Juan* on personal studies with a Central American shaman. Together, the two of them used plant hallucinogens to access an invisible but parallel dream world that had higher status than waking states. Castaneda himself remained somewhat of a mystery. Although he clearly invented parts of his past, his academic credentials were never called into question. His stories about turning into an animal during these shamanic sessions were clearly spurious. Today, we look back at the success of the Castaneda series on dreams and shamanism with amusement, and with some embarrassment, and with more surprise that his stories were once taken so seriously not all that long ago. Once we realize that Castaneda was once considered credible, then it is easy to understand why so many less sophisticated societies believed in the existence of permeable boundaries between sleeping dream and waking life.[21]

EMANUEL SWEDENBORG AND WILLIAM JAMES

Carlos Castaneda was certainly not the first scientist who switched to supernaturalism and promoted his personal dreams as universal truths. Carl Gustav Jung also straddled these two worlds, to the chagrin of his many critics and to the delight of his many devotees. Emanuel Swedenborg made a similar transition centuries before. He, too, had an equally lasting impact, partly because he attracted such prominent artistic and even scientific followers.

The Swedish-born Swedenborg was an assessor for the Board of Mines. First, he published a magnum opus on mineralogy and mining in 1734. He proceeded to publish works on physiology and psychology but became more and more concerned with the mystery of soul-body interaction. He came to believe that the brain is the seat of the soul and attached mystical significance to it. Convinced that every physical object has a corresponding spiritual reality, which could be revealed though a universal symbolic language, Swedenborg coined the concept of "correspondences." Around this time, Swedenborg had a religious crisis that led to his posthumously published and highly influential *Journal of Dreams*. After witnessing a few visions of Christ, he abandoned his scientific work completely to concentrate on theological writings.

Swedenborg never established a church before he died of a stroke in 1772. But Swedenborgian societies began to appear shortly after his death. These societies were most popular in England but appear here and there in America. His influence is felt most acutely through the artists and writers and thinkers he influenced, rather than through his churches. Swedenborg's best-known follower was poet-painter William Blake (though later in Blake's life, his illuminated book *The Marriage of Heaven and Hell* satirized Swedenborg's visions).

Swedenborg's writings also intrigued Balzac, Baudelaire, Emerson, Yeats, and Strindberg, each of whom went on to produce dreamlike or ethereal poetry, prose, or plays. The maudlin French poet Baudelaire adapted Swedenborg's theory of correspondences. Baudelaire changed the world of poetry and art in the process, both through his own poems about *The Flowers of Evil* and through his French translations of the revered dreamer and writer, Edgar Allan Poe. Balzac also vacillated between reality and fantasy and used hashish as much as Swedenborgian philosophy to produce unusual prose. As an American Transcendentalist, Emerson wrote around the same time as Walt Whitman and captured a recognizable Swedenborgian spirit in his exaltation of nature. Strindberg's *A Dream Play* shows evidence of a generic presurrealist intrigue with dreams that is partly attributable to Swedenborgian influence and partly attributable to Strindberg's impending psychosis.

Swedenborg exerted an indirect but important influence on modern psychology through the writings of William James.[22] James was raised as a Swedenborgian and trained as a physician. He was the brother of writer Henry James. William James' best-remembered book, *The Varie-*

ties of Religious Experience, broadcasts his Swedenborgian-like appreciation for transcendent mental states. James makes no distinction between dreams, visions, revelations, and waking life, when he assesses the authenticity of religious revelations. In the very first chapter of his book, he dismisses the utility of neurology in judging religious ideas and condemns "psychologism" overall.

This book has remained in print since its first publication in 1902. Published two years after Freud's *The Interpretation of Dreams, The Varieties of Religious Experience* did not have as much influence on the twentieth century as Freud's work. Still, it is a clear competitor in its own way. With a point of view that is the polar opposite of Freud's, it paved its own unpaved paths in its own way. In *The Varieties of Religious Experience,* James supports personal, experiential religion, and downplays the importance of organized or institutionalized religion. He recognizes the insights of Transcendentalist poets such as Wordsworth, Yeats, and Emerson as true religious sentiments. He puts their religious achievements on a par with the Old Testament prophets, or Catholic saints such as Theresa or Loyola, or Sufi seers such as Al-Ghazzhali. But he does not encourage all religion automatically but, instead, distinguishes between the religion of the "healthy-minded" and the religion of the "sick-minded."

Although he never practiced the medicine that he studied at Harvard, James had an established academic career in experimental psychology when he wrote this book. He chaired the first department of psychology in a United States university. Many of his contemporaries saw his later-life switch from experimental science to experiential religion as a sign of mental derangement. They pointed to his early history of psychological instability but rarely considered the contribution of his long-established Swedenborgian beliefs.

James' interest in the intersection between supernaturalism and psychology had begun long before this ground-breaking publication. In his 1890 text on *The Principles of Psychology,*[23] he wrote about dreams and foreshadowed the path he would take later in life. He said that "most people have probably had dreams which it is hard to imagine not to have been glimpses into an actually existing region of being, perhaps a corner of the 'spiritual world.' And dreams have accordingly in all ages been regarded as revelations, and have played a large part in furnishing forth mythologies and creating themes for faith to lay hold upon." The sentiments expressed in this paragraph are remarkably close in spirit to Swedenborg's *Journal of Dreams.*

James' spiritualistic approach to dreams, with its Swedenborgian spiritual foundation, was vastly different from the path taken by Sigmund Freud, the self-described "Godless Jew." To his dying day, Freud remained skeptical about the "oceanic feeling" that mystics such as

James enjoyed. Yet James welcomed Freud's research on *The Interpreta-tion of Dreams* and invited the Austrian neurologist to lecture at Clark University in Massachusetts in 1909. Few serious scholars openly embraced Freud's theories at this time, although some medical journals reviewed them. James' generous invitation introduced Freud's ideas to American audiences. This act was fortunate for Freud, because Freud's iconoclastic ideas took their most tenacious hold in America, rather than in Europe.

MARTIN LUTHER KING'S DREAM

Swedenborg's *Journal of Dreams* is rarely read in America today, but the Rev. Dr. Martin Luther King, Jr.'s Dream Speech reverberates. King's opening line of "I have a dream" is nearly as well-known as Lincoln's "Four score and seven years ago" that began the Gettysburg Address. King's Dream Speech is especially interesting to students of dream because it situates dream at the intersection of the social and the supernatural. It reaches back to the words and deeds of the prophets of old to meet the needs of mid-twentieth century society. There is a long, long tradition of blending the seemingly ethereal theme of dream with practical political purposes.

A scholar and a clergyman, the Rev. Dr. King, Jr. became the most influential civil rights leader of the twentieth century. In 1964, he delivered his famous Dream Speech to a crowd of 200,000. This speech stimulated the most wide-reaching civil rights legislation enacted since the Civil War. The first words of this speech—*I have a dream*—were emblazoned on black-on-white buttons that appeared on countless lapels for the duration of the decade. King was assassinated four years after this history-shaping Dream Speech.

If someone was not familiar with the dream themes of Old Testament prophecies and with the tradition of the "message dream" in the ancient Near East, King's Dream Speech might have sounded like any other potentially attainable "American dream." At times, it seemed closer to a fanciful "pipe dream," because there was so much resistance to overcome. The average listener could think that King framed his pleas for racial equality in the tentative language of dreams to avoid invoking the ire of a skeptical and possibly even vengeful society.

Yet to those who study dream themes of the past, it was apparent that King embedded his Dream Speech with multiple meanings and that he loaded it with supernatural significance. The Dream Speech was a modern version of the same ancient dream message. It evoked the authority of the dream and hinted that King's goals of racial equality were divinely decreed. It implied that he, as a clergyman and as a man of God, was sent as God's messenger to deliver his people from their bondage in America, just as Moses delivered the Israelites from their bondage in Egypt. Moses also received word of his divine mission during a dream. By foretelling of a time when black men would walk alongside white men, King's Dream Speech recollected the idyllic dream of the prophet Isaiah. Isaiah also envisioned a better world, where the lion would lie down with the lamb and where warring nations would beat their swords into sickles.

It may seem far-fetched to suggest that there was supernatural significance lurking beneath the surface of King's Dream Speech. However, the civil rights movement was laced with religious imagery from start to finish. Clergymen led it, from King on down. Civil rights marchers sang spirituals based on Old Testament themes as they walked through the streets. Someone of King's education and accomplishments and church affiliation was well aware of the potential power of the theme of dream. It was no secret that ancient peoples, from the Egyptian pharaohs to the Israelite prophets, established personal political authority by citing divine dreams.

King's Dream Speech stands at the cornerstone of many different approaches to dreams and cannot be accurately reduced to a single meaning. It became more powerful and more memorable because the imagery of "dream" spoke on so many different levels to so many different people from so many different backgrounds. It reached out and impacted as intensely as it did because it evoked an experience that is common to all humankind: the dream. It referenced religious and literary allusions to dream and allowed each listener to add his or her own associations. Given the way that so many politico-religious movements as well as messianic movements have begun with a dream, it would not be at all surprising if King's Dream Speech acquires even more supernatural significance as time goes on. There is a possibility that it will inspire sectarian religious and messianic movements in the future.

SUPERNATURALISM AND SUPERSTITION

Supernaturalist approaches to dreams did not simply fade away, even after psychoanalysis and science challenged them. They simply morphed into different forms. The supernaturalism that belonged to the past and to preliterate societies of the present has found new life in New Age and neo-Jungian ideas of the third millennium. Dream symbol books proliferate in contemporary times and line the shelves of "mind-body" sections of major bookstores. Many of these publications look astoundingly similar to the ancient Greek, Egyptian, Assyrian, or even alchemical dream symbol books from the very distant past. Often, only their New Age-sounding titles, or their computer-generated graphics, or the crispness of their covers distinguishes these new books from antiquarian works.

Spiritually oriented dream-sharing groups are particularly popular at the turn of the twenty-first century and are said to be proliferating steadily, especially as the Internet makes them accessible to more and more people.[24] Such dream circles attract a broad audience and began to appear in conjunction with the self-help groups of the 1960s and 1970s. Dream-sharing groups fare especially well with members of 12-step chemical dependency programs, because they lace well-established supernaturalist dream traditions with a belief in a 12-step "higher power." Dreams are welcomed because they tap into natural altered states of consciousness that were once accessed artificially through drug and drink.

In a 1999 book on *Visions of the Night,*[25] religion professor Kelly Bulkeley wrote that dream interpretation was slowly but steadily returning to the realm of religion since the late 1960s, after having been co-opted by psychology and psychoanalysis for the first half of the century. To prove his point, he identified 50,000 dream-sharing communities that exist in "real space" across America. One can only wonder how many more groups appeared both in real space and in cyberspace, since the time his book appeared.

There are many reasons for this resurgence of religious notions about dreams and other things. Among other things, it is a direct response to the devaluation of twentieth century psychoanalytic approaches to dreams and to the decline of psychoanalysis' influence as a secular religion. The public's increased awareness of the parallels between psychoanalysis and occultism also facilitates this return to the religious.[26] It almost seems appropriate that dreams would return to their supernatural sources after spending just a short century away from these original roots.

NOTES

1. Kapur, S., and P. Seeman. "The Dream in Contemporary Psychiatry." *American Journal of Psychiatry.* 158:3 (2001).

2. Cohn, Norman. *The Pursuit of the Millenium.* New York: Oxford University Press, 1974.

3. Harner, Michael, ed. *Hallucinogens and Shamanism.* New York: Oxford University Press, 1973.

4. Underhill, Evelyn. *Mysticism,* 12th ed. New York: Signet-Penguin, 1974; Scholem, Gershom G. *Major Trends in Jewish Mysticism.* 3rd ed. Jerusalem: Schocken, 1951.

5. Neumann, Erich. "Mystical Man." Joseph Campbell, ed. *The Mystic Vision.* Princeton, NJ: Princeton University Press, 1968, 375–419.

6. Gay, Peter. *A Godless Jew: Freud, Atheism and the Making of Psychoanalysis*. New Haven, CT: Yale University Press, 1989; Bakan, David. *Sigmund Freud and the Jewish Mystical Tradition*. Princeton, NJ: Van Nostrand, 1958.

7. Charcot, J. M., and Paul Richter. *Les Demoniaques Dans L'Art*. Paris: Macula, 1984.

8. Packer, Sharon. "Jewish Mystical Movements and the European Ergot Epidemics." *Israel Journal of Psychiatry*. 35:3 (1998): 227–239; Goodman, L. S., and A. G. Gilman. *The Pharmacological Basis of Therapeutics*. 4th ed. New York: Macmillian, 1970, 557–559.

9. Berndt, Ronald. "The Dreaming." *Encyclopedia of Religion*. New York: Macmillan, 1987, 479–481.

10. Hamilton, Malcomb. *The Sociology of Religion*. London: Routledge, 1995.

11. Eliade, Mircea. *Shamanism: Archaic Techniques of Ecstasy*. Rev. and enlarged ed. Chicago: University of Chicago Press, 1964; Bourguignon, Erika, ed. *Religion, Altered States of Consciousness, and Social Change*. Columbus: Ohio State University Press, 1973; Lincoln, Jackson S. *The Dream in Primitive Culture*. London: University of London, 1935; Laderman, Carol. *Taming the Wind of Desire*. Berkeley: University of California Press, 1993.

12. Eliade, Mircea. *Shamanism: Archaic Techniques of Ecstasy*. Rev. and enlarged ed. Chicago: University of Chicago Press, 1964.

13. Eliade, Mircea. *Autobiography. Vol. I. 1907-1937: Journey East, Journey West*. Trans. Mac Linscott Ricketts. Chicago: University of Chicago Press, 1981.

14. DeKorne, Jim. *Psychedelic Shamanism*. Port Townshend: Loompanics, 1994.

15. Michael Harner, former chair of the anthropology department of the New School for Social Research and author of *Hallucinogens and Shamanism* started this trend.

16. La Barre, Weston. *The Peyote Cult*. 5th ed. Norman: University of Oklahoma Press, 1989.

17. Erikson, Erik H. *Childhood and Society*. 2nd ed. New York: Norton, 1963.

18. Vale, V., and Andrea Juno. *Modern Primitives*. San Francisco: Re\Search Publications, 1989.

19. Castillo, Richard. *Meanings of Madness*. Pacific Grove: Brooks/Cole Publishing Co., 1998.

20. Devereaux, George. *Reality and Dream: Psychotherapy of a Plains Indian*. New York: Anchor-Doubleday, 1969.

21. Fikes, Jay Courtney. *Carlos Castaneda. Academic Opportunism and the Psychedelic Sixties*. Victoria, B.C.: Millenia, 1993.

22. Bjork, Daniel W. *The Compromised Scientist: William James in the Development of American Psychology*. New York: Columbia University Press, 1983.

23. James, William. *The Principles of Psychology*. vol. 2. Cambridge, MA: Harvard University Press, 1891, 923.

24. Bulkeley, Kelly. *Visions of the Night*. New York: State University of New York Press, 1999.

25. Bulkeley, Kelly. *Visions of the Night*. New York: State University of New York Press, 1999.

26. Crews, Frederick. "The Memory Wars. Freud's Legacy in Dispute." New York: *New York Review of Books*, 1995.

10

Reason and Romance

DISTINCTIONS AND DUALISMS

"The Age of Reason" and "The Romantic Era" were diametrically different from one another, but each made its distinctive mark on history. Each of these eras reverberate in American society to this day, and each has intriguing parallels to human personality styles. Each era produced a unique system of philosophy and economics and theology and protopsychology. Each left an easily identifiable body of art and literature and music and drama, and each had a different approach to dream.

By studying these two eras side by side, we can appreciate why the Romantic Era was so concerned with dream, while the Age of Reason had relatively little to say on the subject. We will also see that the more recent clashes between psychopharmacologists and psychoanalysts reach back to far deeper roots and why contemporary attitudes toward dreams are so conflicted.

A historian of Romanticism said that we would understand each society if we begin by understanding the relationship that society posits between the dream and waking life.[1] It is not surprising that this scholar arrived at this insight through the study of Romanticism. There was no other period in time in Western culture when dream achieved such status and inspired such a unique and enduring artistic legacy. To understand how and why and when the Romantic mind set came into being, we should examine the era that directly preceded it, the Age of Reason.

REASON AND RATIONALITY

During the Age of Reason, rationality reigned. Science and discovery and reason and logic replaced superstitious assumptions and reflexive religiosity of centuries past. Early in the 1600s, faith in God, king, and country was rerouted but not completely derailed. Belief in progress, human rights, the nation, and humanity arrived to replace these older ideals.[2]

The Age of Reason was made possible by two periods that preceded it: the Renaissance and the Reformation. The humanism of the Renaissance strengthened humankind's confidence in its own intellectual abilities. Geniuses such as Da Vinci and Michelangelo closed the distance between the human and the divine. They sculpted sacred subjects in human proportions and endowed heavenly beings, saints, angels, and Satan with a full range of human emotion and muscular movement. The Reformation, on the other hand, challenged the central authority of the Church and acknowledged the importance of an individual's conscience. The Reformation applauded an individual's ability to interpret and experience the Scriptures. This personal approach to the Biblical books led to a more personalized approach to the rest of the world.

Having been primed by the Reformation and the Renaissance, the Age of Reason demanded proof for explanations that were previously accepted on faith. In doing so, it paved the path for the following century's scientific discoveries and the era known as the Enlightenment. The European Enlightenment that followed the Age of Reason is quite distinct from the metaphysical enlightenment described by Eastern meditative systems. One has nothing to do with the other, except for accidental use of the same English word.

During the Age of Reason, innovators such as Galileo, Brahe, and Kepler changed the world of astronomy. Descartes, Newton, Guyens, and Pascal made their marks on mathematics. Sydenham and Harvey altered the theory and practice of medicine. Composers such as Bach, Handel, and Scarlatti—all of whom were born in 1685—imposed order on musical composition and mirrored the era's intellectual attitudes through their art.

Their scientific discoveries made travel and commerce and mercantilism and colonialism possible. Europe's expanding encounters with the New World helped mold Enlightenment thought. Increased contact and commerce pitted Europeans against the "primitives" who inhabited these new territories. Enlightenment-age Europeans were forced to formulate new, nontheological theories to justify the way they overpowered and exploited darker-skinned peoples who worshiped different deities and demons. One way to rationalize these hierarchical relationships with "heathens" was to emphasize their lack of "reason" and to overstate the importance of "reason" in European society.

This "reason" part of the Age of Reason became the hallmark of our Western value system and was used to distinguish civilized human beings from savages. Being reasonable is considered a virtue in the

Western world, whereas being emotional is not. Reason is a mode of thought and action associated with adults (and with males), whereas experience and emotion are imputed to children (and women). Reason is sometimes associated with that catchall and not completely correct phrase, "right-brained thinking." Because dreams defy reason and are often illogical to the extreme, they were not well regarded during the Age of Reason.

DREAMS AND DICHOTOMIES

Finding artistic or academic references to dreams during the Age of Reason is difficult. On the other hand, it is more difficult to stop citing examples of Romantic depiction of dreams. There is a very simple reason for this unequal attention to dream: the Romantics valued dreams and lavished attention and affection on them in art, psychology, and philosophy. The "philosophes" who formulated the philosophical basis of the Enlightenment did not need to devote lengthy discussions to a subject that they more or less dismissed, especially not when they had so many important "real-worldly" political and social issues to discuss.

There was another reason the Age of Reason avoided emphasizing dreams: dreams could be confused with madness, and madness was something that the Age of Reason shunned. Exploring the Age of Reason's attitudes toward insanity can explain that age's dismissive attitude toward dream.

As philosopher Michel Foucault stated in his much-discussed treatise on *Madness and Civilization*, attitudes toward the insane shifted during the Age of Reason. During those years, the insane were separated from the rest of society, previously having been permitted to wander about freely. When economic changes demanded that each citizen prove his or her productivity, these nonproductive insane became intolerable to society and had to be hidden from view (according to Foucault but not according to his critics). The insane were locked away in dark and dank and dirty institutions, where they were deprived of medical care, proper food, sunlight, and ordinary human respect.

Just as one would not want to risk a charge of witchcraft in medieval or even Renaissance Europe, one would not want to be identified with the insane during the Age of Reason. Illogical and incoherent dream thought could be confused with the delirium or dementia of the disenfranchised insane, and that was something to be avoided. Added to that was the fact that dreams were associated with primitive and preliterate cultures or with superstitious and unscientific prophecies of the past.

That does not mean that the Age of Reason or the Enlightenment had nothing important to say about dream. Quite the contrary. Several Enlightenment thinkers identified dreams with memories and thus set the stage for psychoanalytic thought, as well as sophisticated twentieth century neuroscience. Even the Romantic fascination with memory and meaning evolved out of these "enlightened" ideas about dream. When the pioneering neurosurgeon Penfield stimulated patients' brains with an electric probe in the 1950s and found that the temporal lobe of the brain produced a flood of personal memories from the patient's distant past, along with self-described "dreamy states" of consciousness, he inadvertently confirmed this Enlightenment speculation through scientific experiment.

When Freud posited that dreams excavated long-forgotten memories stored from unresolved childhood conflicts, he was drawing upon philosophical connections between dream and memory begun in the Enlightenment and elaborated upon during the Romantic Era. When Jung theorized that dream connected the dreamer with a collective unconscious or with a racial unconscious, he, too, depended on ideas first developed in the Enlightenment, as did French novelist Marcel Proust, who penned three thousand–plus pages of vivid, dreamlike recollections after tasting a single madeleine biscuit. Making the connection between dreams and memory and severing the link between dreams and divination (to foretell the future) was a significant shift in thought, which we owe to the Enlightenment.

The idea that dreams tapped into the past, rather than predicting the future, was a critical shift. European society had been weaned on Biblical beliefs about dreams as prophecy and prediction. Viewing dreams as part of an individual's own internal experiences was equally revolutionary for Christian Europe, when they previously deemed that dreams were messages sent by *external* sources, such as deities or heads of state or communal spirits or external sorcerers. For hundreds of years, cults of saints and hordes of heretics had coalesced around specific individuals who convinced others that their personal dreams revealed universal truths. The Enlightenment introduced the ideas of *self* and *past*. Drawing upon the humanism of the Renaissance, the Enlightenment paved the path to a fuller appreciation of the individual in the Romantic Era and in the postpsychoanalytic age.

BURTON AND VOLTAIRE

The Enlightenment and proto-Enlightenment Age of Reason attitudes toward dreams can be understood by studying the words of two influential and articulate spokespersons of that era.

In the seventeenth century, a clergyman and Oxford don named Robert Burton (1577–1640) wrote a landmark book called *The Anatomy of Melancholy*. Functioning as a protopsychiatrist and drawing upon his personal experiences with both depression and dreams, Burton stated that "The gods send not our dreams, we make our own." Historians of psychiatry hailed Burton's recorded reflections as the forerunner of our contemporary search for internal and individualized sources of mental distress.[3] Such scholars put Burton's diary on a par with Augustine's equally introspective *Confessions* written in the year 397 C.E.

For Burton, frightening dreams were symptoms of "melancholy" that could be banished by a good diet. At a time when supernatural explanations for human emotions and perceptions were more the rule than the exception and when society was willing to send women (and some men) to the stake for bewitching people into behaving badly, Burton's attitude was most unusual. He was, after all, writing in Britain, where Christian-influenced medicine was vastly different from more medically oriented, Greek-influenced Moorish medical systems practiced in Spain, Southern Italy, or North Africa. Burton's attitudes would not have been out of place in Greek medicine or in the Arabic-speaking world that perpetuated those Greek traditions, because both of those medical traditions valued the importance of diet, for both mental and physical health.

There were more immediate reasons to identify dietary deficiencies or spoiled food as the source of mental chagrin in the seventeenth century when Burton wrote. This was a time when ergot epidemics regularly rocked Western Europe and dosed whole populations with the same psychoactive chemicals that would be used to synthesize LSD some three centuries later. Ergotism began with mystical or macabre dreams and could evolve into strokes, seizures, or psychoses, if ingestion continued. Famine was common, and rotted food was more the norm than the exception. Vitamin deficiencies and pellagra could definitely induce dementia and depression and daytime dreams.[4]

Even if specific scientific knowledge about bad food and bad dreams and bad mood would not arrive for another few centuries, there was a well-established folk belief that bad food induced bad dreams. The Jewish Talmud of the third century distinguished between "true" prophetic dreams and the "false prophecy" that followed food and drug-induced dreams. Several European subcultures and sects and sorcerers foraged in the forests in search of perception-altering molds and mushrooms, long before laboratories or scientific studies existed.[5] A century later, British Romantic poets and painters such as Mary Shelley and Henri Fuseli took Burton's admonitions to heart and turned them upside down by deliberately ingesting spoiled food in order to induce—

rather than to avoid—the sort of frightening night visions that Burton endured.

Voltaire, who lived between 1694 and 1778, is far better known to most of us than Burton. An archenemy of ecclesiasticism and superstition, Voltaire was one of the greatest thinkers of the Age of Reason. He laid the philosophical foundation for the forthcoming French Revolution. Voltaire vehemently opposed the prevailing idea that dreams foreshadow the future and saw dreams as the basis of primitive prophecy or prediction. It was Voltaire who posited that people selectively remember those dreams that come true and conveniently forget the content of those dreams whose conclusions do not come to pass. According to Voltaire, it was this error in memory that persuaded people to equate dreams with divination. Centuries later, scientists and statisticians and cognitive psychologists validated Voltaire's theories about selective recall and rephrased his original eighteenth century ideas in refreshingly modern terms.[6]

Voltaire's denunciation of dreams and prophecies struck out against French Catholicism. He voided the colorful claims of France's many mystics and heretics who recounted their daytime dreams and passed them off as religious revelations. Joan of Arc, Therese de Lisieux, and Bernard de Clairveaux were among his "victims." Voltaire's sweeping skepticism bode equally badly for colonized people in the Americas, East Indies, and Africa, where dreams were intricately interwoven into shamanic healing, tribal initiation, cultic myth, or yogic meditation. His ideas were worlds away from sacred history conveyed by the thirteen dreams in Genesis or the dream-based dogma in the New Testament. He made a farce of Emperor Constantine's dream-based, world-changing decision to convert to Christianity.

Voltaire's observations severed ties with the past and molded the climate of his own times and of times to come. We hear echoes of Voltaire's Enlightenment ideas in the nineteenth century theories of anthropologist Sir Edward Tylor (1832–1917), who was Oxford University's first chair of anthropology. Tylor altered the infant science of anthropology when he added his hands-on investigations and observations to Voltaire's historically-based "armchair anthropology" theories. After doing fieldwork in Mexico, Tylor wrote a landmark text on *Primitive Culture*, where he hypothesized that all religious ideas originated in dreams.

REVERIE AND THE FRENCH REVOLUTION

Voltaire's philosophy led the way to the French Revolution. The French Revolution was a pivot point, which both connects and separates the Enlightenment and Romanticism. Occurring in 1789, before Romanticism started, the French Revolution paved the path to Romanticism, both in a positive and a negative way. On one hand, the ideals of the Revolution affirmed the importance of individual freedom, which was an integral element of Romanticism. The excesses of the French Revolution and the violent upheavals that followed during the Reign of Terror also cast a harsh light on the limitations of political processes and fermented disillusionment with the "real world."

William Wordsworth, the first and arguably most important Romantic poet of all, was touring France during the time of the Revolution. Wordsworth saw hundreds of severed heads rolling down the streets, left as sick souvenirs of the revolutionaries' enthusiastic use of the guillotine. Although Wordsworth himself is known for the jubilation and personal renewal he found in nature, many other Romantics redirected energies inward and found solace in the soul, the unconscious, and the dream. The flamboyance of the French Revolution was mirrored in the flamboyant Romantic artistic images.

The French Revolution also impacted directly on the practice of psychiatry, because it led famed psychiatrist Philippe Pinel to "unchain the insane." Pinel is typically credited for his clinical acumen, his courage to challenge the psychiatric standards of his day, and his personal humanitarian impulses. But it is the French Revolution that deserves the most credit for this landmark act. By loosening the bonds that literally tied madmen and madwomen to the institutions that incarcerated them, Pinel was showing proper revolutionary support for the freedom for the human spirit. Pinel's freeing of the insane from the walls of the infamous Parisian insane asylums—the Bicetre and the Salpetriere—mirrored the same symbolic events that were taking place at Paris' nearly empty Bastille prison. Once the most irrational citizens were freed from the bonds that held them prisoner in their institutions, ordinary people were set free to dream, and so began the Romantic mind set.

THEORIES OF MIND AND ROMANTIC THOUGHT

While the French Revolution set the stage for Romanticism, the movement did not start in France. The Romantic spirit stirred first in Germany, and then in France, and eventually spread through Europe, Russia, and even across the sea to America. It spared no nation from its influence. Different nations developed distinctive expressions of Romanticism. A dark side of Romanticism also developed, and the darkest side of all expressed itself though destructive nationalistic movements such as National Socialism, a century later.

The words of the philosopher Gottfried Wilhelm Leibnitz (1646–1716) bridged the Age of Reason and the Romantic Era. As the author of *New Thoughts Concerning Human Understanding,* Leibnitz updated John Locke's staunchly rationalist *Thoughts Concerning Human Understanding.* Locke's book became an unofficial manifesto of the Age of Reason. Leibnitz's book earned permanent fame as the ancestor of Freudian theories about dreams. For it was Leibnitz who stated that dreams stem from accumulated memories.

Before delving into more details about Romantic thought, it is useful to examine some general principles of Romanticism. As mentioned earlier, Romanticism refers to a specific era in European history. This "Romanticism" is not the same as the hearts-and-flowers, bouquets and ribbon bows that we associate with this term today—although those cupids and blossoms did appear in paintings by Romantic artists such as Philippe Otto Runge. Rather than being restricted to the commercialism of Valentine's Day, as it is today, Romanticism with a capital *R* was a far-sweeping philosophical, literary, artistic, and musical movement. It had many different manifestations, all of which shared a certain similarity in thinking, feeling, and sensing. From the start, Romanticism was colored by separate national sentiments, so that British Romanticism could be distinguished from French or German, and so forth.

Unlike the French Revolution, which is celebrated on a specific day (Bastille Day, July 14), and unlike the Reformation, which began on the day that Martin Luther nailed his list of objections on the cathedral door, the Romantic movement had no clear-cut beginning and an even less clear-cut end. The movement appeared somewhere between 1790 and 1830 and surfaced again as Neo-Romanticism between 1880 and 1900 (when psychoanalysis started). Strains of Romanticism persist, as a continuous undercurrent in society, and ripple every now and then in a slightly different guise. Similar sentiments resurfaced in the surrealist movement of the 1920s, and in the 1960s counterculture, and in the New Age principles of the 1990s. For some people—and especially for those people who adore dreams—Romanticism is as much a state of mind as a point in time. Because Romanticism has such important parallels in human personality traits, it is doubtful that the Romantic approach to life and love will ever completely disappear.

Although it built upon the same belief in unalienable individual rights that the Age of Reason and the Enlightenment championed, Romanticism was a direct reaction against the Age of Reason. It privileged the very qualities that the Age of Reason attempted to obliterate. It was a "reaction formation" to the Age of Reason and served the same purpose for post-Enlightenment society that psychodynamic reaction formations serve for individuals. On the surface, Romanticism insulted everything that the Age of Reason represented, but some strains of

Romanticism did not severe the connection with reason completely. Many Romantics attempted to balance reason with an opposing point of view, to create a new and more usable synthesis of both cognitive and emotional qualities, of logic and intuition. This stress on synthesis and reunification set the stage for some psychotherapy techniques of the next century.

Romanticism was much more than just a reaction to the era that immediately preceded it. It was a reaction to specific events in the present as much as it was a reaction to points of view of the past. This movement arose against the backdrop of the Industrial Revolution, which brought unprecedented urbanization and mass migration to cramped and squalid cities. Romanticism reaffirmed the importance of individual experience in an age of mass production and mass movement and mass transportation. Its cult of the individual counteracted the routinization and mechanization and dehumanization and demoralization of daily life, just as much as it perpetuated Enlightenment and Revolutionary ideas about individual liberty. Romanticism permitted people to retreat to their own personal space during their dreams, though they lived in overpopulated and unpleasant locales during the day.

Many Romantics stressed the ethereal over the material, paradoxically perhaps, because the movement evolved at the very same time that the Industrial Revolution produced more and more material goods. Instead of resurrecting the superstitious and spiritualist beliefs that were laid to waste by the Age of Reason, Romanticism forged new secular expressions for these impulses and interests.[7] Although some early Romantics dealt with the here-and-now and dramatized social issues as significant as slavery in the New World, the movement favored exoticism and Orientalism. Romanticism looked to Greece and Spain, as well as the Near East, North Africa, Byzantium (contemporary Turkey), and the Biblical lands.

Romanticism had a special connection with the past and so set the stage for Freud's future "archaeology of the mind." Such concerns were reinforced by the great archaeological discoveries of the nineteenth century: Pompeii and Nineveh. Romanticism sanctified passed time, and formulated a new feeling for history, and conjured up images and associations with past centuries. Several Romantics showed an intense affinity for the Middle Ages. Romanticism's stress on the concept of "becoming" (*werden*), rather than "being," laid the groundwork for future psychoanalytic optimism about curing conditions that were previously thought to be incurable. Overall, Romanticism offered immediate, acceptable alternatives to the fast-forward, future-oriented pace produced by scientific innovation and overseas expansion. Yet the movement in general did not advocate a wholesale abandonment of this new way of life, as the hippies did in the 1960s. Romanticism simply added internal and escapist alternatives.

Romanticism regarded psyche and nature as interconnected and imputed a near-mystical meaning to both. True Romantics attempted to attain *einfuhlung* (empathy) with nature and strived to penetrate the secrets of nature's "fundament" (*grund*). The Romantics make references to the "world soul" (as opposed to the soul of the supernaturalists of the past), and so scholars such as Abrams subtitled Romanticism as the era of "natural supernaturalism."[8] Jung coupled this concept of the "world soul" with Carus' Romantic concept of the unconscious and transformed the two into his quasi-mystical and completely unscientific concept of the collective unconscious. Eventually, the Romantic soul and the psychoanalytic psyche became nearly interchangeable. As a result, there is a surprisingly easy transition between supernaturalist approaches to dreams and the Romantic depiction of dreams.

GERMAN ROMANTICS: FRIEDRICH AND CARUS

This so-called world soul was evident in Romantic painting and was described by Romantic poets such as Novalis and Hoelderlin. Luminaries of the likes of Caspar David Friedrich and Karl Gustav Carus painted penetrating landscapes that looked as though they were alive and animated by a soul. Each man influenced many more generations, each in his own way. Friedrich was a mystical man who was haunted by the death of his brother, who drowned after falling through broken ice while trying to save young Caspar. Friedrich repeated this theme of awesome and overpowering and unpopulated nature over and over again in his paintings. He also repeatedly painted scenes of jagged, broken ice, without a single human soul in sight.

Friedrich eventually suffered a stroke that left him apathetic and alone and forgotten in his final years, but his mystical spirit—as well as his sense of solitary suffering—remain eerily alive through art and film. His twisted, gnarled, agonized trees directly influenced the set design of early German filmmakers, such as F. W. Murnau (*Nosferatu*), Fritz Lang (*Destiny*), and Henrik Galeen (*The Student of Prague*). His work also inspired *The Night on Bald Mountain*, portrayed in Disney's first *Fantasia*. Friedrich's most recent reincarnation came through Vincent Ward's lush, computer-generated images of the afterlife in *What Dreams May Come*.[9] Friedrich himself was influenced by the great Romantic dream writers, whom we will discuss following.

Carus left an equally intriguing legacy. Carus was originally an obstetrician and comparative anatomist, turned thinker and aesthete. His art reflected so much of Friedrich's influence that viewers often confuse their paintings. Carus attained his greatest fame through painting and writing, rather than through science or research or medical practice. He authored *Psyche,* a speculative work that became a seminal example of Romantic psychiatry. Carus was the first person to articulate the concept of the "unconscious." In true Romantic fashion, he based his psychiatric theories on personal introspection, rather than on empirical or experimental evidence. He never attended to a psychotic patient! Yet his Romantic notions filtered into Freudian thought, and perfused psychoanalytic ideas, and embellished Freud's clinical case discussions.[10]

These Romantic themes were important to the future and were critical to making life livable in the present. By positing the existence of a mystical attachment to the land, Romanticism fought the sense of displacement that resulted from leaving one's land to find employment in cities and factories. The world soul became an antidote to the alienation brought about by the division of labor and the piecemeal assembly line process to which Karl Marx called attention. The "world soul" offered a feeling of wholeness for those who were separated from family and friends and familiar fields and forests, as a result of the wholesale exodus to the city. In essence, Romanticism was a retreat from the realities of the day. It offered the same mental respite that medieval mystical movements provided to persecuted Jewish communities or that contemporary action-adventure escapist films offer to economically and socially disenfranchised American youth.[11]

Whereas the Enlightenment and the French Revolution (1789) deliberated about the role of the individual in society and redefined relationships between the citizen and the state, Romanticism focused on the individual's relationship to the self, the soul, the universe, and even the unconscious. Romanticism uncovered the individual's *weltanschauung* (or "world view"), without necessarily concerning itself with the individual's obligation to that world. Such emphasis on individual introspection and a personal unconscious made it possible to appreciate both the uniqueness and the universality of dreams, which were so esteemed by the Romantic mind. The Romantic Era thus ushered in the cult of the individual, which colors virtually every aspect of our contemporary Western world view. This Romantic ideal was intertwined with the frontier spirit, to produce the unique American ideal of rugged individualism. Some sociologists (such as Christopher Lasch) lampooned these traits, because they corrupted into narcissism and self-indulgence by the late twentieth century.[12]

INSANITY AND DREAMS

As science was discovering more and more predictable principles, and as technology was stripping production of human error and

experience, and assembly lines were forcing routinization and regula-
tion, the Romantic movement was applauding the most uncontrollable
events and experiences. Some English Romantic painters, such as William Turner and John Constable and Samuel Palmer, gained fame by
glorifying the stormy seas or skies, which were free from the taint of
technology. Others, such as John Martin or Thomas Cole (who went on
to found the Hudson River School in the United States), portrayed
uncontrollable and overpowering climatic events, such as floods, earthquakes, and fires. They showed technology crumbling from the force of
a cataclysmic climate.

Romantics took this appreciation of the atypical and out-of-control
one step further and lavished similar appreciation on the stormy psyche. They venerated insanity (or simulated insanity), where irrationality completely conquered reason and loosened the rein over inner
impulses. Because dreams are the most immediate and accessible manifestation of the insanity and imagination and individuality, the Romantics adored dreams. But there were many more reasons for the Romantic
deification of dream, as we shall see in the next section.

ROMANTICS AND DREAMS

According to the Romantics, dreams tapped into that universal spirit
or soul that they revered. Dreams transported the dreamer into another
realm of reality—in somewhat the same way that recently-built rail-
roads transported people to completely different realities. It was no
accident that Freud would see dreams as "the royal road to the unconscious," at a time when new modes of transportation were appearing
and changing everyday experience.

The Romantic mind identified two parallel worlds: one was an external visible world of the senses, and the other was an internal world of
the soul and dreams. The Romantics firmly believed that the dream
could connect the dreamer to the unconscious and unearth otherwise
inaccessible memories of the distant past. As the era that put poets on
a par with prophets and started the "cult of the poet" in the process, it
was only fitting that the Romantics posited a connection between dream
and poetry. They felt that the interpretation of dream permitted the
artist to perceive the existence of this magical realm. The true artist
could then convey his impressions of this unique world through his or
her art and make it accessible to everyone.

Whereas the topic of dreams had been but a footnote for the *philosophes* of the Enlightenment, almost all the Romantics had something to
say about a subject as dear to them as dreams. Romantic artists devoted
themselves to "the dreamy landscape" (whereas their Symbolist succes-

sors would illustrate the "landscape of the dream"). Yet early Romantic literature is replete with references to dreams. In 1800, Novalis published his *Hymns to Night*. Friedrich von Schlegel's dreamy *Dialogue on Poetry* appeared in 1803, and Hoelderlin's *Night Songs* were printed in 1805. Later Romantics read these works and translated these impressions of dreams into pictorial or dramatic or acoustic terms.

Among the favorite Romantic writers (and an important influence on prototypical Romantic painter Caspar David Friedrich) was Heinrich von Kleist. Von Kleist lived in isolation and had violent "crises." Striving to cultivate an "inner voice," he wrote that humankind lived in a circular dimension, ever in search of a new grace, which may be granted by the unconscious, a dream, or a new unfolding of the personality.[13] Gotthilf Heinrich von Schubert was another "tormented soul," who published in medicine, theology, natural science, and history. He, too, was a favorite of Caspar David Friedrich. Von Schubert's lectures on the *Nocturnal Aspects of the Natural Science* evolved into his 1714 publication on dream symbolism. In that book, Von Schubert wrote: "In dreams, and already in the delirious state which precedes sleep, the soul seems to express itself in a language all its own." Von Schubert believed that dreams contain innate information and that they are superior to ordinary information because they transcend time.

Another Romantic writer who had much to say about dreams and who influenced Friedrich was Ludwig Tieck. His fairy tales were set in magic forests, filled with symbolic flowers and stones (as in *Fantasia)*. His characters renounced reality and proclaimed that "We grow up, and our childhood is a dream woven within ourselves." What a wonderful way to connect the world of childhood and the world of dream and to explain the special insights of each stage! This same sentiment would resurface in many Romantic works, including *The Nutcracker Suite*, which we will discuss following. This thought planted seeds for psychoanalysts, who coined an entire craft to forage through adult dreams in order to find forgotten childhood experiences.

The Romantics themselves were not concerned with cataloguing the various psychological stages of the dream; they simply *believed* in the interconnection between dreams and the unconscious and the "sleeping soul." These concepts were medicalized and psychologized later in the century. We can trace a straight line between Romanticism and Freud's epoch-making *The Interpretation of Dreams*, where he described dreams as the royal road to the unconscious and where he stated specifically that he was presenting a *scientific* [sic] theory of dream (as opposed to all the speculative or superstitious theories that preceded him). If we try to connect Jung's *Memories, Dreams, Reflections* to Romantic thought, we will find even closer correspondence to Romantic musings. If we try to draw a line between Jung and Romanticism, we will find that we have drawn a parabola instead, which starts with Romanticism and loops loosely around Freud, before turning back on itself to return completely to its Romantic roots.

The Romantics were more or less unimpressed by the biological basis of dreams, and were not in the least concerned with distinguishing drug-induced states from sober states. They were willing to give credence to dreams derived from opium or hashish or other drugs, as well as to dreams that occurred "de novo," because they believed that intoxication and addiction did not obscure, but rather cleansed the lens. Romantics who regarded such altered states as authentic revelations of reality were closer in spirit to many primitive cultures than they were to the European Age of Reason. Their world view had little in common with the attitudes of scientific positivists who came later in the nineteenth century and was completely dissimilar from third-millennial American thought, which makes fine legal as well as psychiatric distinctions between sobriety and insobriety. In contrast to the counterculture of the 1960s, which sought out the "higher consciousness" available through drugs and dreams, the Romantics put dreams on a par with waking life. They accorded equal status to the external visible world of the senses and the internal world of the soul and dreams.

MUSIC AND ROMANTICISM

The Romantics excelled in accessing the artistic imagination. They harnessed the sense of the sublime that existed among the supernaturalists and translated these awesome experiences into creativity. They often depicted the dream, be it through music, ballet, art, prose, or poetry. They portrayed that dream as a special state, suspended in time, located somewhere between earthly existence and paradise.

Many Romantic musicians remain household names today. Beethoven, Bellinni, Bennett, Berlioz, Brahms, Bruckner, Chopin, Donizetti, Glinka, Grieg, Halevi, Liszt, Loewe, Marschner, Mehul, Mendelssohn, Meyerbeer, Mussorskgy, Rossini, Schubert, Schumann, Smetana, Spohr, Tchaikovsky, Verdi, Wagner, Weber, and Wolf are among them. But when it came to depicting dream, none surpassed Tchaikovsky. Tchaikovsky composed for both orchestra and ballet and brought Romantic ballet to new heights.

Ballet proved to be an ideal medium for depicting dreams, because it combines the immediate sensory stimulation of music with the visual appeal that pervades dreams. Since it bypasses dialogue and direct speech and does not demand a linear narrative, ballet can introduce disjointed and spontaneous dance sequences, just as dreams do. Like dreams, balletic pantomime is elusive and requires the audience's active imagination to make sense of the story. Because dance speaks through the language of movement—while the "real" sleep state is characterized by physical paralysis—there is a peculiar paradox to depicting dream through dance. The drama is heightened as a result.

If there is one ballet-based dream that has entered our everyday American awareness, it is surely *The Nutcracker Suite*. With its "March of the Wee Folk" and its child stars, *The Nutcracker Suite* is a favorite of children. It remains a Christmas season staple. The music was composed by the ill-fated Russian Tchaikovsky, and the story came courtesy of a spectacularly talented and spectacularly self-destructive German storyteller, E. T. A. Hoffmann. *The Nutcracker Suite* chronicles the night visions of a little girl named Laura, who fell asleep one Christmas Eve after unwrapping a grotesque wooden nutcracker that was nestled among her holiday gifts. While sleeping, Laura enters an enchanted world that parallels the ordinary waking world. There, the nutcracker turns into a handsome prince. Household mice grow to superhuman proportion and the Sugar Plum Fairy and several exotic dolls come to life and pirouette past the audience's eyes. Most of the stage action takes place in a dream.

The ballet captures the magical melange of childhood and dream that is so characteristic of the Romantic message. Like the Hoffmann story on which it is based, *The Nutcracker Suite* infuses everyday experience with a sense of the extraordinary and blurs the boundaries between sleep and spirit. It is possible that the story drew upon the actual perceptions of an author who suffered from several different medical conditions that alter perceptions. Hoffmann spent much of his life in a drunken state. He was forced to leave town because of his behavior on several occasions, in spite of his widespread recognition for his literary and musical accomplishments.

He developed devastating liver disease as a result of his drinking. Such liver disease alone can cause alterations of consciousness, daytime dreams, and confusion between day and night, through a metabolic condition known as "hepatic encephalopathy." This condition compounds the effects of ordinary intoxication. He presumably endured the hallucinosis and disorientation of d.t.'s (delirium tremens) whenever he decreased his alcohol intake.

Hoffmann also lived during the time and place of the ergot epidemics, when psychoactive fungi infiltrated both bread and beer (which he was known to consume in large quantities). Continuous consumption of such blighted bread and beer causes chronic ergotism, which begins with mystical or macabre dreams and which affects people with pre-existing liver disease earlier and more intensely than healthier people. Late-stage ergotism can also produce "general paresis of the insane" and result in the very same neurological symptoms as neurosyphilis. We know for a fact that Hoffmann died of "general paresis of the insane." What we do not know is whether or not his fatal neuropsychiatric disorder was due to syphilis or ergotism, or both.

Whatever the sources of Hoffmann's inspiration were, the fact remains that the by-products of his brain colored literature, art, dance, and even psychoanalysis in the centuries to come. Freud referred to Hoffmann in his classic 1923 essay on the uncanny.[14] Any number of Hoffmann's other works—including *The Devil's Elixir* and *The Sandman*—tapped into the theme of dream just as intensely as the nearly-canonized *The Nutcracker Suite*. Hoffmann's story about a doll that came to life found its way into the equally beloved ballet, *Coppelia*. Jacques Offenbach's opera *The Tales of Hoffmann* immortalizes this story even more, because it is performed at the Metropolitan Opera children's matinees each Christmas season. The dream-based theme of Hoffmann's *The Sandman* story reappears with a new and less sinister twist, in an ever-expanding series of graphic novels by author Neil Gaiman.[15] Gaiman's *Sandman* returns to even earlier dream myths than Hoffmann's and revolves around the Greek mythological Morpheus, the ancient deity of dreams.

Tchaikovsky produced other equally enthralling examples of dreams-as-art, including *Swan Lake* and *Sleeping Beauty*. His own recurring depressions and eventual suicide synchronized with the soulful melancholy that epitomized the Romantic era. Most major ballet companies perform *Sleeping Beauty* each season. It has inspired several film versions over the years. American audiences know *Sleeping Beauty* best through its animated 1959 Disney version, where Tchaikovsky's original score reverberates against the backdrop of Disneyland's Magic Kingdom.[16]

The crossover between the themes of dream, sleep, and *Sleeping Beauty* is obvious. Beauty endured one hundred years of sleep because of a curse cast by an aggrieved sorceress who did not get an invitation to Beauty's christening. Still, some versions downplay the sleep aspect, and some critics deflect our attention away from Beauty's dreams entirely. It is easy to lose sight of the Romantic message behind Tchaikovsky's *Sleeping Beauty,* after hearing scathing feminist criticism condemning Beauty's dependence on the Prince. True, the *Sleeping Beauty* story revolves around a physically and mentally paralyzed female, who is mobilized only through her association with a male and is unable to act on her own. This parable of 1950s-style feminine helplessness offends those of us who live in a postfeminist era that values action and achievement, but pandered to the Romantic belief in the near-supernatural state of sleep. Rather than disparaging this passive condition of dreaming rather than doing, the Romantics linked the physiological sleep to sorcery and deemed the dreams that occurred during that time to be very active achievements.

Giselle is another Romantic ballet classic that speaks worlds about the Romantic approach to dream and life in general, as does *La Bayadère*. The story of doomed but undying love, *Giselle* tells the tale of young women who were banished to a never-ending netherworld, inhabited by women who died before their suitors married them. These *wilis* avenged their fates by luring passing men to their doom and dancing with them until they died. Like dreams, these young maidens, who were known as *wilis*, were active only between midnight and dawn. They could claim the lives of mortal men who passed by them during those hours only.[17]

In true romantic fashion, this soulful and sorrowful alternative world was made up of the requisite mist, forests, and forced perspective. It combines a naturalistic forest scene with the supernatural world of the *wilis*. Giselle, the heroine of this ballet, was about to enter this supernatural *wili* world, to become a *wili* herself, after she died of madness and a broken heart. Her death occurred immediately after she learned that the nobleman Albrecht had deceived her and had failed to inform her that he was already betrothed to another, when he first won her love.

In the second scene, Albrecht is grieving for Giselle and admitting his responsibility in her death. He enters the forest to place flowers upon her grave. Then the *wilis* emerge to claim him and to dance him to death, as they would do to any other male. But the gracious and all-forgiving Giselle appears and takes it upon herself to dance with her duplicitous lover until four in the morning, when the *wilis* lose their power. Albrecht then exits unharmed. The *Giselle* story ends as the dawn lights up the sky. The story comes to a close in the morning, just as dreams do.

As fanciful as this story sounds on the surface, this fiction reflects a certain amount of fact. Fatal heart attacks are more frequent just before dawn, when dream-laden REM sleep is most intense. This deadly "dancing" may be a metaphor for the sexual act itself, which tends to be a nighttime activity. Or it may allude to the imaginary sex that occurs during an erotic dream, which also carries an increased risk of cardiac arrest and can lead people to die in their sleep.[18]

There are other curious correspondences to consider. The music to *Giselle* was composed by Adolphe-Charles Adam (1803-1856). Theophile Gautier wrote the libretto and based it on a story by the Romantic poet Heinrich Heine. Heine spent the last decade of his life under the influence of morphine, which he used to relieve the pain of his paralysis. But it is Gautier who interests us almost as much as the *Giselle* story. Gautier authored many memorable dream stories, including *The Dead in Love,* which focuses on the confusion between dream and reality and revolves around the erotic acts committed by a priest who is uncertain if he is awake or asleep.[19] Gautier wrote while under the influence of hashish, which had recently been imported to Europe from the "Oriental" lands of the Near and Mideast, Turkey, and the Holy Land.[20]

Gautier was introduced to hashish by Moreau de Tours, an obscure psychiatrist and early pharmacology experimenter.[21] Moreau de Tours' approach did not attract much attention from medical colleagues. Gautier, on the other hand, succeeded in founding the Hashish Club in 1844, so that he and his literary cohorts could explore the hazy boundaries between dreams, drugs, and psychotic states. Gautier's Hashish Club eventually included literary luminaries such as Victor Hugo, Balzac, Maupassant, and Gerard de Nerval. Several of their dream and drug-inspired short stories appear in English translation in Joan Kessler's *Demons of the Night.*[22]

Another favorite Romantic ballet, *La Bayadère,* revolves around opium-induced dreams about the "Kingdom of Shades." This story is set in exotic India, rather than in the misty forest of Europe, and centers around unrequited and avenging love. This time, the victim is a woefully wronged temple dancer or *bayadère.* The real action begins after the dancer is bitten by a poisonous snake that was hidden in a gift basket sent by the amorous high priest, whom she rejected in favor of the affections of a handsome young warrior. The poisonous venom kills her quickly.

In the second act, the grief-stricken warrior whom she loved smokes opium to induce a dream of his lost love. The illusory image from the kingdom of shades brings only temporary and insufficient relief for the warrior-turned-opium dreamer. It is not until the ballet's end, when the temple crumbles and crushes the spiteful high priest and all those in it, that the soul of the deceased *bayadère* wreaks its revenge and reunites with her intended in the kingdom of shades.

The dreamy state of opium permeated much Romantic literature, which did not distinguish between the drug-induced dream state and the spontaneous dream state of sleep. Authors such as de Quincey opened up a new genre of literature when he published his *Confessions of an English Opium Eater.* Opium-intoxicated poet Coleridge penned the most dreamlike poem ever written, *Kubla Khan.* Like *La Bayadère,* both *Opium Eater* and *Kubla Khan* linked the exotic Orient with opium-induced dreams. Each lends an incorrect and even offensive impression of the "Orient," as outspoken literature professor Edward Said pointed out in his often-quoted study of *Orientalism.*[23] Both Coleridge and de Quincey each had very realistic reasons to visualize Asia while under the influence. De Quincey had been visited by a Malay man, shortly before recording his dreamy visions of Asia. He was reflecting upon his own personal, recent memory of Malaysia. Coleridge fell asleep after reading a book about the Mongol conqueror Kublai Khan. Upon awakening, he composed a confabulatory tale about a faraway land called Xanadu, based on these presleep readings. It should be noted that Coleridge had already made several attempts to write the poem, before he finally succeeded through the help of this pharmaceutical stimulus.

Some influential Romantic dream literature was based upon actual journeys to the East. Gerard de Nerval's account of his hashish-induced hallucinosis, in his *Journey to the Orient*, is an excellent example of this genre. Another of Nerval's works, *Aurelia* (also entitled *Life and Dream*), is even dreamier and for good reason. Nerval composed his vivid visual descriptions while confined to a psychiatric asylum. He had been an accomplished writer before his breakdown. Still recoiling from rejection by the singer Jenny Colon and still under the influence of opium, ether, and alcohol, as well as hashish, Nerval had published only part of his dreamy manuscript before hanging himself from a Paris lamppost. The full work appeared in print either hours or days later (depending upon which source one accepts). He influenced both surrealists of the next century, as well as budding psychopharmacologists of his own time, who were eager to point to a written work that could identify ordinary dreams with pathological delirium.[24]

ENGLISH ART AND LITERATURE

There are many excellent examples of dream and drug-influenced Romantic literature. One of the best known is Mary Shelley's *Frankenstein*, which was conceived while the author was under the influence of an alcohol and opium concoction called "laudanum." Mary and her poet-husband Percy Bysshe Shelley were spending time in the country with Lord Byron and their doctor when an enormous electric storm hit. According to Ken Russell's colorful film *Gothic* and according to many popular legends, but *not* according to fact, they set up a contest to pass the time and to see who could compose the best horror story. Mary Shelley won, with her fanciful story about a monster created by man.

Rather than representing a retreat from reality, Shelley's *Frankenstein* fantasy captured prevailing public concerns about electricity and science. Electricity had recently been discovered, and science was forging ahead and threatening to dehumanize society. The lightning bolts in the sky reminded the intoxicated author of these cultural currents. Her clouded consciousness conceived of a way to warn readers about unchecked powers of science and scientists. Her dreamy Romantic premonitions rivaled prophetic dreams and drug-induced oracles of the past.

The story of the creation of the *Frankenstein* story was appealing in its own right and so became the subject of Ken Russell's tongue-in-cheek film, *Gothic*. *Gothic*, in turn, was advertised with a poster of an equally famous nightmare vision, one that was originally created by Swiss-born and Italian-educated Romantic artist, Henri Fuseli. Fuseli had already relocated to England when he painted his quintessentially Romantic image *The Nightmare*. In *The Nightmare*, a sleeping woman lies supine, draped across the bed, her nightclothes falling in the same sort of gentle folds that appeared in the art of Italian masters of old. Gracious curtains, reminiscent of classical Greek togas and flowing Renaissance robes, surround the bed. Peeking out from behind those curtains is a ghostly-looking horse's head. This horse head looks slightly silly to an audience reared on animatronics and computer graphics but is significant because it is a literal rendition of the "night mare."

The small, green, devilish-looking *incubus* that squats on the sleeper's chest refers to sexualized, supernatural beings that appear in the myths of many unrelated cultures. Such incubi are implicated in nightmares, nocturnal emissions, and lesser sexual feelings that surface during sleep. A print of this famous Fuseli painting, with its brazenly eroticized rendition of the sleeping state, hung on the wall of Freud's apartment on Berggasse 19, Vienna.[25] This painting is a perfect restatement of Freud's daring new theories about sexual instinct and the unconscious and dreams. A reprint of this particular painting, as well as other Fuseli paintings, appears in Carl Jung's last and most popular book about *Man and His Symbols*. When Freud's first biographer, the English analyst Ernst Jones, wrote his own book *On The Nightmare* several decades later, he placed a plate of Fuseli's painting on the inside cover.[26]

Fuseli's illustrations of Shakespearean plays are equally well known to the art world. Shakespeare's *A Midsummer Night's Dream*, with its "flower-juice"–induced visions of fairies, inspired Fuseli's meticulously detailed, highly realistic renderings of utterly unreal worlds. Because *A Midsummer Night's Dream* bridges several different approaches to dreams, it offers a wide and wonderful opportunity for artistic and dramatic interpretations. It is a place to portray erotic little fairies, who are scantily clad, yet rendered innocuous by partially concealing wings. On the other hand, this dream scene appealed to those Romantic and post-Romantic poets who equated night visions with drug-induced images.

Shakespeare's insights about dreams and psychological conflict anticipated psychoanalytic concerns of the late nineteenth and early twentieth centuries. Yet attributing dreams to chemical causes, such as flower juice squirted in the eye, was a far cry from psychoanalytic searches for the internal, rather than external, origins of dreams. On the other hand, this approach was perfect for late nineteenth-century laudenum users, such as John Anster ("Fairy") Fitzgerald, or the tragic Richard Dadd, and many others. Fitzgerald painted so many fairies that he earned the nickname "Fairy Fitzgerald." Dadd's personal and professional stories are even more complex.

Richard Dadd was already an accomplished artist before he murdered his father while in the throes of a drug-induced, psychotic state. He spent the rest of his years as a patient in an asylum as a result of this heinous act. While confined, he painted intricate little fairies and dream scenes from *A Midsummer Night's Dream*. In spite of his obvious infirmity, Dadd continued to produce appealing art that found its way into charming little children's books. Later generations were apparently not aware that these lovely illustrations had such an unlovely origin.

Dadd's work appears in a beautiful book on *Victorian Fairy Painting*, published to accompany an art exhibit of the same name.[27] In that same volume, one can find "Fairy" Fitzgerald's renditions of *A Midsummer Night's Dream*, and his own version of *The Nightmare* (1857), and the *Artist's Dream* (1857), and *The Pipe Dream* (1870). Also in that volume are several versions of *The Stuff That Dreams Are Made Of* (1858), which owes its title and its theme to Shakespeare's *Tempest*. Although Dadd's life history is far more sensational than Fitzgerald's, Fitzgerald's paintings caused more controversy, because of his prominent portrayal of drug equipment. Those parts of his painting were edited out and painted over before being publicly displayed. Yet other artists of this same school inspired Disney's delightful little Tinkerbell!

These Victorian fairy painters fused Fuseli's original dreamy imagery with the spiritualist influences that were popular during their own times. Fuseli's night visions live on, through the fairy paintings that populate the pages of children's books and through Disney classics. Sadly, Fuseli himself is not as well known as his heirs, and he is certainly less well known than his contemporary and countryman, William Blake. Blake's blatantly dreamlike visions are far better recognized, partly because Blake left a distinctive collection of "illuminated painting," replete with poetry. This poetry was rediscovered by the Romantic poet Yeats, who, in turn, influenced other pillars of poetry, such as William Wordsworth, Allen Ginsberg, and others. The public and poets alike returned to Blake to view his art and to read his text.

Unlike Fuseli, whose fantasies drew upon secular inspirations, Blake was at his best when he was spiritual. He devoted himself to dreamy books of the Bible and added the mystical influence of Swedenborg, who also recorded religious visions that appeared to him during his dreams. Yet he drew muscular Michelangelesque figures that contrasted with Fuseli's finely-rendered and fastidiously draped fairylike figures.

Blake excelled when he interpreted the prophet Daniel's apocalyptic dreams of four-headed monsters. He recorded King Nebuchadnezzar's terror-struck visions of the city of Nineveh before its destruction, and before the king fell into a psychotic state of lycanthropy, when he devoured human flesh under the belief that he was a wolf. Blake illustrated Milton's visionary epic *Paradise Lost*, as well as Dante's *Divine Comedy* (which speaks about a semisleep state). Blake created his own imaginary realm of *Urizen* and tapped into the realm between dream, imagination, and religion. He accessed a universe that is available only to persons of a very unusual mental state.

Blake embellished his preprinted text and engraving with watercolor to produce "illuminated painting."[28] He claimed that his dead brother disclosed this unique technique when he appeared to him in a dream. Blake first experienced such waking visions when he was four. His dreamlike world inspired the symbolists later in the nineteenth century and served as an example for some "outsider artists" near the end of the twentieth century. But Blake was no ordinary dreamer. He could blend his idiosyncratic visions with more universal themes to create artworks that resonate in every human soul, yet still stand out as being distinctly and idiosyncratically "Blake." His artistic approach and his isolated life separated him from his fellow Romantics, but he was nevertheless typically Romantic in the way that he fused dreams, the written word, and graphic art.

Two other contemporaries of Blake and Fuseli had a major impact on the Romantic rendition of dreams. Those people were John Martin and his brother Jonathan. An opium smoker, John Martin became known as "Mad Martin." This nickname stuck partly because of his own eccentricities, but mostly because he was confused with his brother Jonathan, who set fire to the York Ministry after receiving instructions in a dream. John Martin was a well respected illustrator and engraver. His panoramic apocalyptic scenes are populated by dead souls, heavenly angels, fireballs, earthquakes, and floods. Reprints of these disasters appeared on popular calendars in the nineteenth century. John Martin also painted scenes of Pompeii, Nineveh, Babylon, and Sodom and punctuated them with unique touches excavated from his own imagination and intensified by his smoking opium. The far-reaching panoramas that Martin painted are chillingly similar in form to the panoramic vistas described by some temporal-lobe epileptics, who hallucinate while in a dreamy, seizure-induced state.

John's stature as an illustrator increased, rather than decreased, after his older brother's trial. The trial attracted widespread attention. It set off psychiatric debates about the nature of insanity, after Jonathan portrayed himself as one of many prophets who acted in response to dreams and expressed conviction about the truth of the dream that directed him to commit his crime. Jonathan was eventually declared criminally insane and was incarcerated in Bedlam. While in Bedlam, Jonathan pursued his art and drew robust humans and imaginary animals, set in a disjointed space that was easily distinguished from John's carefully-crafted and mathematically-precise panoramas.

Jonathan left diaries and drawings, replete with descriptions and interpretations of dreams that could rival transcripts from Freudian psychoanalytic training sessions. He became the best-studied madman of the nineteenth century. His dreams and dream-inspired art were deemed to be the perfect portrayal of insanity. At the same time that science and society agreed that he was psychotic, Jonathan also fulfilled the Romantic ideals of the insane artist (albeit a criminally insane one). He affirmed the newly-established Romantic belief in art as a form of a self-expression. Some say that he foreshadowed Freud's fascination with dreams as revelations of mental derangement and interior states. Jonathan Martin clearly stood at the crossroads of two distinctly different approaches to dream, each of which retains its adherents to this day.

Ironically, Jonathan's less refined and more psychotic art attracts wider audiences at the cusp of the twenty-first century than his brother's more academic style. This changing preference reflects the late twentieth century's intrigue with the outsider art of the unschooled insane. It may also reflect the impact of John MacGregor's chapter on Martin's art and life, in his highly influential volume *The Discovery of the Art of the Insane*.[29]

GOYA AND THE SPANISH SCHOOL

These examples of English Romantic artists and the dreams they depicted represent the author's favorites. However, it should be noted that Francisco Goya's depictions of dreams, madhouses, and acts of violence are regarded as the true forerunners of Romanticism. Originally a tapestry painter who turned professional portrait painter, Goya lived through the brutal Napoleonic invasions of Spain. He had been reared in an era that adhered to the values of the Age of Reason and only inadvertently came to epitomize the value shift of the next century. In his later years, he painted the inmates in the madhouse at Saragossa, Spain. The anguished and expressionist poses in this painting revolted adherents of the Age of Reason but inspired symbolists and expressionists of subsequent centuries. In his later years, Goya created a terrifying image of Saturn devouring his son. He also favored witches' sabbaths as subjects.

Goya's bleak black-and-white lithograph *The Sleep of Reason Produces Monsters* restated the Enlightenment's horror at the thought of unleashing uncontrolled images and imagination. This often-reproduced work represents a turning point between Reason's and Romance's approaches to dream. It shows owls and bats flying out of the head of a man who has fallen asleep. These night creatures hover around the dreamer to haunt him. Like Pandora's box, which could not be closed once it was opened, the dreamer's brain is forever changed, once reason has departed and dreams appear.

The cause of Goya's slippage into "black romanticism" and his preoccupation with violence, witchcraft, and madness has always been unclear. Some say it was simply a reflection of the outer world and Spain's corruption by the ravages of war. However, there is ample evidence to suggest that Goya would have suffered an inevitable mental decline on account of the lead poisoning he acquired from "pointing" his paintbrush in his mouth, when it was covered with lead-based "flake white" oil paint. He experienced intermittent paralysis, organic brain syndrome, deafness, and a course tremor that demonstrably affected his paint strokes. Cut off from communication by his hearing loss and constantly besieged by the strange psychiatric symptoms caused by this brain disease, Goya lapsed into a nightmarish world, where dream intruded into daily life. Goya's dramatic life story and his horrific inner experiences are brilliantly dramatized in the 2000 film, *Goya in Burgos.* This is one foreign language film that achieves more, rather than less, through its subtitles. The absence of understandable speech allows the spectator to enter Goya's wordless world more directly and offers an opportunity to witness his visual hallucinations with more immediacy and potency than might otherwise be possible.

There is more irony to Goya's personal decline and his departure from reason and the artistic conventions of his day. Even though his decorative tapestries and precise portraits brought him commercial success in his early years and ensured a solid reputation at the time, they would not have brought him enduring fame. They are not the reason why he is remembered today. It was Goya's descent into the underworld of madness and dream, coupled with his ability to translate these experiences into art, that appealed to later generations. Goya's dark side or his "shadow side," so to speak, paved the path to early nineteenth century Romanticism, late nineteenth century Symbolism, early twentieth century Surrealism, mid-twentieth century Expressionism, and late twentieth-century visionary and video art. Romanticism as a whole receded over the course of the nineteenth century, but its sprit resurfaced in wholly new forms over the next two centuries. The discovery of psychoanalysis and the reinvention of the dream was just one of the many ways that Romanticism was reinvented.

NOTES

1. Beguin, Albert. 1939. "L'Ame Romantique et le Reve" ["The Romantic Soul and the Dream"]. Chaudon, Francis. *The Concise Encyclopedia of Romanticism.* Secaucus, NJ: Chartwell Books, 1980.

2. Europe's Age of Reason of the seventeenth and eighteenth centuries was not the first point in time when doubts about the supernatural or "sentimental" interpretation of dreams surfaced. Some early Greeks and Romans were just as adamant about the importance of reason. See Dodds, E. R. *The Greeks and the Irrational.* Berkeley: University of California Press, 1951.

3. Alexander, Franz, and S. T. Selesnick. *The History of Psychiatry.* New York: Harper, 1966; Mora, George. "Historical and Theoretical Trends in Psychiatry." Harold I. Kaplan, Alfred M. Freedman, and Benjamin Sadock, eds. *Comprehensive Textbook of Psychiatry.* 3 vols. Baltimore: Williams and Wilkins, 1980, 4–98.

4. Rosen, George. *Madness and Society.* Chicago: University of Chicago Press, 1968.

5. Harner, Michael, ed. *Hallucinogens and Shamanism.* New York: Oxford University Press, 1973; Schultes, Richard Evans, and Albert Hofmann. *Plants of the Gods.* Maidenhead, U.K.: McGraw-Hill, 1979.

6. Voltaire, Marie Francois Arouet de. "Somnambulists and Dreamers in the World of Dreams." Ralph L. Woods, ed. *The World of Dreams: An Anthology.* New York: Random, 1947.

7. Abrams, M. H. *Naturalism and Supernaturalism: Tradition and Revolution in Romantic Literature.* New York: Norton, 1971.

8. Kirschner, Suzanne. *The Religious and Romantic Origins of Psychoanalysis.* Cambridge, U.K.: Cambridge University Press, 1996.

9. 6 July 2000. http://www.cinematographer.com/magazine/nov98/dreamsFX/pg1.htm.

10. Ellenberger, Henri. *The Discovery of the Unconscious.* New York: Basic, 1970.

11. Packer, Sharon. "Jewish Mystical Movements and the European Ergot Epidemics." *Israel Journal of Psychiatry.* 35:3 (1998): 227–239; Scholem, Gershom G. *Major Trends in Jewish Mysticism.* 3rd ed. Jerusalem: Schocken, 1960; Underhill, Evelyn. *Mysticism,* 12th Ed. New York: Signet-Penguin, 1974.

12. Lasch, Christopher. *The Culture of Narcissism: American Life in an Age of Diminishing Expectations.* rev. ed. New York: Norton, 1991.

13. Sala, Charles. *Caspar David Friedrich and Romantic Painting.* Paris: Editions Pierre Terrail, 1993.

14. Freud, Sigmund. "The Uncanny (1919)." *Studies in Parapsychology.* ed. Philip Rieff. New York: Collier-Basic, 1963, 19–62.

15. Gaiman, Neil et al. *The Sandman.* Book 3. New York: D.C. Comics, 1995.

16. Disney's Magic Kingdom is modeled after European castles built by Mad King Ludwig. Allan, Robin. *Walt Disney and Europe.* London: John Libbey and Company, 1999.

17. Kaye, Elizabeth. *American Ballet Theatre: A 25-Year Retrospective.* Singapore: American Ballet Theatre, 1999.

18. Although Ernest Jones' book *On The Nightmare* does not mention *wilis,* when it catalogues the recurring theme of sexual activity with night demons it

is clear that the *wilis* in Giselle represent one more mythological version of night succuba, who copulate with men during their sleep.

19. Kessler, Joan. Introduction. *Demons of the Night*. Chicago: University of Chicago Press, 1992, iv-xxii.

20. Said, Edward W. *Orientalism*. New York: Vintage Books, 1979.

21. Moreau, J. J. *Hashish and Mental Illness*. New York: Raven Press, 1973, 17.

22. Kessler, Joan. *Demons of the Night*. Chicago: University of Chicago Press, 1992.

23. Said, Edward W. *Orientalism*. New York: Vintage Books, 1979.

24. Kessler, Joan. *Demons of the Night*. Chicago: Univesity of Chicago Press, 1992.

25. Powell, Nicolas. *Fuseli: The Nightmare*. New York: Viking Press, 1972.

26. Jones, Ernst. *On The Nightmare*. New York: Liveright, 1951.

27. Martineau, Jane, Jeremy Mass, Pamela White Trimpe, Charolotte Gere, et al., ed. *Victorian Fairy Painting*. London: Merrell Holberton, 1997.

28. Chaudon, Francis. *The Concise Encyclopedia of Romanticism*. Secaucus, NJ: Chartwell Books, 1980.

29. MacGregor, John M. *The Discovery of the Art of the Insane*. Princeton, NJ: Princeton University Press, 1992.

11

Symbolism and Surrealism

SYMBOLISM, SURREALISM, AND THE FIN DE SIÈCLE

Symbolism and surrealism both dealt with dream, each in its own distinctive way. Symbolism was the first of these two amazing art movements. It began in the nineteenth century, trickled into the twentieth century, and disappeared after World War I. The other movement—surrealism—was situated frankly and firmly in the twentieth century. Surrealism was a thoroughly modern movement, one that broke with the past, yet still paid tribute to symbolist and Romantic—and even medieval—precursors.

The symbolist movement was in place *before* Freud "discovered" his psychoanalytic dream theory and so does not show the concerns with the deep meaning of dreams found in post-Freudian and post–depth psychology art. Symbolism arose in French-speaking regions and was rooted in the French heritage of hypnotism and occultism and mesmerism, which were quite different from Freud's later psychoanalytic theories. However, we cannot forget that Freud used hypnosis to treat his hysterics, early in his career. He also went to France to study hypnotic techniques and theories with Bernheim and Charcot. So he had a chance to come into contact with French symbolist art influences during his sojourn there. Jung also studied in Paris.

Surrealism, on the other hand, superceded psychoanalysis and followed in its footsteps. In fact, surrealism was a direct response to Freud's fully formulated dream theories and stated as much in its published "surrealist manifestos." In spite of its impressive debt to psychoanalytic treatment techniques, surrealism remained an art and literary movement. It takes some stretch of the academic imagination to tie symbolism to psychoanalysis. Symbolism is more closely connected to Jean-Martin Charcot's experiments with hypnosis or Pierre Janet's research with dissociative states and multiple personalities.

Symbolism and surrealism depicted the theme of dream in very different ways. The symbolists emphasized the dreamer, while the surrealists stressed the dream itself. The symbolists often portrayed a person lost in internal and ill-defined reverie. The spectator identifies with this vague but evocative symbolist subject but has few clues about what the dreamer is dreaming. So the spectator fills in the blanks with his own thoughts or feelings, and treats the symbolist portrait as though it were a Rorschach or thematic apperception test (TAT). The symbolist spectator is free to decide if the subject's dazed state is the result of dreams, drugs, hypnosis, spiritual possession, or any permutation of the preceding. Since the symbolists have not yet learned that dreamy states arise from the unconscious (as the post-Freudian spectator assumes), they have more explanations at their disposal.

The surrealists' dream themes were not nearly so ill-defined, and were presented in sharp focus, often in excruciatingly exacting detail. The surrealists forced the spectator to identify with the artist, rather than with the artist's subject matter, and pushed the spectator's gaze into alignment with the artist's gaze—in much the same way that cinema does. The surrealists' spectator sees the same scene that the artist saw and is free to add his or her own associations, or to act as a psychoanalyst and interpret the dream depicted on canvas. But the surrealist spectator arrives *after* the action of the dream has been completed. So surrealism is static, because it portrays a frozen moment in time. Surrealist paintings provide a "photograph of a dream state," and so are souvenirs of events that already took place. In contrast, symbolism is dynamic and shows the subject while he or she is still in the throes of the dreamstate.

There were other important differences between the symbolist and surrealist depiction of dream. The symbolists were interested in collective and culturally-based dreams. They preferred myth, with its system of symbols and stories that society as a whole acquires. Myths, by definition, are not the property or product of a single individual, though they can be adapted by any individual. The surrealists were not concerned with this shared story, but instead emphasized the idiosyncracies of the individual dreamer and of each individual dream. That is because surrealism started after psychoanalysis had arrived and shifted the focus away from the group and onto the individual.

The symbolists produced their dreamlike art without the self-consciousness of the postpsychoanalytic surrealists, although some symbolists did augment their dreamstates with drugs and others enlisted the aid of hypnotism or spiritualism. Surrealist attempts to plumb the unconscious were willful and contrived. There was nothing accidental or inadvertent about surrealist efforts to exploit "spontaneous writing" and "spontaneous talking" to generate spontaneous images. Surrealists were well aware of what they were doing, when they presented random images in irrational ways. Only their untutored audiences are confused about their intent.

It is equally important to know that symbolism began before the Great War (which we now know as World War I), whereas surrealism started after World War I and was a direct reaction to that war. The movement came to full flower between the two world wars and left a lasting influence that continued throughout the twentieth century and into the third millennium.

Contrarily, symbolism disappeared after World War I, because it was seen as a throwback to the nineteenth century and to the premodern era that ended with World War I. As a relic of the old world, symbolism carried unwanted memories of the people and nations who engineered this devastatingly destructive event. It was something to be forgotten, once modernism reared its head, and would not make a full-fledged reappearance until the latter part of the twentieth century. By that time, most of those who recollected symbolism's sad associations were too old or infirm to object to its resurrection.

It is curious that Freud's pioneering theories about psychoanalysis and his influential *The Interpretation of Dreams* were sandwiched between these two different artistic approaches to dreams. This chronological correspondence was not coincidental. It is difficult to prove beyond a reasonable doubt that symbolism had a direct connection to Freud's formula for interpreting dreams. It is easy to show a connection between symbolism and Jean-Martin Charcot, the neurologist who taught Sigmund Freud. It was well known that artists attended Charcot's popular public lectures on hypnotism and hysteria. Charcot's connections with art are less well known, but equally well documented. Charcot was not only familiar with the symbolist art of his time (and expressed disdain for that art), but he was an artist himself in his youth and retained an affection for art overall, for visual displays, and for drama, throughout his career.[1]

UNDERSTANDING SYMBOLISM

Identifying a specific symbolist approach to dreams is difficult, because the symbolists were never a cohesive school, in the way that the surrealists were. They were never organized in a fraternity, like the British Pre-Raphaelite Brotherhood of the late nineteenth century or the German Nazarenes. Some say that art critics constructed the entire concept of symbolism by looking backward in time and artificially demarcating the boundaries and beginnings of an artistic approach that had no clear-cut start and no self-identified members.

Because the origins of symbolism were so vague and the names of its "members" are often disputed, it has been the task of scholars, rather than the artists themselves, to identify who was a symbolist and who was not. It is generally agreed that symbolist art was intended to suggest, rather than to make a direct statement. The movement (if it should even be called a movement) tended to be as diffuse as its goals and its accomplishments. Symbolists were most skilled at portraying subjects that were equally diffuse and ethereal. Symbolism performs best when presenting spiritualism and occultism and dreams and somnambulism.

The symbolism art movement was further complicated by the fact that it began with poetry (which we will not discuss here) and produced visual art only secondarily. There was a strong link between symbolist art and symbolist music, because the symbolists believed in "synesthesia." In synesthesia, perceptions from one sensory organ are experienced through an entirely different sense organ (as actually happens while using LSD). The symbolists believed that music could be translated directly into visual image and vice versa, and so they blurred the boundaries between different art forms. They bypassed the direct, linear, literary inspiration that uses cognitive, coherent thought worked into words. They thereby reproduced the dreamstate, which also blends image, emotion, sensation, and story, and connects several senses simultaneously.

It has been said that the symbolists depicted the landscape of the dream but that the Romantics, who came before them and influenced them, depicted the dreamy landscape. The Romantics glorified nature and took it to new heights, but the symbolists preferred settings that existed outside nature. That lent an otherworldly aura to their art. When symbolists borrowed elements from nature, they removed those natural elements from their natural habitat and placed them in an unreal and often eerie space. For instance, leaves and flowers and rocks and feathers find their way into symbolist art, not as part of an organic whole, but as detached and displaced objects. These objects, in turn, augment the sense of the spiritual and the sublime. Some symbolists, such as Odilon Redon, distorted nature, and disguised nature, and turned it into a menacing presence.

Whereas Romanticism arose in Protestant countries such as Germany, where personal inspiration and interpretation were part of the Protestant approach, symbolism took hold in Catholic countries. In Catholicism, religion intertwined with art and music and drama and often used mythic symbols that had multiple meanings. This sense of collective myth and a shared past expressed itself in secular form in symbolism. The Industrial Revolution arrived later in Catholic countries than in Protestant ones and did not take hold as quickly or as intensely. When it did appear, it prompted a retreat from reality that paralleled the earlier Romantic protest in Protestant regions. Symbolism permitted a retreat from those real-world pressures of change.[2]

In spite of its spiritualist and occultist bent, symbolism retained some connection to the material world. For instance, the great pastelist and printmaker, Odilon Redon, who was the forerunner of the symbolist school, based his fantastic art on scientific illustrations of strange botanical plants and microorganisms. Redon was dubbed "The Prince of Dreams" for several reasons: because of his phantasmagorical subject matter, because of his special ability to transport his viewers into a dreamy state, and because he himself named his lithograph series "Dans Le Reve" or "In the Dream."[3] Redon was equally impressed with the achievements of Louis Pasteur, the controversial French chemist who discovered the role of microorganisms in communicable disease. Redon went as far as to send Pasteur a copy of his "dream" lithographs. Perhaps this was a way of saying that he and Pasteur were both aware of a world that was invisible to the naked eye and that each was ready to change the world in his own way, by tackling that invisible reality.

Redon's credentials in the dream world were unparalleled. During his twenty-year "noir" period, when he worked exclusively in black and white, he illustrated the works of the grea American fantasist and dream merchant, Edgar Allan Poe. Redon captured the crazed world of a man who went mad from a mixture of opium and alcohol and who died of lost love and untreated tuberculosis. Like Redon, Poe delved into the literary world of dream and delirium and wrote several odes to dream. Unlike Redon, who lived long enough to have a religious awakening that changed his dark palette into the softest and most beautiful pastel hues, Poe died at forty (1809-1849). Poe was a victim of his own drinking and drugging, but his art lived on. He spawned several more generations of artists, filmmakers, and writers, including stop-motion puppet animationist George Higham, who based his phantasmagorical puppet film on Poe's "Annabel Lee."[4]

The work of both Poe and Redon revolved around the concept of the "uncanny" and epitomized the uneasy feeling that arises when the familiar is made unfamiliar. This sense of the uncanny permeates symbolist art, where images of the man-beast Sphinx, of humanoid fetuses, and half-dazed dreamers abound and lead the viewer to believe that he or she has entered that otherworldly reality of the dream. Freud elaborated on the uncanny in a famous essay that remains required reading for many film and literature classes to this day. In this essay, Freud classified dreams, insanity, automatons, and puppets as equally "uncanny."

When we consider the crossovers between symbolism and the uncanny, we start to understand why symbolism was never as popular as impressionism, which also emerged in nineteenth century France. Championed by such luminaries as Van Gogh, Manet, and Pissaro, impressionism concerned itself with the sensory impressions of individual artists. It concentrated on the world that existed between the object and the artist's eye and added individual interpretation to these sensory impressions. Impressionism's focus on retinal images of the eye retained a semblance of reality, while the symbolists presented images from the mind's eye or that hypothetical and mystical "third eye" and so jarred the spectator's sense of solidity and reality.

For the symbolists, the eye turned inward, to an internal reality and onto a spiritual reality. The symbolist view looked in a very different direction than the impressionist gaze. The symbolists explored perceptions that the senses did not perceive and that could not be verified by secondary sources. To this day, many symbolist artists remain difficult to interpret and so elude our understanding. Our present day awareness of the unconscious makes it even more difficult to understand works that were produced so far before people learned to think in these terms.

One symbolist artist whose work is easier to relate to and easier to react to is the Belgian painter Fernand Khnopff. Khnopff was intrigued by sleep, dreams, and somnambulistic states, as were many of his contemporaries. He lived and worked at a time when people believed that dreams and hypnotic trances and seances could tap into a parallel universe to produce personal memories, recollections of past lives, and connections to dead souls. Such beliefs were common in preindustrial cultures and were typically intermingled with religion. Symbolist art secularized these age-old ideas about sleep and dreams and souls and spirits.

Khnopff himself saw somnambulism as a conduit between the mind and the occult. He was enamored enough of the idea of "hypnos" to keep a statue of the Greek god Hypnos in his studio. In some of his paintings, Hypnos appears on a pedestal, standing in the midground, to suggest that the artist's imagery evolved out of the somnambulistic trances of hypnosis or seances. He often painted enraptured women, standing immobile, wearing armor, as they stared off toward "inner space." His imagery implied that his subjects were trapped in the physical reality of the body, but that they were preoccupied by something that exists outside the picture plane or by something that does not really exist at all. Their dreamy stances and their ambiguous surroundings invite the viewer to speculate about the experiences of these subjects. Spectators become active participants in the painting when they identify with the model and wonder whether their own experiences are similar or dissimilar to the subject's experiences in the picture plane.

Another nonspiritual source of Khnopff's ladies' dreamy states deserves mention. The fixed, pinpoint-sized pupils of Khnopff's models suggests that they were under the influence of opium, which has the power to constrict pupils to the size of a pin—the medical sign known as pinpoint pupils. Opium's effects on eyes are totally different from the better-known effects of belladonna, which are also recognizable in other European paintings. Belladonna (which means "beautiful lady" in Italian) dilates the pupils and imparts a very distinctive appearance, because it acts on the brain and the iris of the eye. Belladonna produces a dreamy, dissociated expression in its users because it truly does impair concentration.

A concoction of alcohol and opium known as laudanum was quite popular during Khnopff's time and was sold without prescription, just as aspirin is today. Laudanum served more than medicinal purposes. Since the Romantic era, opium was valued for its alleged ability to unearth buried memories and to produce dreamstates of immense personal significance. One could say that opium's mnemonic function in the nineteenth century bore certain similarities to psychoanalysis' memory-excavating effects in the twentieth century.

The symbolist intrigue with opium, alcohol, ether, chloral, or other drugs did not impress everyone. Max Nordau, a psychiatrist-turned-journalist, published a very influential book about the drug-addicted "degenerates" who created this art. Nordau dismissed the symbolist intrigue with dreams, spirituality, and other ethereal things as another manifestation of mental degeneration. Nordau's book *Degeneration* alleged that degeneration was an inheritable and incurable mental condition passed from one generation to the next. Degeneration supposedly grew more severe with each successive generation. Degeneration could result from neurosyphilis, which they believed was transmitted transgenerationally, rather than through infection, or it could come from drug or alcohol use. This term took on sinister overtones in the next century, when the Nazis co-opted this concept to justify the extermination of the mentally and physically disabled and races and individuals that they deemed to be degenerate.

Not every generation was as condemning of drugs and dreams as Nordau's. The 1960s counterculture was an extreme example of a generation that venerated both dream and drug experience and promoted them as pathways to higher consciousness. Not surprisingly, the 1960s and 1970s witnessed a temporary rekindling of interest in symbolist art. Philippe Julien's book *Dreamers of Decadence*, along with a few well-timed museum shows, spurred that interest as much as the zeitgeist. *Dreamers of Decadence* emphasized the decadent strain of symbolist art and elaborated on the characters chronicled in Huysmans' novel *A Rebours*.[5]

Kenneth Anger took his inspiration from the nineteenth century symbolist painters, and mixed this sensibility with the opulence of Max Reinhardt's theater and film. The author of *Hollywood Babylon*, Anger became one of the most influential filmmakers of the 1960s, even though he began directing much earlier. He also added touches of the remarkable surrealist poet, author, and auteur, Jean Cocteau, whom he would join in Paris later in life. Max Reinhardt's visually sumptuous cinematic rendition of Shakespeare's *A Midsummer Night's Dream* figured into Anger's rendition of *Inauguration of the Pleasure Dome* in several significant ways. Young Anger made his film debut as an actor when he appeared in Reinhardt's film, at the age of three. Anger's mother was a costume mistress for the film. She dressed angelic-looking little Kenneth as a fairy and possibly sowed the seeds for Anger's adult preoccupation with gay sadomasochistic leather costumes seen in his cult classic, *Scorpio Rising*. Anger's *Inauguration of the Pleasure Dome* also looked back to the Romantic Era, when the opium-addicted poet Coleridge wrote about the "pleasure dome" in his Orientalist ode to Kublai Khan while in a drug-induced dreamstate.

Above all, Anger's symbolist and Orientalist excess tapped into the sumptuous art of protosymbolist painter, Gustave Moreau. Like Anger, Gustave Moreau merged myth and dream and Orientalist fantasy onto a single surface. Moreau posed Biblical figures, such as John the Baptist or Salome, or Greek mythological figures against the backdrop of complicated South Indian temple carvings. These impossible juxtapositions remind the viewer of the arbitrary associations of a dream. By painting writhing serpents slithering across his canvases, Moreau makes spectators wonder if he himself hallucinated these atavistic images during d.t.'s (which are well known to induce such visions).

A reclusive man who had little contact with his fellow artists, Moreau appeared in Huysmans' novel about the decadent fin de siècle spirit. It was through this book, *A Rebours,* that Moreau and others, such as Redon, became better known. Moreau's magnificent but iconoclastic art was underappreciated by subsequent generations. The Parisian townhouse where Moreau lived and worked eventually became a museum that can still be visited today. But legend has it that no one had visited this idiosyncratic space for a period of twenty years when Andre Breton returned to Moreau's mansion and reignited interest in this odd art of the imagination.

Andre Breton's visit to the Moreau Museum was fortuitous, for Breton was destined to become the impresario of the surrealist movement. Surrealism reinterpreted symbolism and recycled the idiosyncratic and introspective spirit of Moreau's work, by adding timely political, scientific, and even medical messages to this otherwise personal approach. As profound as Moreau's influence was for Breton and his circle, Moreau was just one of many equally interesting stimuli for Breton's surrealist society.

Psychiatry and neurology played as strong a role in Breton's artistic movement as art itself. Some serious scholars say that Breton was inventing another psychoanalytic school when he "invented" surrealism and that he could have produced a fourth major direction in psychoanalysis (to rival Jung, Adler, and Sullivan) had he returned to medicine and not remained with art. Mental states were as important to the surrealists as the artistic productions that they inspired. Moreover, dreams were important to Breton for the same reason that they were important to Freud: because they permitted closer contact with the unconscious. Breton aped Freud's methods of free association and excavated dream imagery. Yet his goals were diametrically different from the goals of the founder of psychoanalysis. Breton did not intend to cure patients or to explain the reasons behind their distress. He used art and literature and cinema as vehicles to make the unconscious as accessible as the conscious and to alter ordinary human experience.

World War I itself and the profound despair that followed in its aftermath was an important and indispensable impetus to the surrealist sensibility. Confidence in the "real world" was shattered, and preexisting values were devalued, now that the powers that be had destroyed the world around them and claimed countless lives in the process. By default, one had to look inward to find new meaning in existence. Communist and collectivist ideals, which also surfaced in the twentieth century, made a profound impact on the surrealist "society." The "Surrealist Manifesto" mimicked the "Communist Manifesto" in name, although not necessarily in content. In this manifesto, the surrealists spelled out their goals and their methods, with the same authoritarianism displayed by other totalizing political systems that were popular at the time.

The real key to understanding why surrealism took the direction that it did lies in the facts of Breton's life and the twisted and tangled role that World War I played on his own personal aspirations. Breton had not begun life intending to be an artist or writer. Rather, he planned to be a doctor. He was a medical student, before enlisting in the French military during World War I. As a student, Breton studied with Dr. Pierre Janet, the French philosophy professor-turned-psychiatrist. Janet was renowned in France at the time, but his retiring personality prevented him from becoming better known elsewhere.[6]

Janet specialized in the study of dissociative disorders and automatic movements. He lectured on the relationship between psychiatry and religion, and on psychiatry and spiritualism, and on automatisms. Breton heard these lectures and became familiar with this uniquely French approach to psychiatry. Moreover, as a Frenchman, Breton grew up in a milieu that had once been receptive to Franz Mesmer and "mesmerism." This controversial Austrian doctor had been banned from practicing "animal magnetism" in his native Vienna but successfully transplanted himself in France, to the chagrin of other medical societies. When he was a medical student, Breton also heard about the unusual research of a still obscure Viennese neurologist named Sigmund Freud.

Armed with information about Janet's automatic writing and Freud's free association, Breton enlisted in the French army, not as a physician but as an ordinary soldier. He was assigned to work on a ward of brain-injured patients. There were many such patients during World War I, because the casualties were astounding. Physical injuries were dramatic. Mental breakdowns were common among soldiers who spent a year or two at a time cramped in foxholes, squatting alongside the bodies of their dead buddies, listening to the deafening sounds of constant shelling. The term "shell shock" entered the everyday vocabulary.

The war made strong impressions on sensitive souls who later became artists. Many of those who did not suffer complete nervous collapses nevertheless left the war permanently changed. Their value systems lay in rubbles, like the destroyed cities. These young men had not found ideals that could replace their faith in the old world, save for a vague hope in "modernism." These were the future members of the "lost generation."

Breton was one of those changed men who did not return to his prewar existence. Rather than picking up where he left off, and completing his medical degree, and pursuing further formal study in psychiatry or neurology, Breton took a dramatically different turn. He did not discard what he had learned from his medical studies and his field experience. He simply reworked his intellectual inheritance and his wartime work experiences and added a unique twist of his own, when he wrote the *Surrealist Manifesto*.

Still concerned with madness and dream and the unconscious, Breton shook off the formalism of medicine and psychiatry. Instead, he wrote: "Dear imagination, what I especially like about you is that you do not forgive. . . . Only imagination makes me aware of the possible, and that is enough to lift a little of the terrible restriction; enough also for me to surrender to imagination without fear of being mistaken. . . . Hallucinations, illusions, are not a negligible source of pleasure. . . ."[7] He went on to speak of the "the confidences of madmen," saying that "I would spend my life provoking them. They are people of a scrupulous honesty, and whose innocence is equaled only by mine. Columbus had to sail with madmen to discover America. And see how that folly has taken form and endured."

This admiration for madness set Breton apart from practicing asylum psychiatrists, who sought to suppress madness and to isolate the mad from society by containing them in institutions. This attitude put Breton closer to the sentiments of the "modern" psychoanalysts, such as Jung, who himself had spent seven years in an essentially psychotic creative crisis. Like Freud, Breton saluted the dream's ability to access the unconscious and to mirror the psychotic process. Breton also anticipated "antipsychiatrists" such as R. D. Laing, whose unconventional approaches to schizophrenia attracted attention (and eventual condemnation) in the 1960s and 1970s.

Writing in his *Surrealist Manifesto*, Breton expressed his opinions about dream directly. He said, "From the moment that we succeed in realizing the dream in its integrity . . . when its contour will develop with unequaled regularity and breadth, we can hope that mysteries— which are not really mysteries—will yield to the great Mystery. I believe the future resolution of these two states, so contradictory in appearance—dream and reality—into a kind of absolute reality, of *surreality*, if one may call it so." So the concept of surrealism developed directly from this fusion of personal nighttime dream and consensual waking reality.

Breton's writings make it is clear that he saw a higher purpose to surrealism. He aspired to produce much more than mere art and literature and film. Its purpose was psychiatric as much as it was aesthetic. Surrealism offered an entirely new outlook on the world and a different way of experiencing life. Surrealism, as Breton saw it, could reduce the fragmentation of consciousness and achieve a psychological reconciliation for the total human being.

Yet Breton did not purport to produce model citizens or perfectly healed people, as practicing psychoanalysts did. Breton specifically spoke of the "prosecution of the real world" and of "breaking free of the tyranny of the unconscious." Surrealism advocated irresponsibility and recommended escape from the imperatives of a moral order and from the control of reason. Because of these goals, it is not surprising that the surrealist movement admired the Marquis de Sade, the monstrous sadist who spent his latter years confined to both prisons and mental asylums. For the surrealists, Sade epitomized the person who was persecuted by the state, precisely because he escaped its moral, sexual, legal, and cognitive control. What was more was that Sade was a writer, who produced massive novels, recounting his real and imaginary excesses. He served as inspiration for emerging surrealist writers, such as Breton himself.

Breton preferred states of psychological surrender, such as the dream, and orchestrated other techniques to enter altered states. Unlike many of their Romantic and symbolist predecessors, most (but not all) surrealists did not resort to drugs to attain surreal states of mind. This general disinterest in drugs did not affect their admiration of the visionary poet Rimbaud, who advocated a "disordering of the senses" through drug or drink to "make oneself a seer." Rimbaud also epitomized the surrealist ideal of amorality, because he abandoned his poetry career at age twenty and began life anew as a slave trader in East Africa. They also remembered Rimbaud for his turbulent affair with fellow poet Paul Verlaine. Later, Verlaine spent time in prison for stabbing Rimbaud.

In contrast to their indulgent hero Rimbaud, the surrealists sought their visionary states from automatic writing, speaking, and dream. Breton devised new techniques to access the unconscious. His method was novel enough to provoke the esteemed historian of psychiatry, Dr. Henri Ellenberger, to say that Breton could have started his own separate school of psychoanalysis, had he remained in medicine and not defected to art.

Breton had another favorite, who straddled the nodal point between insanity and art and who blended dream and life. That favorite was the symbolist writer Gerard de Nerval. Nerval's best-remembered writings about dreams were produced while he was confined to an insane asylum. Despondent over his rejection by singer Jenny Colon and possibly even delusional about the nature of their relationship from the start, Nerval hanged himself just hours before the publication of the second half of his manuscript *Aurelia* (also titled *Dream and Life*).[8]

Nerval's confusing and disconnected novels, with their abundance of fleeting, visual images, dramatize the blurry boundaries between dream and mental disease. His writings also betray the hallucinogenic influence of opium, alcohol, ether, absinthe, and hashish, all of which contributed to his mental decline. Nerval himself had been influenced by the eighteenth century German Romantic author and composer, E. T. A. Hoffmann, as well as by Theophile Gautier. Gautier started the Hashish Club in 1850s France, with the expressed purpose of introducing writers and artists to the creativity-enhancing effects of the herb.

Another hero of the surrealists was the fifteenth century Belgian artist, Hieronymous Bosch. Bosch's amalgams of esoteric symbols and familiar figures are constantly confusing, but endlessly entertaining. Works such as *The Temptations of St. Anthony*, *The Garden of Earthly Delights*, and *Ship of Fools* spoke to the surrealist aesthetic in the early twentieth century, just as they continue to appeal to anyone who appreciates imaginative art. Their enigmatic iconography was ideal for artists who came of age after the publication of Freud's *The Interpretation of Dreams* and who gleefully combed Bosch's juxtapositions searching for the same meaningful symbols that Freud found in dreams. Paintings such as *Ship of Fools* depicted madmen who were set asail on a ship. Bosch's renditions of *The Temptations of St. Anthony* illustrated the hallucinations that occurred while Anthony lived alone as an ascetic in the desert.

Unlike Nerval, whose life history was well known to the surrealists and was much discussed by the psychiatrists of his own day, Bosch's life history remains a mystery. Much more is known about the social climate of his times. Perhaps that aura of the unknown made Bosch's paintings even more appealing and permitted more elaborate and more fanciful and more personal interpretation of Bosch's symbols.

One look at a Bosch painting makes it easy to see how his wild imagery functioned as Rorschach test. His crowded canvases encouraged the surrealists to comb their own memories and imaginations, as they searched for explanations for these fantastic creations. For the Surrealists, who put dream life on equal footing with conscious perception, what could be better than the world depicted by Bosch's *Garden of Earthly Delights*? There, candy-colored castles and enormous birds and hybrid beasts live in the same landscape as realistically rendered humans.

It is now known that Bosch painted during the heyday of the ergot epidemics, when LSD-like chemicals infiltrated the food supply and produced bizarre visions, strange sightings, and waking dreams in those afflicted. Perhaps Bosch himself was exposed to ergot, as were many of his countrymen. This fact may be interesting to us today, now that we are more aware of the biological basis of behavior, but it held little appeal to psychoanalytically-inspired surrealists, who were more concerned with content than with cause.[9]

Besides appreciating specific artists and writers of the past and the dream state itself, surrealists also admired the altered psychological state of the medium. The surrealists did not appreciate spiritualism for the same reasons that the nineteenth century symbolists did. The symbolists came of age when the world was mired in spiritualism and seances and even Satanism. They accepted and even welcomed the unseen supernatural sources that guided the medium. The surrealists substituted a more modern, and more scientific, and more psychoanalytically-inspired twist to this intrigue with spiritualist messages. The surrealists specifically stated that they sought out messages "sent not from the spiritualist hereafter, but from the actual self, hidden by consciousness."

There were striking similarities between the surrealist experiments with "mediumship" and Jung's medical school dissertation on the psychological states of mediums, although the surrealists clearly favored Freud. Before coming into contact with his mentor (and future rival) Freud, Jung researched the mediumistic trances of his cousin Helene, who was a well-known clairvoyant. He concluded that the medium's messages arose from her own unconscious, which became accessible to her during these dissociative spiritualist states, just as it does during the dreamstate.

The early surrealists imitated this spontaneous, unconsciously-driven speech of the mediums, and combined it with Freudian techniques of free association, and called their technique automatic talking. They contrasted automatic talking with the automatic writing of the nineteenth century spiritualists. Unfortunately, automatic talking was too powerful, when used by the inexperienced or untrained. It produced a temporary psychosis in several members of the circle. Stabbings and suicide attempts occurred at surrealist gatherings.

Perhaps those people who experienced such extreme reactions to automatic talking were already psychologically unstable and needed just a gentle nudge to go over the edge entirely. Perhaps the surrealists' open admiration for artists and writers who met with violent or psychotic ends—such as Lautreamont or Rimbaud or Sade or Nerval—encouraged this dark twist. Perhaps the early surrealists simply did not have the expertise needed for safe journeys into unchartered psychological terrain. Automatic talking fell out of favor, and was officially outlawed in France, and bitterly condemned by official psychoanalytic journals. It was not until Breton entered the surrealist fold and introduced more medically-oriented techniques that the surrealists resumed their collective excursions into the unconscious.

The second time around, though, the surrealists substituted the far safer automatic writing for automatic talking. They devised a technique that they called the *Exquisite Corpse*, in which they passed around a folded napkin to each participant. Each person wrote his or her thoughts on the visible section of the napkin, without reading what the last person had written. The result was a disjointed, dreamlike journal.

By this time, psychoanalytic circles were too skeptical of surrealism to give much credence to this strange schism. Freud himself refused to collaborate with Breton, though Breton approached him and openly expressed his admiration for his new "science" of psychoanalysis. However, Freud did agree to meet with Salvador Dali, many years later, and praised Dali's artistry and creativity. Most other psychoanalysts followed Freud's lead and spurned the surrealists. One notable exception was French analyst Jacques Lacan, who was unorthodox in many other ways as well.

Ironically, though Freud disdained the surrealists overall and Breton in particular, it was the surrealists who translated and published

Freud's dream theories in French. They used their official journal to make the French-speaking world aware of Freudian dream theories, at a time when *The Interpretation of Dreams* was more or less marginal to the medical world and was of even less interest to the French. It was curious that the surrealists showed such high regard for Freud, the Austrian import, though Paris' Pierre Janet made a career of studying altered states of consciousness. It was more ironic that the surrealists favored Freud, when the rest of France preferred the existentialist explanations offered by philosophers such as Jean-Paul Sartre. France resisted the psychoanalytic ideas coined by the German-speaking culture and contented itself with French philosopher Henri Bergson's book *On Dreams*.[10]

In fact, France as a whole remained indifferent to psychoanalysis, until Jacques Lacan filtered Freud's voice. After hearing Lacan's interpretation of Freud, the French finally embraced psychoanalysis, and turned it into a powerful force in French psychiatry, politics, and culture by the 1950s. By the 1970s, French Lacan-based psychoanalytic theories about cinema led the world and inspired new vistas in film criticism. This same Jacques Lacan had published articles in surrealist journals at a time when Freud refused to speak with Breton. Lacan also married a woman who was once married to a well-known surrealist writer and publisher and pornographer, George Bataille. It was Lacan who would collaborate with the flamboyant surrealist painter and lithographer, Salvador Dali.[11]

Dali's influence endured longer than Lacan's. Dali painted self-described "photographs of his dreamscapes." He quickly became one of the most recognized surrealist artists and was far more financially successful than other members of this school. He developed a "paranoid-critical" approach to art in collaboration with Lacan and published his theories about the explorations into the unconscious in an often-republished paper by that name. Unfortunately, this paper about the paranoid-critical approach to painting was as disjointed and incoherent as Dali's much-celebrated paintings. Dali's skill as a painter and printmaker far exceeded his ability to write. Like his paintings, the exact meanings of Dali's theories are elusive and evoke the reader's personal associations more readily than they convey the author's actual intent.

He became even more controversial because of his political views, after he voiced support for the fascist forces that were coming to power. Responding to his right-wing ideas, the surrealists removed Dali from their tight-knit, politically sensitive circle. Yet Dali was indirectly instrumental in publicizing psychoanalytic dream theory, through his stunning contribution to Hitchcock's film *Spellbound*. In *Spellbound*, a handsome young psychiatrist (Gregory Peck) loses his memory and is suspected of a murder that he did not commit. He attracts the attention (and affection) of an equally attractive young physician/analyst, Dr. Constance Peterson, played by Ingrid Bergman. By dissecting the dreams of the troubled young doctor, the female physician uncovers the clues to the identity of the real murderer and restores the lost memory of the amnesic medic. She also reveals the treachery lurking behind the psychoanalytic asylum, when she elicits a confession from the true killer (Leo G. Carroll), who had headed the hospital but who was about to be replaced by a younger rival.

As compelling as Hitchcock's plot twists are and as appealing as the actors' performances may be, it was (arguably) Dali's surrealist dream scenes that gave the cinema its enduring strength and that made it so unforgettable, even after everything else in the film seemed dated. Dali's images of detached eyes, plastered across a stage screen, become inseparable from the screenplay. This riveting imagery intrigued an otherwise skeptical audience and practically hypnotized people into believing in the power behind psychoanalytic dream interpretation. While few viewers can remember the details of the convoluted plot, virtually every viewer leaves the theater with vivid recollections of Dali's dream scenes.

Interestingly, Dali's original dream scene lasted a full thirty minutes but was cut down to two and one-half minutes, because it was considered pornographic. Although the original was destroyed and the exact content of Dali's dream scene is not available, one can safely surmise that Dali's sexual scenarios mirrored Freud's own emphasis on the sexual symbolism of dream imagery. Other dream scenes in *Spellbound* were created by Hitchcock himself.

Dali also collaborated with director Buñuel on a strikingly short but remarkably influential surrealist film about dream scenes, entitled *Un Chien Andalou (The Andalusian Dog)*. This film foreshadows the unforgettable eye imagery found in *Spellbound* but perverts it in an intensely unpleasant way. *The Andalusian Dog* begins with a bizarre scene of a woman's eyeball being slit open. This disturbing and sadistic close-up symbolizes the violent opening of the physical eye, to reveal the more important mind's eye lurking behind. The scene and its female victim may also have latent sexual symbolism as well, because it shows the symbolic defloration of the artificially-opened eye, which was concealed by the labialike eyelids.

Un Chien Andalou is distasteful to many spectators but is as familiar to film students as *Spellbound* is to the general American public. Buñuel went on to create other films that rivaled *The Andalusian Dog*, both in their perversity and in their exploitation of dream as framing devise. *Belle de Jour*, a film about the sadomasochistic fantasies and daytime dalliances of a bored, beautiful doctor's wife (Catherine Deneuve), opens with an equally violent scene that turns out to be nothing but a dream. Other Buñuel films mix dream and waking reality just as potently and continue to exploit paraphilic themes, as was befitting a filmmaker who was a foot fetishist himself.

Over the years, Dali's imagery and the imagery of several other surrealists found their way into the American advertising industry. Dali's painting about *Memory* was used to sell liquor. Belgian surrealist Rene Magritte's painting of an eye whose pupil opens to expose the sky outside has become a nonspecific advertising icon for museums, universities, and other assorted mindscapes. Surrealism's disconnected dream imagery infiltrated the fashion scene when it inspired designer Elsa Schapiarelli to create a hat from a shoe. By entering these two forms of "art for the people"—fashion and advertising—surrealism became familiar to almost every American.

Because it was based upon psychoanalytically-inspired dream theories, surrealism became the vehicle by which the unschooled became familiar with the psychoanalytic concepts. Freud's ideas about dreams entered American pop culture, partly because of this dream-inspired advertising imagery. Like dreams themselves, these dream theories seeped into society in disjointed and convoluted and unpredictable ways. The "science"of psychoanalysis often arrived by way of cinema, surrealism, advertising, and art. With that insight, we can look at psychoanalysis' new and novel interpretations of dreams in a new light.

NOTES

1. Goetz, Christopher G. Michel Bonduelle, and Toby Gelfand. *Charcot: Constructing Neurology.* Oxford, U.K.: Oxford University Press, 1995.

2. Huysmans, Joris Karl. *Against the Grain [A Rebours].* New York: Dover, 1969; Gibson, Michael. *Symbolism.* Colonge, Germany: Benedikt Taschen, 1995.

3. Art Institute of Chicago. *Odilon Redon: Prince of Dreams 1840-1916.* New York: Abrams, 1994.

4. 11 Sept. 2001. <http://www.poepuppet.com>.

5. Jullian, Philippe. *Dreams of Decadence.* New York: Praeger, 1975.

6. Ellenberger, Henri. *Discovery of the Unconscious.* New York: Basic, 1970.

7. Waldberg, Patrick. *Surrealism.* New York: Thames and Hudson, 1997.

8. Kessler, Joan. *Demons of the Night.* Chicago: University of Chicago Press, 1992.

9. Packer, Sharon, and Warren Dotz. "Epidemic Ergotism, St. Anthony's Fire and Jewish Mysticism." *Dermatopathology: Practical and Conceptual.* 4:3 (July–Sept. 1998): 259–267.

10. Bergson, Henri. *On Dreams.*

11. Lacan's life did not flow smoothly. Lacan's controversial practices precipitated a split between French and international psychoanalytical circles. He was banned from other psychoanalytic societies because of his unor-

thodox beliefs and practices. In retrospect, we can see traces of these early forays into surrealist studies in Lacan's mature theories. We can also see how Lacan's unorthodox embrace of surrealism foreshadowed later unorthodox attitudes in other areas.

12

Psyche and Soul

THE CULTURAL CONTEXT OF PSYCHOANALYSIS

If each different approach to dream followed a linear, logical pattern, and advanced from one to the next, and represented a greater achievement than the last, this study would be much simpler. But that is not the way things work. Different approaches to dreams are simply *different*, not necessarily *better*. Even ostensible advances in the understanding of dreams often turn out to be not so advanced at all. Some advances have stronger connections to older ideas than anyone would have realized, had they not taken the time to dissect those advances and trace their sources and stand them side by side, next to those older approaches. Psychoanalytic approaches to dreams are an excellent case in point.

Granted, attitudes toward psychoanalysis have changed drastically over the decades, and contemporary college students do not share the same respect for this subject as those who came of age shortly after World War II. Yet even skeptics expect to find a significant schism between "modern" twentieth century psychoanalytic approaches to dreams and the ancient approaches admired by anthropologists. Psychoanalysis was, after all, a modern movement, and it was a product of the twentieth century rather than the second century. So it should theoretically operate on a different plane from bygone preliterate or superstitious societies. But theory is not the same as fact.

Similarly, most people expect to find a continuum between the psychoanalytic science of the early twentieth century and the sleep laboratory science of the second half of that century, if only because psychoanalysis speaks in the language of science and portrays itself as a science. It did, after all, evolve out of the medical speciality of neurology and was taught through psychiatry departments of medical schools. Thus, there was no reason to believe that psychoanalysis was anything other than science.

Yet the experimental approaches of mid-twentieth century sleep laboratory scientists were an abrupt departure from the methods of fin de siècle psychoanalytic depth psychology. Moreover, the most important sleep laboratory studies were not possible until 1928, when the EEG (electroencephalogram) was invented. Before then, brain waves could not be measured. Without the ability to measure brain waves, there was no way to distinguish the different stages of sleep. Curiously, the dawn of contemporary sleep laboratory studies (post-1928) overlapped with the twilight years of Freud's life. Freud died in 1939, a decade after the first EEG. Kleitman's groundbreaking book on *Sleep and Wakefulness* appeared in 1939,[1] the year of Freud's death. The sleep laboratory studies that followed in the wake of the EEG returned to pre-Freudian experimental techniques that had been neglected since Freudianism took center stage.

This disappointment at learning that psychoanalysis is not particularly scientific is especially acute for those who took Freud at his word and believed his promises to deliver a scientific basis for dream interpretation, as stated on the first page of *The Interpretation of Dreams*. But by the 1990s, even heads of major psychoanalytic institutions conceded that Freud's "scientific" discipline of psychoanalysis lay closer to the arts and humanities than to the sciences. On the other hand, readers who expect *The Interpretation of Dreams* to be a useless morass of outdated dream theories are in for a pleasant surprise when they find so many marvelous references to the arts and letters of Freud's own time and from past times.

THE START OF PSYCHOANALYSIS

When Freud coined the concept of psychoanalysis in 1895, he had years of experience as a neurologist behind him and had already achieved acclaim as a research scientist. He had two published books and many articles to his credit. His research had revolved around serious neurological topics, such as aphasia or the loss of language. He pursued his studies of dream with the same serious-mindedness that he applied to his earlier endeavors.

Today, *The Interpretation of Dreams* sometimes appears in the occult section of bookstores, sitting alongside volumes on tea leaf reading, the *I Ching*, and palmistry, sometimes wedged between wrapped packs of tarot cards. *The Interpretation of Dreams* is rarely used as a reference in academic psychology courses, except when it is examined for its historical interest and as a foundation for the serious scientific and scholarly studies that it inspired. Freud himself would be shocked to see the company his book keeps in the twenty-first century. Then again, Paracelsus would be equally dismayed if he saw that his alchemical studies are not taken seriously by contemporary chemists.

Still, *The Interpretation of Dreams* remains the cornerstone of psychoanalytic studies, a subject whose popularity has waxed and waned in the Western world. At one time, psychoanalysis was essential to the training of psychiatrists. All top-ranked psychiatry departments were chaired by physicians certified in psychoanalysis, and "good" psychiatrists pursued advanced training in psychoanalysis even if they did not intend to use it. This status changed as biological psychiatry advanced, and as psychopharmacology eclipsed psychoanalysis, and as the "brain" replaced the "mind" as the major paradigm. Ironically, psychoanalysis is being revived in Eastern Europe, where it had been dismissed by communists who stressed the social determinants of behavior over the psychological.

For most, *The Interpretation of Dreams* remains a relic of another era, never to be forgotten, but never to recapture the enormous influence it enjoyed in the twentieth century. No matter how flawed this book is and no matter how dated it seems today, this book constantly begs to be rediscovered and reread in a different light. It was this book that changed Freud's career and that transformed the cultural climate of the twentieth century (in conjunction with many other forces and discoveries and thinkers). *The Interpretation of Dreams* put the study of dreams on the front pages of peoples' imaginations. It also paved the path to late twentieth century postmodernist philosophy, because it elevated the importance of dream's disjointed fragments, with their multiple simultaneous meanings and varieties of interpretations—which is exactly what postmodernist thinking does.

Published a little more than one month before 1900, Freud's *The Interpretation of Dreams* is considered to be his most influential book. That is an amazing accolade, considering that Freud was one of the most influential thinkers of the twentieth century. He also he remained remarkably prolific for nearly another 40 years and produced many, many more books and articles that could conceivably compete with this book. Freud himself argued that *The Interpretation of Dreams* was his most important work.

Though he was repeatedly accused of authoritarianism, and was known to cast out followers who questioned his core ideas, Freud was not as completely convinced of the correctness of his theories as his followers were. Freudians who followed in his footsteps were more adamant about preserving his original ideas than was Freud. He was not one who could rest easy with his research without reexamining it, and so he continued to refine his ideas until he died of throat cancer in 1939.[2] He made minor revisions to his original dream theories. He published a book *On Dreams* for the public, two years after *The Interpretation of Dreams* appeared. But he never released a revised edition of the original *The Interpretation of Dreams.*

Freud was a pioneer, a provocateur, and also a false prophet. When he published *The Interpretation of Dreams* at the sunset of the nineteenth century, dreams were not a proper subject of serious scientific study. Dreams were the province of occultists, who were in ample supply at the time and who were popular with the public. Maury, whose dream studies he cites at the start of his magnum opus, was an archivist and a historian of magic, rather than a scientist per se. Scientists of Freud's day were "positivists" who demanded experimental proof for theories and would not squander time on topics that could not be proven by accepted scientific standards.[3]

The late nineteenth century scientists—as well as experimental psychologists—disdained the speculative explanations of philosophers and turned to laboratories and dissection tables instead. The practice of sitting in an armchair or standing behind a podium and theorizing by thinking and talking, as the philosophes had done in the past, had fallen by the wayside. Freud's biographer Peter Gay referred to him as "the last of the philosophes."[4]

Freud was as familiar with academic standards as anyone, if not more so, having been a respected laboratory researcher with an international education. Freud worked in the same century as Darwin and saw himself as a man of science, in the fashion of Darwin. Darwin's revolutionary theories about evolution cleaved biology from belief and were worlds away from the quaint creation stories of Genesis. They still ignite controversy in some circles to this day and were nothing less than incendiary in their own time.

Freud made a point of saying that he did not recognize religious truth and reiterated this position in several different essays. When Freud wrote to the acclaimed author and Himalayan traveler Romain Rolland, who inspired Somerset Maugham's novel *The Razor's Edge,* he admitted that he never experienced the "oceanic feeling" sought by mystics such as Rolland. Freud was nothing less than daring in his willingness to offend religious sensibilities, both of his own Jewish coreligionists and of the Austrian Catholics who controlled the country where he lived and worked. Freud's late-life book on *Moses and Monotheism* stood as testimony to a spiritual skepticism that never wavered, not even as advancing age and incurable illness loomed their ugly heads. He blatantly blasphemed the beliefs of his Catholic countrymen in his 1923 essay on *A Case of Demonic Possession,* where he wrote about a monk who served at Mariazel, Austria's greatest Catholic healing shrine. He equated religious ritual with obsessive-compulsive symptoms and disparaged faith altogether in a book about *The Future of an Illusion.*[5]

In spite of his antireligious and antisuperstitious bias—or was it because of his antireligious attitudes?—Freud's *The Interpretation of Dreams* bridged the gulf between the scientific and the occultist approaches. Here was a scientist who was willing to acknowledge the existence of an unseeable sphere of the unconscious, which had first been described by the Romantic-era physician, artist, and anatomist Carus. Freud believed that this unconscious was always present and all-important. One might say that this psychoanalytic unconscious was as powerful and pervasive as the Old Testament's omniscient and omnipotent Jahweh. Although this unconscious was just as invisible as the ether or the spirit world that superstitious people spoke about, it could make itself manifest through dreams, humor, slips of the tongue, and loose associations.

Freud grafted the concept of sexual instinct and infantile sexuality onto this quasireligious concept of the unconscious. This physiological twist situated Freud firmly in the Darwinian camp and prompted one of his less laudatory biographers to describe him as a biologist of the mind. Freud's Darwin-like readiness to view man as one of the beasts sent him searching for further evidence of humankind's animal instincts, this time concealed in their dreams. Freud's theories also reflected the influence of Helmholtz, the reigning physicist of his day.

It was Freud's physiological emphasis, more than anything else, that distinguished his psychoanalytic approach from the early nineteenth century German Romantic view and from supernaturalist approaches in general. For the Romantics, dreams were part of an ethereal netherworld that existed on a separate spiritual plane. Like the Romantics, Freud regarded each person's dreams as important expressions of that person's individuality. Like the philosophes of the Enlightenment, Freud recognized the role that personal memory plays in dreams. Like the structuralists of his own era, Freud searched for a common substructure to dreams, one that was shared by all human beings and perhaps even by the beasts. Like the supernaturalists of old, Freud felt that dreams served a higher purpose, although for Freud that purpose revolved around human, rather than divine, drives.

It has been said that Freudian psychoanalytic dream theories focus on the past and offer insights about the past, whereas supernaturalist soothsayers focus on the future and foretell the future. While this generalization is superficially accurate, it turns out to be too simplistic. If we look beneath the surface, we see that both Freudian dream interpretation and supernaturalist assumptions are future-oriented. Freudian ideas about psychological determinism claim that early childhood experiences mold a person's personality and set a pattern that is so strong that the past does indeed predict the future. If humankind is doomed to repeat earlier, unresolved conflicts through a process known

174 Dreams in Myth, Medicine, and Movies

as the repetition compulsion, then it follows that a dream that draws upon the past simultaneously opens a window to the future. One could say that Freudianism views dreams as prophetic in this distinctive way.

There are many interesting articles and books that compare the Freudian concept of the unconscious with the Romantic concept of the "soul" or "seele," as it is known in German. Freud's writings left no doubt that he considered this unconscious to be the most critical attribute of humankind. *The Interpretation of Dreams* contains as much information about the unconscious (or his theories about the conscious) as about dreams. Dreams were important to Freud, not because he found the theme of dream so endearing for its own sake, but because he believed that dreams were the conduit to this precious psychological commodity, the unconscious. Dreams were, as he said, the "royal road to the unconscious" (the *via regia*, in Latin). Freud elaborated on the ways that the unconscious (ostensibly) composed dreams, not because he wanted to gain insight about the end stage of dreams, but because he wanted to understand the unconscious wishes concealed within the dream. It was fortuitous for Freud that he himself was such an avid dreamer and so was able to use one thousand or so of his own dreams while working out his theories. But he was not driven by the need to decipher his dreams, as so many dreamseekers are today.

It is shocking to learn that the man who wrote such an influential and enormous text on *The Interpretation of Dreams* was not fascinated by dreams in and of themselves, but it is essential to appreciate this point. To repeat: it was the unconscious that intrigued Freud. Freud's desire to unearth the conscience conflicts that supposedly stimulated dreams drove him to theorize about dream and to use dreams in his clinical treatment of patients. For Freud, the dream was a clinical tool, rather than a beauty to be beheld. In this way, he was the polar opposite of artists and dramatists, who focus on the imagery or symbolism or the unfolding of the plot and who delight in the "free film" that appears after the eyes close shut. It just so happened that Freud inadvertently saturated the twentieth century with the theme of dream, because he wrote an enormously influential book about *The Interpretation of Dreams*.

Freud theorized that each dream represents a wish fulfillment and dramatizes a fantasy that the individual hopes will be enacted in the future. According to Freud, these hypothetical wishes arise from each individual psyche and are *not* implanted inside the mind by external sources such as demons or deities, as the supernaturalists claimed. Nor are these dreams a reflection of external material circumstances, as the equally influential Karl Marx might have opined. Later, Freud acknowledged that there are exceptions to this generalization about dreams as fulfillment. He admitted that combat veterans who suffer from recurring nightmares do not wish to return to their war traumas.

Even though he recognized that internal somatic or even external physical stimuli can influence dream content, Freud had little interest in these nonpsychological sources. He dismissed the importance of the magicianlike studies of Maury. Maury had held perfumes in front of a sleeping subject, who then dreamed of a perfumed Oriental bazaar. Freud made other omissions as well. Though he was fascinated by culture as a whole and wrote whole books on this topic later in his career (such as *Civilization and Its Discontents, Totem and Taboo, The Future of an Illusion,* and *Moses and Monotheism*[6]), he was relatively indifferent to the cultural contribution to individual dreams. He left this job to Jung, his intended successor and eventual competitor.

When we examine Freud's psychoanalytic "discoveries" side by side with events and trends and dialogues that took place at the time that this embryonic field was forming, we easily see that popular and academic dialogues helped shape Freud's theories about dreams. Freud's formulations about dreams and about all other things reflect far more than mere clinical data or laboratory discoveries or medical school studies. Freud drew upon his extensive education, which familiarized him with the Greek and Latin classics and with some Biblical studies as well. He could assimilate insights from centuries of the past and could simultaneously stay attuned to cultural currents and new discoveries, such as archaeology and Darwinian evolution and Helmholtzian physics and even the cinema. He could add knowledge accrued from years of experience as a neurology researcher, from formal studies of hypnotism and hysteria, and from insights inspired by patients, professors, and philosophers such as Brentano. Some say that his firsthand encounters with cocaine and the sexually charged perceptions and dramatic dreams induced by that drug added even more to this already interesting melange.

Perhaps Freud's genius sprang from his ability to synthesize so many different sources. Even if all of his theories do not hold up to scientific scrutiny and even if his totalizing theory about the psychosexual origins of dreams are too constricting to satisfy twenty-first century audiences, Freud's syncretic skills are still an achievement. We can compare his abilities to the alchemists of old, who mixed raw materials together to create a novel chemical product. Freud also composed a wide variety of ideas, information, and clinical experiences and transformed them into something new and distinctive.

FREUDIAN IDEAS ABOUT DREAMS

While Freud's theories about dreams have been hotly contested, most people freely admit that his descriptive vocabulary makes it far easier

to describe these otherwise difficult-to-describe events. Freud introduced terms such as "dreamwork," "latent and manifest meaning,"
"day residue," "condensation," "dramatization," "displacement," and
"symbolization." The labor-intensive job of embroidering and encoding
dreams became the dreamwork, in "Freudianese." During dreamwork,
unconscious impulses are translated into images and ideas, before
being strung together into some semblance of a story. Because these
unconscious urges and impulses are not acceptable to the ego when it
is awake and alert, they are blocked from consciousness during the day.
So the dreamwork must communicate these messages and meanings in
code.

Dreamwork puts tools such as displacement, condensation, dramatization, and symbolization into motion to convey emotion-laden and
socially unsanctioned messages in veiled form. These techniques can
transmit many messages simultaneously, since a single symbol can
stand for several different ideas or objects or people or places. This
"multitasking" makes dreamwork economical, also. These mental editing techniques produce an end product that is more acceptable to the
ego and that, according to Freud (but not according to later researchers),
serves to preserve sleep, by protecting the sleeper from being awakened
by disturbing ideas.

As the author of a neurology text about a language dysfunction
known as aphasia, Freud was familiar with the way that the brain
behaves when language abilities are impaired. He saw that something
inside reacts to words on a concrete and literal level, to produce
unintentional puns and paraphasias and "plays on words." He was
prepared to compare the speech of the brain-injured to the dreams
of ordinary people. Freud believed that dreams contain both latent
and manifest meanings. The manifest meaning of a dream is readily
identifiable and is a literal retelling of the story. Decoding the latent
meaning of a dream to find the meaning that resides beneath the
surface is more difficult and is best achieved (according to Freud)
when augmented by Freud's insights about psychosexual development and the patient's free associations.

Like other nineteenth century structuralists, such as Marx and
Durkheim, Freud perceived the presence of an underlying structure
around which self or society is organized. His psychoanalytic theories
attempted to identify these deeper principles or structure. At the same
time that he replicated the trends of his times, Freud also mirrored the
methods of Biblical commentators, as he sought out layers of meanings
behind a single dream. Long before Freud was born, rabbis, such as
Rashi and Maimonides and Nachmonides and Ibn Ezra and
Gershonides, searched each word and punctuation point of the Old
Testament for both esoteric and exoteric significance. Several of these

Biblical scholars were also physicians. These medieval hermeneutical techniques attracted renewed attention in the nineteenth century, as Protestant theologians employed similar methods to probe the Bible.

Even though Freud organized a highly structured and often authoritarian psychoanalytic circle, Freud was not nearly so authoritarian in interpreting the meanings of his patients' dreams as one might expect. In fact, just the opposite was true. Freud *did not* offer his own interpretation of his patients' dreams immediately. Instead, he asked the dreamer for his or her personal explanation and encouraged the dreamer to elaborate on the dream by adding extraneous and uncensored and spontaneous associations. He called these free associations and valued them more than the dream itself. Freud did not pressure his patients to remember every word and image and sequence of the dream. What mattered to Freud were the selective memories that remained on the day after the dream, which he referred to as the "day residue." This imperfect memory of the day residue reveals the issues that are important to the dreamer and is more relevant to Freudian theory than the actual details of the dream.

For Freud, dreams and their interpretations were just one part of the psychoanalytic process. Interpreting the dream was not his goal, as it was for the occultists. The cure and catharsis of psychological conflicts that supposedly inspired the dream were critical to Freud. Furthermore, Freud *did not* use dream interpretation as a sole diagnostic or therapeutic technique. He delved into dreams to help his patients free associate and to facilitate his talking cure. Dreams were never the primary means of Freudian psychoanalytic treatment, although Hollywood films lead us to believe otherwise. In other words, dreams were the appetizer that led the way to a more complicated and carefully constructed entree. Freud's disciple, Carl Gustav Jung, developed a different approach to dreams and treated dreams with far greater reverence than Freud.

Freud's interest in dream peaked after he observed that patients themselves mentioned their dreams spontaneously during their therapy, as they were trying to unearth other memories. Even patients who were unable to produce spontaneous associations during their psychoanalytic sessions were often able to discuss their dreams.[7] Delving into dreams seemed to be a time-consuming and cumbersome detour, when one really wanted to access the unconscious source of conflicts and symptoms. Yet this detour into dreams proved to be the "royal road to the unconscious" that deftly bypassed other roadblocks.

There is another important but ill-understood point worth noting about Freud's approach to dreams. Freud interpreted his patients' dreams while conducting analysis. Because these patients had already revealed their memories and associations, as well as their social and medical histories, Freud (and most—but not all—of his followers) knew a great deal about their personal lives *before* he addressed their dreams. Unlike the storefront psychics, who promise to interpret a single dream for a set price during a single session, Freud did not interpret dreams blindly, nor did he base his assessment of the patient's problems on the dream material alone.

This information-intensive, highly personalized, text-bound approach of the psychoanalyst differed from the approach of occultists, who attributed their dream interpretive abilities to unseen spiritual sources that they alone could access. Psychoanalysts also claim to possess special privileges and unique knowledge and have been accused of functioning like shamans by Freud's critics such as neuropsychiatrist E. Fuller Torrey.[8] Yet psychoanalysts generally use the dream as a document, before filtering that dream text through the lens of their chosen psychoanalytic theories. It should be noted that Freud described some universal dream symbols in a way that was reminiscent of both spiritualism and supernaturalism.

MUSEUM DREAMS

Those who have studied standard laboratory techniques and are familiar with the scrupulously scientific methods of experimental psychology are bound to be shocked by the physical setting where Freud conducted his dream studies. Freud's lavish home office was worlds away from B. F. Skinner's infamous "Skinner Box," where Skinner isolated and observed his young son and kept him free from all external environmental influences that could alter his behavior. In contrast, Freud conducted his talk therapy in his home, first on 19 Berggasse Street in Vienna, until he fled Austria to escape the Nazi's occupation. Freud relocated his home office to the largely Jewish section of North London, near the Swiss Cottage Road tube (subway) station, where it is preserved as the Freud Museum. There, he took tea with his patients, before they retired to the couch and emptied their unconscious of recollections and described their dreams. While en route to this new kind of examining room, Freud's patients gazed at the elaborate contents of his home and library and collections, just as museum visitors do today.

This home office deserves its "museum" designation. It houses elaborate archaeological collections, displayed in glass cases that recollect the meticulous displays in Vienna's Museum of Natural History. Ancient Egyptian, Roman, and Etruscan artifacts dot the room, standing upright on tabletops or lying flat under glass. Portraits and paintings and photographs line the walls, hung by ribbons and bows, in haute-Victorian style. In other places, a gargantuan library boasts book titles that boggle the mind and the memory.

Busts are perched on pedestals and scattered about the room. "Dismembered" heads, salvaged from the sculptures of several different civilizations, stand upright on shelves, silently proclaiming that it is possible to separate the head from the body, and to dissect it, and to appreciate it for its own sake. Elsewhere, Michelangelesque sculptures of full frontal nudes stand tall and undoubtedly inspired seething sexual sensations that crept into consciousness during psychoanalytic sessions.

Persian rugs drape over the couch. They invite associations about the Silk Road or Marco Polo's voyages to dreamy and distant lands. The scene reminds one of nineteenth century Orientalist odalisque paintings, where seminude women stretched out invitingly on similar carpets and sofas and beckoned to sexually repressed spectators. Surrounded by this wonderland of ancient artifacts, classical coins, books, and Egyptian antiquities, a patient was primed to recall a rich and pregnant and sensual past. Each of the hundreds of relics provided yet another symbol and stimulus for the dreamer who entered this office. There was nothing neutral about this "clinical setting."

It is no wonder why laboratory researchers were so skeptical of Freud's findings. It is also no surprise that the dreams reported by early psychoanalytic patients were so much more elaborate than the rather mundane dreams recounted to sleep researchers working in more contemporary and less provocative settings.

SOURCES OF SEXUAL SYMBOLISM

Freud's office decor broadcast his admiration for archaeology. This intrigue was understandable, for Freud lived and wrote at a time when amazing archaeological discoveries were made. Taking his cue from contemporary culture, he spoke in the language of his generation and identified himself as an "archaeologist of the mind." He delighted in peeling away layers of later civilization, to reveal the more primitive core concealed at the center. His metaphor made the ambiguous goals of psychoanalysis easier to understand. A public that recently learned about the treasure chests buried beneath the Egyptian sands was more willing to believe that equally enthralling secrets existed in the interior of the mind, where caverns of dreams hid beneath the surface.

But it was sexual symbolism that Freud was known for and with which his name will always be associated. It is commonly—although erroneously—assumed that the only secrets that Freud plumbed were sexual secrets and that the dream symbols that he sought were exclusively sexual symbols. This requires clarification. While it may be true that Freud emphasized the sexual side of human development and that he attributed everyday problems to unconscious sexual conflicts, he nevertheless recognized that other elements contributed to dreams. He specifically acknowledged that nocturnal stimuli as well as day memories made their way into these night visions.

Yet even the most casual observer can recognize Freud's "sexual preoccupations" running rampant through his theories. Some critics suspect that Freud's personal indulgence in (medicinal) cocaine contributed to his intensely erotic insights. Cocaine increases libido and intensifies sexual pleasure and produces erotic ruminations in users. Cocaine's potency at enhancing sexual pleasure can lead to its abuse. It also produces unusually vivid dreams.

Freud was so impressed with this "nonaddicting" and "harmless" cocaine that he wrote about his experiences in his "cocaine papers." Later, when he recognized how much he underestimated the adverse effects of cocaine, he had these papers purged from his collected writings.[9] He used cocaine as an experiment. There was no overt reason to suspect that he abused the drug to enhance sexual sensation or to increase his literary productivity or his overall energy, even though this drug is now known for these effects. Still, Freud undoubtedly experienced some psychotropic effects of cocaine, and it is quite possible that cocaine colored his own dream imagery. This point can be important, because Freud drew conclusions about dreams from his own self-analysis as well as from his patients' clinical material.

Not everyone attributes Freud's sexual preoccupations to this powerful coca powder. One of the more interesting (but controversial) explanations is found in psychologist David Bakan's book *Sigmund Freud and the Jewish Mystical Tradition*. In that much-maligned, but often-read book, Bakan traces Freud's theories of dreams and other things to Cabalistic (Jewish mystical) sources that peaked in the Middle Ages. This underground system of mystical thought unearthed secret meanings in the Bible and came complete with specialized dream decoders. Cabala became particularly popular during the Middle Ages, when it spread from secluded groups of Jewish scholars to more modestly educated Jewish masses, who often misinterpreted its messages. Jewish Cabala was studied by mystically-inclined Christians, including the contentious physician and alchemist, Paracelsus. At one point in history, Jews were saved from mass exile and possible murder, because a Christian defender persuaded his compatriots to spare the Jews on behalf of the potential power of the Cabala. At other points in time, Jewish dabbling in Cabala and dream-decoding led to accusations of sorcery and even greater persecution.

Cabalism catalyzed eighteenth century Chasidic mystical movements in Eastern Europe. Chasidism spread in those regions and remained strong, until Hitler killed half of the Chasidim during World

War II. Some Chasidic sects lived near Freud's birthplace of Moravia, which was further east and less economically developed than his family's second home in Vienna. Even Jung, who was renowned for his intrigue with mysticism and denounced for his occasional anti-Semitism, made direct references to Cabalistic treatises in his texts.

Writing in the early 1950s, at a time when it was unfashionable to link Freud to Jewish tradition, Bakan presented impressive anecdotes about the similarities between Freudian theories and Jewish esotericism. For instance, he noted that the inherently bisexual nature of humankind had been documented by esoterically-inclined Biblical commentators as early as the second century C.E. Yet academicians frowned upon Bakan's theories when they were first presented and pointed to the fact that Plato also wrote about physical and psychological androgyny.

There were several reasons why Bakan's ideas were not accepted. At the time that Bakan wrote, Freud was considered to be a secular, rather than a religious, Jew. He showed his scorn for religious ritual in several essays. His first biographer, Ernest Jones, believed that Freud was reared without traditional Jewish religious observance in anti-Semitic Austria. It was also politically incorrect to link Freud's psychoanalysis to Jewish tradition so soon after World War II and so soon after Hitler and the Nazi party had dismissed psychoanalysis as "the Jewish science" and banned Jews from practicing psychoanalysis. Connecting Freud to Judaism could be construed as giving credence to the Nazi's nefarious assertions. Furthermore, most Jewish scholars and psychiatrists of the time were trying to assimilate and to be "American" and to adapt to the "New World." They wanted to secularize psychoanalysis, and to separate it from any religious roots, and to present it in the language of science rather than of superstition. They could undermine their purposes if they acknowledged that this master of modernism and the forerunner of the future was nothing more than a throwback to the Middle Ages, and to such a strongly sectarian Middle Ages at that.

However, as happens with all things academic, newer research challenged the assumptions that led to the wholesale dismissal of Bakan's ideas. It has now been proven beyond a doubt that Freud was more familiar with Jewish culture and learning than previously recognized. Researchers such as Rice and Yershulami showed that Freud had early formal Jewish education and that he spent enough time with religiously observant relatives in Moravia to acquire some informal ideas about Jewish mysticism and tradition. He did not study these concepts as assiduously as a dedicated Yeshiva scholar, but he was certainly smart enough to have incorporated insights from passing discussions and to shuffle them into the storehouses of his otherwise awesome intellect.

It is quite conceivable that some of Bakan's arguments were overstated, but it is still reasonable to compare Freud's ideas about dreams with Jewish concepts of dreams found in the Bible, Talmud, more esoteric Cabalistic writings, and generic Jewish folklore. We cannot lose sight of the fact that Schlomo Almoni's book on *The Interpretation of Dreams and Magic* was still circulating at the time that Freud was born in eastern Austria. Superstitious beliefs about dreams had not completely disappeared from the Jewish ghetto that his family occupied in more urbane Vienna. We have no record of the rabbinical sermons that young Sigmund heard when attending a Bar Mitzvah in a synagogue. However, considering how commonly dream themes appear in the Hebrew Bible and how commonly rabbis refer to Biblical stories during their sermons, it would be virtually impossible for Freud to have been as sheltered from these ideas as some biographers would like us to believe.

The similarities between Freud's dream techniques and the approaches recorded in the Aramaic Babylonian Talmud from the first and second centuries are particularly striking. Like Freud, the scholars who wrote this extensive Biblical commentary sought meaning in dreams and regarded a "dream uninterpreted as an unopened letter." They recognized that some dreams resulted from fasting or indigestion and that some dreams were essentially meaningless. Most interestingly, the Talmudists asked the dreamer for his interpretation of the dream before offering their own interpretations. Their willingness to incorporate the dreamer's personal reflections, without imposing a preset, symbol-specific explanation, strongly anticipates Freud's approach.

We do not have convincing evidence to show that Freud was specifically familiar with this Talmudic technique or if he consciously—or unconsciously—used it, after hearing about it through his Jewish education or his personal associations or at cultural gatherings. He could have forgotten the source of this insight, or he could have thought it up de novo, or he might have avoided crediting his Jewish sources for any number of reasons. He did not cite all of his intellectual influences and even omitted footnotes from his forerunner, Nietzsche.

We know for a fact that Freud was familiar with the Biblical figure of Joseph. He discussed Joseph and his dreams directly in *The Interpretation of Dreams* and made it abundantly clear that he had no intention of imitating Joseph. Joseph was willing to credit his dream-interpreting ability to his deity, rather than to claim credit for it himself. For Freud, it was essential to prove that dream interpretation was a science. He had no desire to align himself with the supernatural sources for which Joseph stood.

Although there are many, many differences between the motivations and techniques and circumstances of Joseph and Freud, there are too many personal and political parallels between their lives and careers to overlook. Like Joseph, Freud earned a permanent place in history because of his involvement with dreams. Had it not been for Joseph's self-aggrandizing dreams about his father and his brothers, he would not have been sold into slavery and sent into exile in the land of Egypt. Joseph regained the favor of the Pharaoh and won his freedom from his unfair prison sentence because of his skills in interpreting dreams. He would have been denied an opportunity to prove his leadership abilities to the powers that be, and to change the destiny of the Children of Israel, and to alter the course of both Jewish and world history were it not for those dreams and his ability to decipher them.

Similarly, Freud made his mark by publishing a book on dreams. This book could just as easily have been called "Accessing the Unconscious," but Freud fortuitously focused on the dream theme and gained a far wider audience as a result. This book turned out to be the most influential book of the twentieth century and the most important work of Freud's life. At the time he wrote the text, Freud had no way of knowing that this book would meet this fate and so parceled out only a small space to the ancestor who foreshadowed his future.

Like Joseph, Freud was also a stranger in a strange land (to use the words that Moses used in the Old Testament). Freud felt like an interloper, living in an anti-Semitic Austria, where Jews' opportunities for academic advancement were somewhat constricted, although not outlawed altogether. He was scorned by his "brethren" physicians (or at least he complained that he was), when he proposed his psychosexually-based psychoanalytic theories. Like Joseph, who welcomed the Hebrew tribes into Egypt when Canaan entered a famine, Freud also paved new paths for Jews, by inventing psychoanalysis and inviting other Jews to participate. Like Joseph, Freud gained a loyal following outside of his immediate fold, once his studies on dreams became known to foreigners, particularly to those in America and eventually South America.

It is curious that several eminent scholars have labored to prove parallels between Freud and Moses, largely because Freud's final book was written about *Moses and Monotheism*. But, upon reflection, we must wonder if it was Joseph, rather than Moses, with whom Freud really identified, because they both made their marks through the serious study of dream.

FREUD'S INFILTRATION OF FILM

We would need an entire encyclopedia to identify and deconstruct all of Freud's influences and to track down all the scientific, psychoanalytical, artistic, and anthropological works that were directly influenced by Freud's dream theories. Rather than attempting to tackle this impossible task, we can examine a few ways in which Freudian dream theory infiltrated American movies.

One of the most moving of those movies is Alfred Hitchcock's 1945 *Spellbound*. Produced and directed by the master of suspense, *Spellbound* was not just another mindless thriller or formulaic detective film. It used both word and image to educate (or miseducate) the viewer about the psychoanalytic "science" of dream interpretation. Hitchcock hired world famous surrealist Salvador Dali to create signature Daliesque stage designs and costumes and art direction. Dali, in turn, used his self-described "paranoic-critical method" to make a melange of melting wheels, eye-covered curtains, and human-rabbit hybrids that recollect his paintings of *The Landscape of Memory*. Hitchcock added more dream scenes of his own, but it is Dali's disjointed dream scene that leaves an eidetic image indelibly etched in memory. This surreal scene influenced countless other cinematic dream scenes for decades to come.

Dali's images are so striking that only the rare spectator realizes that they last only two and one-half minutes. Hollywood legend says that Dali produced thirty minutes of dream scenes, but the censors edited the rest because it was obscene. It sounds as though Dali played upon Freudian sexual symbolism to the extreme, but it is not known exactly how he did this, because the original footage was lost and the scenes have not been seen since.

Spellbound's story revolves around a female psychoanalyst, portrayed by the quietly attractive Ingrid Bergman. It is she who drives the plot and plays opposite a tall, dark, and good-looking Gregory Peck. As Dr. Peterson, Bergman evokes the same love-smitten, dewy-eyed, heart-driven character that she played in *Casablanca*, which had been released just two years before. In *Spellbound*, Bergman begins as a sexually-repressed, professionally-consumed, personally-unfulfilled woman who becomes unraveled by her unanticipated attraction to the hand-some but troubled man who came to head the psychiatric institute, where she serves as a staff psychoanalyst.

Luckily for the plot, but unfortunately for the character, Peck's male psychiatrist arrives with substantial character flaws as well as impress-ive academic credentials. He eventually becomes a murder suspect, once it becomes known that the man whose name he uses has disap-peared and is presumed dead. When pressed, Peck can not remember who he really is or what happened between the time that he and the missing man were last seen together.

Bergman becomes fascinated by this presumed impostor and puts her psychoanalytic skills to work. Deploying dream detective work, she uncovers the cause of the doctor's crippling amnesia. Eventually, she cures the man of his memory lapses and clears him of pending murder charges, but not until after she has forsaken her professional position to run away with him on a train and collude with concealing his identity once again. In the end, Bergman not only clears her lover of suspicion, but also implicates an older analyst, played by Leo G. Carroll, as the real murderer. She does all this by using dream-based clues that were unavailable during conscious cognition.

Like any Hitchcock film, *Spellbound* works its spell on many different levels, and it would be completely wrong to say that it deals with the theme of dream and nothing but. The synergistic effects of Dali, Hitchcock, Bergman, Peck, Carroll, and many others contribute to this classic, as do psychoanalytic theory and dream interpretation, train scenes, detective motifs, and so much more. For our purposes, it is important that the film convinces the viewer that dream interpretation can produce near-miraculous cures of amnesia and other psychiatric ills. Films such as *Spellbound*—and many others—instilled the idea that recovered memories cure emotional and mental affliction almost instantaneously.

Mesmerized by messages sent by Hollywood's dream factory, the public began to believe that the psychoanalytic couch of the mid-twentieth century was as powerful and potent as the healing shrine of the medieval saint. Dream cures that were once the province of deities— such as those who appeared during sleep incubation rites at the ancient Asculepian temples—could now be had for the asking, through the secular rites of psychoanalysis. Proselytizing psychoanalytic schools aided and abetted this faith in Freudian cures but eventually felt the need to form organizations to protect the image of "screen psychiatry" and to condemn increasingly common portrayals of sinister screen psychiatrists.[10]

Although cinema made enormous claims for psychoanalytic cures, films such as *Spellbound* did not necessarily idealize the psychiatrists who practiced psychoanalysis. *Spellbound* portrays the institution's doctors as either loved-crazed, amnesic, or murderous. These professionals are little different from the patients whom they confine. Psychiatrists may be capable of controlling their patients but perhaps cannot control themselves or their colleagues, their emotions, or their impulses. According to this film and according to many others (such as Fritz Lang's *Dr. Mabuse* and Robert Weine's *The Cabinet of Dr. Caligari*), psychoanalysts are potentially dangerous and diabolical and are very much like the medieval magician.

Ironically, by reducing therapists to human terms and by belittling their personal contributions to the "science" of psychoanalysis, the film makes the practice of dream interpretation even more appealing and more potentially powerful. If a method such as this could succeed, even when left in the hands of emotion-driven incompetents, then it must be a miraculous method indeed!

Other Hitchcock films featured more subtle dream scenes. In *Vertigo*, Jimmy Stewart plays a mentally disabled detective who retired from the force because of his crippling fear of heights. His phobia began after he failed to rescue a colleague from falling off a rooftop. Stewart was unable to maintain his grip, as the other officer struggled and flailed about and dangled from the edge. Instead, he helplessly watched the other officer drop to his death, several stories below. He was just as inept at saving himself during a departmental hearing. He could not come to his own defense when his shortcomings were shamelessly trumpeted before him and left his police position in utter disgrace.

Rather than receiving the hero's medal that would have been his had he managed to hold the man's hand for a minute longer, Stewart comes away with another permanent reminder of the event: vertigo that comes on whenever he does so much as climb a ladder. He is doomed to relive this event forever through flashbacks and dreams. Unable to handle heights of any sort, he avoids heights entirely and develops a phobia. This phobia would probably be diagnosed as post-traumatic stress disorder, if the film were made today.

But Hitchcock is not concerned with diagnostic dilemmas. This avoidance of heights, this phobia, is the "McGuffin" that drives the plot. Because of this acrophobia, poor suffering Stewart is exploited by a scheming, unscrupulous, and adulterous murderer. This rich man hires Stewart as a private detective to follow his supposedly mental unstable and ultimately disposable wife. Stewart is set up as a patsy, and is planted as a witness who will testify about the "suicide" of this blonde woman, and who will unwittingly take the blame for the wife's death. Before this happens, Stewart will fall in love with this lady, who is played by Kim Novak.

The past predicts the present in both Hitchcock and in Freud. Stewart's vertigo stops him from climbing the watchtower stairs as Novak ascends to jump to her death. He sees her fall but cannot prevent her from jumping, any more than he could stop his colleague from falling. Again and again, Stewart relives this same scene. Again and again, he is struck with vertigo.

To escape his memories, he takes refuge in a small town, where he rents a modest room in a hotel. Just by chance, he meets a shopgirl who looks remarkably similar to the elegant Kim. But this cheap-talking substitute has none of the bearing and manners and speech patterns of the woman whose memory she evokes. Growing more and more mentally unstable himself, Stewart courts her just the same and attempts to effect a Pygmalion-like change. He buys her clothes, shoes, and a new hairdo to make her look exactly like the dead woman whom he loved and lost. Stewart's bizarre behavior convinces the spectator that he is indeed mentally unfit, as was said at his hearings.

However, just as happened with *Spellbound*'s male lead in 1945, Jimmy Stewart's character also has a lifesaving dream. Like the *Spellbound* dream, this dream rescues the hero from an equally evil end that awaits him. Were it not for this dream and the buried memories it unearthed, Stewart would have had to endure more and more layers of psychological suffering, and another damning trial, and further damage to his already scared reputation. Instead, an animated "talking head" appears while Stewart sleeps and alerts him to unconscious clues. The "talking head" turns into a vertiginous image of rotating lines that remind the viewer of the hypnotist's "magic eye." This talking head from 1953 was absorbed into the imagery of the 1960s drug culture and reworked into 1970s rock posters. It appeared on the cover of cult publications such as *Psychotronic Video*[11] and is still imprinted in the cultural consciousness of America.

During the dream, Stewart enters a vertiginous abyss. He "awakens" into a sleepy state of "higher consciousness." He realizes that this Kim Novak look-alike is not just a physical double of his lost love but that she really is the same woman whom he met before, because she owns the same necklace as the wealthy woman who supposedly died by suicide. By deciphering this dream, Stewart saves himself from an impending breakdown brought on by his sense of failure and by his near-psychotic fixation with this alluring, but ultimately evil, femme fatale. He regains both his health and his honor. The Kim look-alike reveals that the real wife was already dead and hidden in the tower, ready to be pushed off the top, even before Stewart arrived at the "suicide scene." Thanks to that confession, the true culprit—the husband—is convicted.

Stewart comes close to reconciling his love for this duplicitous lady but is saved by fate. She admits that the husband hired her to deceive Stewart and to impersonate the wealthy wife, but that she unwittingly fell in love with Stewart in the process, and has been on the run ever since. In an ironic twist of fate, Novak slips and falls to her death just before the film ends.

Many more Hollywood films added dream themes and echoed the approach of *Spellbound* or *Vertigo*. Psychoanalytically-inspired dream themes were especially prominent in film noir of the 1940s and 1950s. By the late 1990s, dream themes were spoofed in comedies such as *Analyze This*, which starred Robert De Niro as a troubled mobster and Billy Crystal as his psychiatrist. *Analyze This* became a box office hit for the month of March of 1999 but quickly disappeared without evidencing any of the staying power of *Spellbound*. Parallels can be found in a television drama about a mob family named *The Sopranos*, whose patriarch also seeks out psychotherapy.

Analyze This plays upon a much earlier film noir, *The Dark Past*, which itself was based on a popular play from the late 1930s. In *The Dark Past*, an escaped convict bursts into a nearby house and interrupts an otherwise ordinary dinner party as he flees from the law. The home conveniently belongs to a psychoanalyst, played by Lee J. Cobb, who went on to play Eve's psychoanalyst in *Three Faces of Eve*. Earlier in the film, the psychoanalyst had professed belief in his ability to cure young criminals, if only he had the chance to analyze their childhood traumas before those traumas progressed to adult criminality. Cobb soon has an opportunity to test out his theory, when the convict holds him and his dinner guests hostage in his home.

Eventually, the criminal falls asleep on the psychoanalyst's home sofa (which symbolically substitutes for the analyst's couch). Then he wakes up screaming, when another of his constantly recurring nightmares begins. The analyst inquires about the convict's dream, and deftly deciphers the thinly concealed vision, and convinces the Cagneyesque character that his adult need for criminal power stems from the powerlessness he felt as a child, as he witnessed his father's death. The analysis of this single dream is so successful that it strips the criminal of his lifelong drive to commit crimes. When the authorities arrive and storm the house by surprise, the criminal cannot pick up his gun. Unable to defend himself, he dies in the crossfire in a self-aware, but not necessarily contrite, state. For the psychoanalytically-informed audience, the psychoanalytically-inspired insight of the dying analysand substitutes for the deathbed confession made to a priest.

Analyze This spoofs this dark theme of *The Dark Past* and adapts it for a much more sophisticated audience that is prepared to laugh at such overstatements. The comedy starts when Billy Crystal backs into a car that belongs to a crime boss, played by Robert De Niro. It turns out that De Niro is clinically depressed and cannot function at work anymore. After he learns that Crystal is a therapist, De Niro sends his henchmen to Crystal, who coerce him into listening to De Niro's recurring dream about "black milk." The film-literate spectator wonders if the milk theme is a homage to the spilled milk scene in *Spellbound*.

Using levity, rather than the heavy-handed approach that appealed to audiences in the 1930s and 1940s, *Analyze This* plays upon contemporary skepticism (but continuing intrigue) with dream cures and with Freudian psychoanalysis in general. Perhaps the American public had become too self-conscious about Freudianism by the end of the twentieth century to accept this theme as anything other than funny. But a quick cure through dream interpretation is still enduring enough and recognizable enough to make for a hit film, especially when coupled with a familiar fascination with gangster caricatures and organized crime. Unlike *The Dark Past*, *Analyze This* has a happy ending, as Crystal calls upon advanced psychoanalytic concepts about transference, displacement, and father figures to talk De Niro out of shooting him.

Not all film noirs presented such a positive picture of dream interpretation as the preceding examples. One of the noirest of noir films—*Nightmare Alley*—was a scathing indictment of the entire process and of the professionals who practiced it. Released in the 1950s, near the end of Hollywood's short-lived romance with psychoanalysis, *Nightmare Alley* unveiled the links between twentieth century psychoanalysis, nineteenth century spiritualism, and eighteenth century mesmerism. The film compared psychoanalytic dream interpretation with sideshow scams. Viewers who are aware that Dr. Mesmer's once-serious psychiatric treatment turned into a popular parlor pasttime are better able to appreciate the plot. The film reached even further into film history and recollected a long line of sinister cinematic psychiatrists, such as Dr. Mabuse and Dr. Caligari.

In *Nightmare Alley*, an unscrupulous female "consulting psychologist" teams up with a shady male mentalist who performs at a nearby carnival. The mentalist "reads minds" by watching for clever hand cues delivered by his long-term female partner and mentor. He eventually deceives this first female in order to set up an even better scheme with the woman psychologist. The latter records her patients' dreams and transmits this sensitive information to him, so that he can appear to read their minds during his new and improved mentalist acts in nightclubs. Using this dream data, the two evildoers extort large sums of money from bereaved patients, who expect their loved ones to appear in the flesh during "seances" that are staged by the colluding carnival performer.

In the end, the man is deceived by the deceptive "psychologist" (who bears the name of Lilith, like the legendary demonesses who appear to men in their dreams to cause them to commit sinful sexual acts as they sleep). He suffers a fate far worse than her unassuming patients. Without the help of a female partner in his scams, he is driven to drink and ends up as the despised carnival "geek." He lives in a cage, and behaves like an animal, and performs for nothing more than a bed at night and a bottle. Like many film noir femme fatales, this snakelike Lilith keeps the proceeds for herself and leaves the scene unscathed.

Like all successful art, this deeply depressing film peered into the future, long before science and scholars could see so clearly. It presented a point of view that would be developed to perfection several decades later, when Freud-bashing became both popular sport and serious academic pursuit. In particular, the film foreshadowed books about Jung and occultism, such as Richard Noll's *The Jung Cult*, F. X. Charet's *Spiritualism and the Foundations of C. G. Jung's Psychology*, and Sanu Shamdashani's *Cult Fictions*, as well as Frederick Crews' New York Review series about the occult origins of psychoanalysis.[12]

JUNG AND DREAM

Freud may have started the twentieth century's fascination with dream, but it was his disciple, Carl Gustav Jung, who closed the century's intrigue with dream. Jung's psychoanalytic studies on dream remained popular at the turn of the twenty-first century, and attracted newer and younger audiences, at the same time Freud's fervent admirers became older and fewer. Jung formulated related, but distinctive, theories based on the "science" inspired by Freud. Unlike Freud, Jung never attracted nearly so many detractors, largely because he was not taken so seriously as Freud. Jung's legacy is largely preserved by the scholars of religion, myth, and drama.

The story of Jung's relationship with Freud is interesting in its own right. Jung met Freud in 1907, and soon became Freud's star pupil. The energized and enmeshed relationship ended bitterly, seven years after it began.[13] Like Freud, Jung was a native German speaker who was well versed in the classics. He was the first non-Jew to join Freud's inner psychoanalytic circle. Freud hoped that Jung's presence would legitimize the all-Jewish and socially-marginalized psychoanalytic movement and permit its acceptance by a wider audience.[14]

Freud went beyond merely welcoming Jung as the token Gentile. There are suggestions that he expected his younger Swiss-born student to become his successor. Never did Freud anticipate that Jung and he would part company as abruptly and acrimoniously as they did. It is equally doubtful that Freud foresaw how prominent Jung would become in the Nazi machinery, as a result of his accepting Goering's invitation to head the German medical society for psychoanalysis. Jung's willingness to accept this post, after the Nazis expelled all Jewish psychiatrists and psychoanalysts from the committee, continues to cause bitter debate among his followers and detractors alike.[15] This shadow on Jung's career has never been fully removed.[16]

The son of a Zwingli Protestant clergyman, who himself was the son of a clergyman, Jung never abandoned belief in the significance of the spiritual. In contrast to his mentor Freud, who emphasized the biological basis of human behavior, Jung retained a Romantic, as well as a religious, reverence for the ethereal. Whereas Freud boasted that he never experienced the oceanic feeling indulged in by mystics, Jung literally lived with the spirits. He left his home for seven years to flee from perceived poltergeists. Even before he met Freud, Jung was intensely intrigued with the occult, which was a more suitable subject of study in the nineteenth century than it is today. For his medical school thesis, he studied his cousin Helene, who was a well-known medium who regularly went into trances. These studies prepared Jung for further research into dreams, psychoanalysis, and the netherworld between psyche and soul.

Jung turned both to organized religion and to esoteric mystical sects from both East and West to add to his understanding of the interaction between the human spirit and depth psychology. Ironically, Jung was repudiated by organized Christianity, who found his spiritual searching offensive. Jung's dream about God the Father, which he described in his autobiography, captured his ambivalent attitude toward mainstream religion. In this dream, he saw God the Father sitting on His majestic heavenly throne, before passing fecal material. Jung both deified and defiled the archetypal father figure, his own father figure, and God Himself—and perhaps even Freud—in this dream.

When Jung parted ways with Freud, he did so because he opposed Freud's position on the sexual origin of human experience. Jung believed that his personal patients—who tended to be affluent and established people in their forties—were suffering from a religious crisis of midlife. According to Jung, most of these people were motivated by a "pathogenic secret" that arose from an event that took place in reality, rather than in imagination. In contrast to his mentor, who believed in psychological determinism, Jung was convinced that people could continue to grow and evolve and change throughout their lifetimes. To this day, many people turn to the more metaphysical and future-oriented Jungian approach after they become disenchanted with Freud's sexual reductionism and his psychological determinism.

Jung saturated his theories with ideas about dreams. For Freud, the dream was just a footnote, but for Jung, the dream was the text. He punctuated his lectures with so many examples of dreams that it is difficult to catalogue his writings about dream. To highlight the contribution of dreams in Jung's own development, he dedicated his autobiography to his "memories, dreams, and reflections." One-third of Jung's lavishly illustrated, general audience publication *Man and His Symbols*, written near the end of his life in 1961, was devoted to dreams. Jung often wrote about dreams in vague and general terms, almost as though he was trying to make it easier for the reader to free associate to his ideas and to add their own ideas about dreams to his basic outline. He made it clear that there were few inviolate rules about deciphering dreams.

Like Freud, Jung introduced a new vocabulary to express his ideas. Terms such as *collective unconscious, racial unconscious, archetype, imago, persona,* and *shadow self* assumed new meaning in "Jungianese." To analyze dreams, Jung turned to terms and techniques from the classical Greek theater. He borrowed directly from the dramatists who wrote thousands of years earlier. Like his classical predecessors, Jung examined five elements in the dream: the *situation* (which describes the time, location, and players), the *exposition* (the representation of the problem), the *development* (or the plot), the *peripatea* (the critical event when something decisive happens), and the *lysis* (the resolution or the solution).

Jung never hid his classical influences. He freely acknowledged his sources, and footnoted his writings in Greek and Latin, and punctuated almost every page with quotes from these antiquated languages. His erudition is evident to everyone who reads his collected works. Jung borrowed other terms from drama and spoke of the *persona* donned by each person in public. The persona was the actor's mask, worn on stage only. The persona depicts the public personality of the character and hides the real and vulnerable human being behind it. The very dreamy film by Ingmar Bergman bears the name *Persona*, because it deals with the secret identity of the self and presents the entangled relationship between a female psychiatric nurse and her patient, through a series of interlocking dreams.

In contrast to Freud, who focused on the associations provoked by the dream rather than on the dream itself, Jung preferred to "remain within the dream" and to discuss the dream for its own sake. Some contemporary Jungian therapists encourage their patients to relive their dreams and to enter the dreamstate during their analytical sessions. This technique has made Jungian analysis enormously popular with drama students, who strive to create a self-sustaining alternative reality when they are on stage and who often appreciate any opportunity to rehearse their roles. But there are serious drawbacks to this approach, because the early stages of schizophrenia or temporal lobe seizures can cause "oneroid" states that resemble dreamstates. Such pathological states must be recognized for what they are and treated appropriately, to avoid prolonging them unnecessarily and interfering with future opportunities to participate in the "waking world."

Besides these clinical concerns about the hazards of overly zealous Jungian-inspired dream therapy, there are major concerns about Jung's indebtedness to the *völkisch* philosophy that led to Nazi ideology. This völkisch or folk philosophy traced its roots to pre-Christian Teutonic mythology and was particularly popular during the Romantic era. While seeking out these mythological connections to the past, Jung identified recurring visual symbols in dreams, films, art, and architecture. He attributed these symbols to inheritable racial characteristics (or a racial unconscious), without foreseeing the dangers inherent in such hypotheses and without considering that this belief in a biologically-inherited trait smacked of the same racism that propelled Germany's extermination of Jews during World War II. Such concepts were throwbacks to outdated, pre-Darwinian, Lamarckian anthropology.

Ironically, as destructive as these ideas were, many contemporary people continue to seek out the sense of kinship and belonging and connectedness that comes from identifying personal dream images with Jung's wider racial unconscious or collective unconscious.[17] Many of his followers see Jungian universalism as an antidote to the sense of alienation and separation that cloud the late twentieth century and early twenty-first century experience.

Mythologists such as Joseph Campbell also looked for recurring motifs in folk tales. Campbell looked to Jung's writings for intellectual and personal inspiration and personally compiled his work into an easily accessible anthology. Campbell also studied Sanskrit, as well as the Arthurian legends about the Knights of the Round Table, and translated important Hindu religious texts into English to produce an alluring melange of Indian myth, Jungian concepts, and European legend. This mix was perfectly suited to the New Age, as were Jung's other writings about the irrational, the dreamworld, alchemy, gnosticism, the *I Ching*, *The Tibetan Book of the Dead,* and the (Taoist) *Secret of the Golden Flower* and *Modern Man's Search for the Spiritual*.

Most medical schools refuse to teach Jung's ideas, not because of his reputed link to the Third Reich, but because his ideas cannot be tested and refuted through standard scientific techniques. His concepts, as they relate to dreams and most other things, lie closer in spirit to religion than to science. Freud's ideas, on the other hand, were so easy to test that they provided a field day for experimental psychologists, and fueled wide-ranging research, and ignited lasting debates about his contribution to (or detraction from) culture.[18]

Jung's writings on Eastern religion endeared him to spiritual seekers, from the 1960s through the 1990s. Many people assume that Jung expressed unequivocal acceptance of Asian ideas about dream and daily life, simply because he devoted so much space to Eastern thought and because he freely mixed Eastern mystical ideas about "synchronicity" with standard psychological theories. Most of his admirers are not psychologically prepared to read the actual words of his writings and to find a spirit that is very different from the all-embracing acceptance advocated by the New Age.

Jung's essay *The Dreamlike World of India* is an example of the case in point. Rather than rejoicing in the idea of dream in Romantic fashion and identifying the many Indian mythological figures who morph into different forms, as figures do in dreams, this narrative reminds the reader of Kipling's colonialist writings from the nineteenth century. True, Jung extolls India for introducing dreamlike symbols into ordinary waking life, and he paints a lively portrait of a lively place. But he also makes unsettling generalizations about the daily lives, dress, and rituals of people who were colonized by Europeans until 1947. He tells us that Indian men dress in infantile pajamas and that overweight Indian women have surprisingly high sexual appeal.

There is a reason why Jung's essay sounds more like an entry in a travel journal than a serious psychological study. This piece was based on his three-week stay in the subcontinent, most of which was spent on board ship. In the end, we find that this essay, with its inviting title, resembles cotton candy more than serious substance. Unfortunately, unlike real cotton candy, it leaves the reader with a bitter, saccharine taste, instead of the cloying sweetness of the real thing.

In spite of the unease induced by some of his actions and attitudes, Jung's approach to dreams retains a certain appeal and makes even the reluctant reader rethink his overall contribution. Jung dared to delve into topics that others of his education and experience avoided, and that is to be commended. Though he is often infuriating (as was his mentor, Freud), both Jung and Freud act as tour guides to inner and outer and past and present worlds. They point out panoramas that the casual observer might overlook had they not directed our attention to them, so that we can see the view for ourselves and choose our own interpretation. It is impossible to predict future generations' reactions to Jung's work, for Jung scholarship is only in its infancy, whereas Freud criticism is already old and arthritic. Critics such as Richard Noll expect there to be the creation of a Jungian religion or at least a Jungian cult. It will be interesting to see if Noll's predictions come to pass.

There is no doubt that Jungianism is still alive and well in some circles. Because Freud died in 1939, just at the outset of World War II, and because his psychological studies began in the 1880s, Freud's life and work reflect the concerns of the late nineteenth century and the first third of the twentieth century. When Freud biographer Peter Gay claimed that Freud represents a "life for our times," he was talking to the generation that came of age between the World Wars. Jung's death in 1961 situated him squarely in the 1960s, and made him an icon of the baby boom generation, and connected him to the turbulent times around the Vietnam War. By outliving Freud by nearly a quarter of a century, Jung turned into a transitional figure for the twentieth century. The "fin de millennium" intrigue with dreams and spiritual searches and syncretic religion and psychological spirituality is woven from the same fabric as Jungian thought.

OTHER IDEAS ABOUT DREAM

Freud and Jung were undeniably the most significant psychoanalytic dream theorists, but they were hardly the only ones who hypothesized about dreams. Freud's *The Interpretation of Dreams* set off a frenzy of psychoanalytic dream theories and demanded comments from all serious students of psychoanalysis. The early decades of the twentieth century brought several significant psychoanalytic publications in this area. Erich Fromm wrote about dreams in *The Forgotten Language*.[19] The son of an Orthodox rabbi who co-authored *Zen Buddhism and Psychoanalysis* (and many other books) and the onetime husband of psychoanalyst Freida Fromm-Reichmann (model for *I Never Promised You a Rose Garden*), Fromm was well on his way to prominence when he wrote about dreams. Havelock Ellis and Krafft-Ebbing, who studied strange sexual fantasies, also wrote about dream. Werner Wolfe published a broad historical review about dreams to which this study is deeply indebted.[20] French philosopher Henri Bergson published his book *On Dreams* at the start of the twentieth century and referred to Freud's still obscure studies in his highly-respected university lectures. The list goes on and on.

This trend continued until the mid-1950s and might have continued even longer, were it not for the fact that sleep scientists at the University of Chicago discovered a physiological link between dreams and REM (rapid eye movement) sleep and redirected cutting-edge dream studies away from the sanctum sanctorum of the analyst's couch and into the sleep laboratory of "real" scientists. From that time forward, psychoanalytic dream theories and scientific studies were on a collision course. One would have to wait until the start of the twenty-first century to attempt to reconcile these two divergent paths.

The irony is that dream dissection does not necessarily relieve personal distress. Some people actually get worse if they delve into their dreams, and some improve if their dreams are suppressed. But Freud never denied this possibility. When asked if psychoanalysis would relieve human misery, he explained that it would only help someone understand their distress better. Freud also never anticipated that relaxation techniques could relieve the nightmares of sexual assault victims and perhaps other trauma survivors as well. Intriguing new data suggests that "imagery rehearsal" techniques can lessen patient distress by having them rehearse new endings for recurring nightmare themes, without exploring the deep-seated fears behind such dreams.[21]

Having said this, let me conclude this chapter by stressing that psychoanalytic ideas about dream must be distinguished from psychoanalysis as a treatment technique. Psychoanalysis or depth psychology can stand alone as a philosophy and can be compared to Romantic or Enlightenment or even medieval thought. Psychoanalytic philosophy claims that humans act and perceive on two levels, on the conscious level and the unconscious level, and that dreams offer the most direct route to the more valuable realm of the unconscious. Psychoanalysis' greatest importance lies in its impact on culture and on the culture of the twentieth century in particular. This importance remains, regardless of the effectiveness of psychoanalytic treatment techniques.

Psychoanalysis is a "heuristic" method that explains and offers meaning, without proving cause or effect. It does not need to establish its own truth. As a heuristic approach, psychoanalysis can be compared with religion, which is the most established medium for providing meaning. We can refer to the twentieth century as the psychoanalytic century, in the same way we call the twelfth and thirteenth centuries the Age of Faith.[22]

These parallels between twentieth century approaches to dream and the supernaturalist approaches from centuries past are both obvious and inviting, and explain why psychoanalysis has had such a tenacious hold on the twentieth century, and why it also continues to evoke such acrimonious debate. Psychoanalysis democratizes the privileges previously restricted to the priestly caste and turns every individual into a priest or a prophet or a shaman or a seer. It accomplishes this through the medium of dream.

For instance, in psychoanalysis, the patient sanctifies each individual dream and reveres it, as though it were a divine message. This dream is brought to the shrine of the psychoanalyst, for priestly interpretation. The individual who dreams that dream is also sanctified, because of his or her association with the sacred. The sense of alienation that pervades postindustrial society is temporarily abated, as the individual distinguishes himself from the group and achieves greater significance and self-esteem through this ability to dream this "sacred dream." Psychoanalytic thought allows ordinary people to share the status that only designated dreamers enjoy in shamanistic societies.

With these opportunities to offer, no wonder psychoanalysis attracted so many adherents in America and no wonder why practitioners are so forgiving of the clinical limitations of this ideology. No wonder why it is so disappointing to think of dreams as being biologically-based and nothing but. Some people say that thinking of dreams as being biologically-based dehumanizes them. That is incorrect. Thinking of dreams as being biologically-based, and nothing but, desanctifies them and returns the dreamer to human status. This is clearly a lower status than he could have enjoyed if each dream were deemed to be a sacred message dream with a meaning. It is the loss of divinity, rather than the return to biology, that humans mourn when they are confronted by the biological basis of dream.

NOTES

1. Ehrman, Milton K. "Sleep Architecture and Its Relationship to Insomnia." *Journal of Clinical Psychiatry* supp. 10 (2001): 62.
2. Saying that a book or a theory is influential is not the same as affirming that it is accurate. Ideas gain importance in history for reasons that go far beyond

fact or truth or proof. For instance, ideas that sorcery caused disease were very influential even though they were not necessarily accurate. Ideas that the earth was flat were influential and guided everything from political policy to religious belief, before these ideas were proven to be inaccurate. These influential but inaccurate ideas are important in their own right, because of the impact they had on people and culture, but they should not be confused with straightforward, scientific fact.

3. William James was criticized for his forays into the realms of religion even more severely when he published *The Varieties of Religious Experience.* See chapter 10, "Reason and Romance."

4. Gay, Peter. *A Godless Jew: Freud, Atheism and the Making of Psychoanalysis.* New Haven: Yale University Press, 1989.

5. Freud Museum, North London, England.

6. Freud, Sigmund. *Civilization and Its Discontents.* Trans. and ed. James Strachey. New York: Norton, 1989; *Totem and Taboo.* Trans. James Strachey. New York: Norton, 1950; *The Future of an Illusion.* Std. Ed. Trans. and ed. James Strachey. New York: Norton, 1989.

7. Rothgeb, Carrie Lee, ed. *Abstracts of the Standard Edition of the Complete Psychological Works of Sigmund Freud.* Northvale, NJ: Aronson, 1973.

8. Torrey, E. Fuller. *Freudian Fraud.* New York: Harper, 1992.

9. Strausbaugh, John, and Donald Blaise, ed. *The Drug User Documents 1840–1960.* New York: Blast Books, 1991.

10. Gabbard, Glen O., and Krin Gabbard. *Psychiatry and the Cinema.* Washington: American Psychiatric Press, 1999.

11. Weldon, Michael. *The Psychotronic Video Guide to Film.* New York: St. Martin's, 1996.

12. Noll, Richard. *The Jung Cult.* Princeton, NJ: Princeton University Press, 1994; Charet, F. X. *Spiritualism and the Foundations of C. G. Jung's Psychology.* Albany: State University of New York Press, 1993; Shamdasani, Sonu: *Cult Fictions.* London: Routledge, 1998; Crews, Frederick. "The Memory Wars. Freud's Legacy in Dispute." New York: *New York Review of Books,* 1995.

13. Donn, Linda. *Freud and Jung: Years of Friendship, Years of Loss.* New York: Collier, 1988.

14. Klein, Dennis. *The Jewish Origins of Psychoanalysis.* Chicago: University of Chicago Press, 1985.

15. Cocks, Geoffrey. *Psychotherapy in the Third Reich.* 2nd Ed, rev. and exp. New Brunswick: Trans/Action Publishers, 1997.

16. Maidenbaum, Aryeh, and Stephen A. Martin. *Lingering Shadows: Freudians, Jungians and Anti-Semiticism.* Boston: Shambala, 1991.

17. Kirsch, Thomas B. *The Jungians: A Comparative and Historical Perspective.* London: Routledge, 2000.

18. Roth, Michael, ed. *Freud: Culture and Conflict.* New York: Vintage, 2000.

19. Fromm, Erich. *The Forgotten Language: An Introduction to the Understanding of Dreams, Fairy Tales, and Myths.* New York: Grove, 1957.

20. Wolff, Werner. *Dream, Mirror of Consciousness.* Westport: Greenwood, 1972.

21. Krakow, Barry, et al. "Imagery Rehearsal Therapy for Chronic Nightmares in Sexual Assault Survivors with Posttraumatic Stress Disorder." *Journal American Medical Association* (August 1, 2001) 286: 5; " 'Imagery Rehearsal' Can Control PTSD-Related Nightmares." *Psychiatric News.* Sept. 11, 2001: 23.

22. Durant, Will. *The Age of Faith.* New York: Simon & Schuster, 1950.

13

Body and Brain

Our last chapter talked about the *psyche* and *soul*. These two terms, one secular and one sacred, are abstract, metaphysical, and metapsychological and are preferred by supernaturalists and psychoanalysts, poets, and painters. This chapter will address the concrete, physical, and tangible realms of *body and brain* that concern psychopharmacologists, experimental psychologists, neuropsychiatrists, and other scientists. The methods and goals of these different approaches could not be further removed from one another.

To understand why psychoanalytic approaches to dreams have so little in common with science, in spite of early attempts to categorize them as science, we must first understand how and why science sets itself apart from nonscience. Once we accomplish that, we will understand why renowned psychoanalytic leaders recently admitted that psychoanalysis belongs to the arts, rather than the sciences. We will also begin to see why some psychoanalytic approaches to dreams lie even closer to religion and why critics predict that they will spawn their own religion in due time.[1]

SCIENCE, RELIGION, AND PSYCHOANALYSIS

Religion starts with absolute—but unprovable—truths. Religion tries to prove itself right to both believers and nonbelievers. Science, on the other hand, strives to prove itself wrong. Science improves itself by correcting its errors and revising its theories to fit added information. Religion, on the other hand, risks taking a tumble whenever its tenets are challenged. Still, disproved religious idea can be revived, if its adherents resuscitate it and add even more inventive explanations to explain away the holes in the original theory.

The best scientists discard theories that fail to meet science's demanding tests, because science (theoretically) holds nothing sacred. Science, unlike religion, is (or at least should be) unafraid to break its own idols.[2] When scientists refuse to act in this professional manner (as they occasionally do), they run the risk of being compared to churchmen or cultists or zealots or quacks.[3]

"Modern" psychology that evolved after the 1850s modeled itself after science and introduced laboratory experiments to test out hypotheses. Philosophers of science such as Thomas Kuhn claim that contemporary social scientists are more concerned with the "scientificity" of their studies than their "hard science" counterparts in physics or chemistry or biology. But things were not always this way. Until Professor Wilhelm Wundt began this experimental psychology in the nineteenth century, psychology was closely aligned with philosophy and was content to theorize and hypothesize, without testing its theories through clinical studies.[4] Some of the most significant concepts in protopsychology—such as Carus' concept of the unconscious—were crafted by an anatomist and artist and obstetrical researcher who never treated a psychiatric patient![5]

Psychoanalysis' origins were completely distinct from those of experimental psychology. The two fields came from very different evolutionary trees, so to speak, and had completely different ancestors, even though they concerned themselves with very similar subjects. Psychoanalysis was borne from the clinical speculations and extensive erudition of neurologist Sigmund Freud. It was based on Freud's personal observations of several selected patients and his own self-analysis. It was peppered by anecdotes from a uniquely turn-of-the-century type of armchair anthropology.

Late in the nineteenth century and early in the twentieth century, both the public and the medical profession were shocked by Freud's emphasis on sexual symbolism and by his audacious speculation about childhood sexuality. Later in the century, experimental psychologists were more shocked by Freud's flagrant disregard for standard, scientific experimental technique. His hubris in insisting that his studies were scientific galled his critics even more and made them even less sympathetic to the fact that his clinical research techniques were no worse than those of his nineteenth century peers.

One of the most irrefutable criticisms of Freud's studies revolves around the lack of a representative sample. Representative samples are de rigueur in scientific research. Subjects are carefully selected to represent a broad segment of the population and to avoid overrepresenting a skewed segment of society. If a scientific study is not based on a representative sample, then its findings cannot be applied to the general population.

Freud based his psychoanalytic theories on a very, very small psycho-analytic patient population of twenty-six! That is a mere handful, when compared with the thousands or tens of thousands of subjects who are studied in contemporary psychological and psychiatric studies. The few patients whom Freud treated were relatively unique, compared to the world at large. They were mostly wealthy, largely Jewish, European-educated women (and some men) who reflected the values and conflicts of the sexually repressive and sexually duplicitous, fin de siècle, central European society.

Being a bit of a dreamer himself, Freud did not let his limited sample size stop him from making sweeping generalizations about dreams, the unconscious, and civilization as a whole. Something said by a single patient or something that he himself thought or dreamed was sufficient to fuel Freud's ever-active imagination. Ironically, Jung, who is so closely aligned with the occult, collected 4,000 dreams to make his point.[6]

These problems with Freud's experimental methodology could have been sufficient to invalidate Freud's findings automatically or, at the very least, prompt rigorous reexamination of his theories, as actually happened. But sleep researchers working in sophisticated laboratory settings made a landmark discovery in the early 1950s, and challenged psychoanalytic claims about the unconscious and its contribution to dreams on completely different grounds, and sent sleep and dream studies on an entirely different trajectory. After these and other discoveries, one pithy textbook writer recommended that students "wake up from Freud's dream studies."[7]

SLEEP LABORATORY RESEARCH

Sleep scientists were far more practical-minded people than the early psychoanalysts. They did not seek to learn the meaning of life through their sleep studies. Instead, they concerned themselves with basic biology and how it affected human behavior and bodily functions. The most important discovery in sleep and dream research arrived in the 1950s, when two scientists identified REM (rapid eye movement) sleep. This discovery would not have been possible before 1928, when EEGs (electroencephalograms) were invented to monitor electrical changes in the brain. This invention proved that brain waves changed during sleep and that dissimilar states of sleep exist.

Then, two scientists saw their subjects' eye balls darting back and forth as they slept. Their eyelids were closed. Nothing could be seen, and yet they seemed to be sighting something. These scientists awakened subjects from their sleep and questioned them about their perceptions. They learned that their subjects were dreaming intensely during this stage of rapid eye movement sleep (or REM sleep). To the world's amazement, even people who claimed that they never dreamed were able to describe dreams at these times.

Classical philosophers and speculative scientists such as Aristotle thought that there was a physical basis to sleep and dreams, twenty-three centuries before this discovery. Maury, a researcher whose studies sparked an interesting section in Freud's *The Interpretation of Dreams*, had also followed Aristotle's lead, when he studied the impact of external physiological stimuli on dreams. Back in the first century C.E., the rabbis who wrote the Talmud were certain that indigestion could cause bad dreams and concluded that such dreams did not deserve interpretation. Then, in 1953, after so many centuries of speculation, there was scientific proof of dream's biological basis. Dreams were linked to physiological, rather than psychological, changes. A new era dawned in sleep research, one that reverted to the pre-Freudian era.

The academic market for psychoanalytic dream theories dried up for a while, after witnessing decades of expansion. Until the mid-1950s, one psychoanalyst after another published a book about dreams, eager to emulate the findings of the master Freud and to improve upon the product. Then the books suddenly disappeared. Even cinema psychiatry soon lost its love for dreams and their interpretation, now that the credibility of dream interpretation had been attacked. Yet interest in the subject of dreams did not disappear, even if these discoveries partly debunked some Freudian "facts." If anything, this surprising research drew even more attention to dreams, and ignited more heated debates about Freud's *The Interpretation of Dreams*, and made a broader segment of society aware of a controversy that otherwise escaped their attention.

As time went on, sleep researchers added more and more sophisticated machinery to their armamentarium. Polysomnograms, electromyelograms, and other mechanical measuring devices accompanied the original electroencephalograms. Studies of brain biochemistry augmented awareness of the *internal* physiological forces that shaped and stimulated dream form and content. As advances in psychopharmacology skyrocketed, more and more was learned about the chemical induction of dreams. Sleep laboratory studies became more innovative, when researchers entered patients' homes and compared the dreams experienced in their natural environments to the dreams described under the artificial laboratory conditions. Over the next decade or two, during the 1960s and 1970s, research and recreational experience with LSD solidified this emphasis on the biological basis of dreams and upstaged Freud's fin de siècle findings about the unconscious control of dreams. Rather ironically, this forward-reaching research sent scientific dream studies back to the concerns of the nineteenth century and basically bypassed the detours taken by psychoanalysis one-half century earlier.

REM SLEEP AND CHILDREN'S SLEEP

For a while, it seemed that these remarkable discoveries about REM sleep would unravel the mysteries surrounding children and their dreams. Since the cult of childhood surfaced during the Romantic Era, it was presumed that children had a special fascination with dreams and a special means to access dreams and the imagination overall. This belief was captured in E. T. A. Hoffmann's story "The Nutcracker Prince,"[8] which became Tchaikovsky's beloved ballet *The Nutcracker Suite*. In the "Nutcracker" stories, young Laura had an enchanted dream about an unsightly nutcracker who morphed into a handsome prince and slew the human-size mice who invaded her bedroom as she slept.

Sleep laboratory studies showed that infants and very young children spend more time in REM (rapid eye movement) sleep than adults do and that newborns spend sixty percent of their first few weeks in REM sleep. By the end of the first year of life, only forty percent of the total sleep time is REM sleep. By two years, these REM periods occur regularly and uniformly and do not last throughout the night. Sometime between the ages of three and four, REM sleep decreases to twenty percent of all sleep, which is close to the adult ratio.

On the surface, these findings suggested that little babies were busying themselves in dreamland, and enjoying every adventure, and lapping up every lullaby. The delightful ideas of Romantic poets and playwrights and composers were about to be confirmed by sleep laboratory studies about REM sleep. Then cognitive psychologists entered the scene and reminded the world that "real" dreams require more than simple "sleep architecture" and REM sleep cycles. Researcher David Foulkes found that abstract reasoning and visual-spacial abilities are prerequisites for experiencing "fully-formed" dreams. Without the ability to think in words and to recognize the position of one object in relationship to another and without a sense of the self as a separate person, one cannot script a dream, even if the brain waves and the eye muscles are moving in the right ways.

Foulkes found that children have simple, rather than elaborate dreams, and that they certainly do not dream of the Sugar Plum Fairy pirouetting across the stage backed by fully costumed and choreographed dancers from India and China and Europe, as happens in the *The Nutcracker Suite* ballet. Nor do children see themselves acting in their dreams, before they are school age, because they have not developed a sense of "personhood" and cannot conceive of themselves as individuals. Many of the vivid and fanciful ideas about dreams relayed by young children are implanted in them by well-intended adults, according to Foulkes. He further suggests that children describe these "dreams" to please their parents, who themselves were conditioned by a long literary, artistic, spiritual, and philosophical tradition about children's dreams.[9]

Cognitive psychologists also have a facile and novel explanation for children's nightmares. Without denying the existence of nightmares (or nocturnal panic attacks, as they are known in some circles), these theorists propose that children embellish their dreams, when they retell them, and add details about the dark and mysterious bedroom environment. They confuse the shadows and scary forms that they see as they open their eyes and look around in the dark, while in this confused and frightened state. Unable to recognize the difference between their sleep dream and real experience because of their intellectual limitations and because of their grogginess, they weave wonderful tales together, which they attribute to dreams.

However, no one disbelieves in the existence of children's night terrors, which are different from nightmares and take place during a different stage of sleep and involve different EEG changes than garden-variety nightmares. The small percentage of children who suffer from night terrors typically awaken with bloodcurdling screams and have difficulty recalling their dreams. Night terrors are almost always confined to children between the ages of four and twelve and strike a mere one to four percent. Nightmares are quite different, both in form and frequency, and are more common than pleasant dreams.

When night terrors occur in adults, they usually show that something is seriously amiss. Even ordinary nightmares are a cause of concern. Neurology textbooks warn that the sudden occurrence of nightmares of any sort in an adult should always raise suspicion of drug or alcohol use or of drug withdrawal. Unfortunately, many people attempt to self-medicate these sleep disturbances with the very substances that can cause them and so begin a downward spiral. By taking a nip of "the hair that bit the dog," they postpone withdrawal symptoms but perpetuate drug or alcohol dependence.

REM AND NON-REM SLEEP

Soon, another mystery of sleep surfaced. Scientists who had been so self-confident about the immutable link between REM sleep and dreams discovered that dreams are not limited to REM sleep, but can occur during non-REM (NREM) sleep. Moreover, NREM sleep is not as uniform as once thought. But there are a few caveats here. NREM dreams are not so numerous as the dreams of REM sleep, and they are qualitatively different from REM dreams. NREM dreams are more linear and logical with a more direct narrative, whereas REM dreams are more visionary and symbolic and thus more enigmatic. NREM dreams are more likely to occur in the very early morning, just before awakening.

For serious dream seekers, there is a great temptation to fall back asleep in the morning to experience these intense and easy-to-remember and late-appearing NREM dreams. But there is a serious psychiatric drawback to this practice (besides the obvious disadvantage of over-sleeping morning appointments). People who habitually sleep past their regular wake-up time may develop depression, because of incompletely understood hormonal and neurochemical changes that accompany such sleep. Those who are already too depressed to leave their beds in the morning and who bury their heads and their problems in their pillows may be particularly prone to such consequences. Those who awaken with a hangover and are doubly disinclined from pulling themselves away from sleep also put themselves at risk.

DANGERS OF DREAMS

There was a time when scientists believed that prolonged REM sleep deprivation, with resulting dream deprivation, could cause psychosis, as well as death, as occurred in laboratory rats. While not everyone goes insane from sleep deprivation, people with tendencies toward bipolar disorder (manic-depression) can set off manic episodes through sleep deprivation. On a less serious note, behavioral neurologists observed that patients with impaired REM sleep may awaken with both daytime fatigue and with painful muscle and joint symptoms that resemble fibromyalgia.[10] The relationship between dream deprivation and these adverse effects is not as clear as it once seemed, but there are new concerns today.

Recent research has called attention to the dangers of excessive dreaming and sounded a warning siren about hazards faced by participants in nonprofessionally supervised dream-telling groups or in casually conducted psychoanalytic treatments. Such self-help groups— which are growing in number—tend to attract people who are already dissatisfied with their lives and who may be clinically depressed or suffer from post-traumatic stress disorder or even more serious disturbances.

People who have a clinical depression (which is different from generic depression or dissatisfaction with one aspect of one's life) have a good chance of improving from appropriately-prescribed medications that suppress—rather than enhance—dreams and REM sleep. Persons suffering from post-traumatic stress disorder, which causes recurring nightmares of the traumatic trigger event, also do better by avoiding the recurring nightmare, instead of confronting it. Sometimes dream suppression, rather than dream promotion, helps heal a condition more quickly. Still, attempts have been made to teach people to change their nightmares and to imagine a positive ending to the traumatic event that triggered these disturbing dreams, to the point that the dream content actually does change. Early studies of such imagery rehearsal have been promising, but it is still unclear if these techniques are as effective as judiciously used medication or if some combination of the two approaches will work better than either one alone.[11]

The use of sleep deprivation to treat clinical depression is especially interesting, on both a theoretical and practical level. Some depressions that do not respond to high doses of antidepressant medication and intensive psychotherapy can improve dramatically if the patient is awakened—and forced to stay awake—before entering the last and longest stage of REM sleep, which starts before four in the morning. This finding is particularly curious, because early morning awakening is a classic accompaniment of depression. This technique contradicts nearly a century's worth of psychoanalytic practice, when dream states were cultivated for their curative effects.

Unfortunately, forced early morning awakening is not a very useful technique at this time, because the remission from depression lasts only one day. The symptoms of depression return once normal sleep restarts, which is usually the next night. Because constant supervision by a staff member is necessary to prevent the patient from falling back to sleep, hospitals prefer less labor-intensive and more long-lasting treatment techniques. Of course, hospitals are hardly the only place where people are awakened from their sleep. Some rigorous religious groups also require very early awakening for prayer or meditation and so are inadvertently practicing this clinical technique of dream deprivation and are relieving their members' depressions through these rites and rituals.

It can be dangerous to forget that some dreamlike states are not dreams at all. The d.t.'s (delirium tremens) of alcohol withdrawal start with dreamlike states or daytime dreams that can progress to life-threatening seizures—as happened with Freud's case study from the monastery at Mariazel. The dreams of d.t.'s are not as dramatic as depicted and are certainly not as amusing as the pink elephants that incorrectly came to be associated with them—d.t.'s are far more likely to be frightening, rather than funny. Because these monstrous apparitions can seem so real, they have led people to jump out of windows to escape them. When we look at the slithering snakes and reptiles found in some paintings by symbolist painter Gustave Moreau or at the imaginary bestiary illustrated by known opium addict Gustave Doré, we must wonder if these artists had firsthand knowledge of the devastating effects of d.t.'s.

Though d.t.'s or withdrawal symptoms in general are remarkably common, these dreamy states of early stage d.t.'s can be difficult to diagnose. In general hospitals, it is not uncommon for internists and surgeons to request psychiatric consults for nonalcoholic patients who grow troubled by strange dreams and insomnia while recuperating from completely unrelated conditions. It is typically learned only after the fact that these patients were using steady but seemingly insignificant amounts of alcohol or drugs before entering the hospital. The sudden deprivation of alcohol or drugs was enough to send them into withdrawal. To many people's surprise, complete cessation of alcohol or drugs is not necessary to bring on d.t.'s. Simply lowering the customary amount of drugs or alcohol can cause d.t.'s.

The delirium that accompanies several serious medical conditions (such as fevers) is also a cause for concern. Confused, dreamy states of delirium begin with disrupted sleep and eventually induce nightmares or perceptual distortions that intensify at sundown. Unlike real dreams, which are benign, these delirious states can signal the presence of serious medical problems and can lead to disastrous, even deadly, consequences if they are not identified and treated appropriately. Unfortunately, delirium is often overlooked, even in hospitals.

Alcoholics and drug addicts are not the only ones who can enter potentially dangerous dreamy states. Someone in the early stages of schizophrenia may appear to be lost in a daytime dream. The *International Classification of Disease-10 (ICD-10)*, a commonly-used compendium of physical and mental disorders, refers to a syndrome known as "oneroid schizophrenia," which literally means "dreamy schizophrenia." Ironically, real schizophrenics have dull and boring dreams, which contrast with the dramatic delusions and hallucinatory voices they endure during the day.

Temporal lobe epilepsy, which lacks the characteristic tonic-clonic movements of grand mal seizures, can also cause transient dreamy states in some people. Temporal lobe epileptics are also more likely to experience hypnogogic and hypnocampic hallucinations of fully-formed beings, that appear as they fall asleep or as they awaken. These vivid visions, which Romantic artist Henri Fuseli depicted in his painting *The Nightmare*, also occur in perfectly "normal" people who have never been diagnosed with epilepsy. Such sleep-associated visions are also prominent among narcoleptics, who fall asleep spontaneously during the day, and enter REM sleep immediately, without the usual latency period that normal people experience.

It cannot be stressed enough that such people will get worse rather than better, if they remain in this "oneroid" state of dreams. The Surrealists experimented with inducing psychosis and with elevating the dreamstate to complete consciousness and almost lost the lives of some of their members as a result of these unbridled experiments. The Jungian-inspired technique of encouraging people to relive their dreams during the therapy session has the potential to cause—rather than cure—psychosis in people who are hovering at the cusp. Interestingly, Jung himself expressed concern about reorienting his patients to reality, before subjecting them to his dream therapies. He recognized that his "analytic-hermeneutic" treatment would not benefit everyone equally and so screened potential patients carefully before accepting them for therapy.

On a more mundane note, people who study dreams report that they dream more and that they remember their dreams better than before, but that they remember more disturbing dreams. That effect reflects the fact that unpleasant dreams occur more often than pleasant ones. Consequently, an increase in dream frequency also causes a proportionate increase in unpleasant dreams. While these unpleasant dreams are often unwelcome, those people who enjoy interpreting their dreams often look forward to an opportunity to discover concealed conflicts and to resolve them while in a conscious state. Then again, some people are simply "better dreamers" than others, no matter what they do, and will experience more of these effects.

DREAMS AND PRESCRIPTION DRUGS

One need not be seriously ill with schizophrenia or epilepsy or narcolepsy or end-stage alcoholism to experience biologically-based, pathological dreams. It is common knowledge that many recreational drugs produce profound dreamy states while their users are awake. It is less well-known that some of the strongest stimulants also impact on dreams, though they are used for wakefulness and alertness and energy and sleep avoidance. Cocaine, amphetamine, methylphenidate (Ritalin), and MDMA (Ecstasy or X) are all classified as stimulants. They all alter sleep architecture in their own ways.

Drugs need not be illegal to induce intense or unusual dreams. Many ordinary, over-the-counter medications affect dreams. Some newly minted antiallergy medications are notorious for such unwanted effects. Nicotine patches, used for smoking cessation, can intensify dreams to the point of distraction, as can melatonin, the natural sleep aid that is still sold over the counter. Some prescription medications that affect the endocrine system, or blood pressure, or various neurological disorders play havoc with dream form, content, and frequency.

As the population ages and develops more age-related medical conditions that require treatment with such medications, such biologically-based dream changes will become more common. At present, "alpha-one blockers" that are used to treat hypertension are prominent among medical medications that cause nightmares. Hypertension is an incredibly common condition that affects a high portion of the American population. Several anti-Parkinson's disease drugs, such as L-dopa, bromocriptine, and selegeline, have intense nightmare-producing potential. Unlike the antihypertensives, the anti-Parkinson's drugs can cause psychosis as well as bad dreams. Half of all users stop treatment when these psychiatric side effects become intolerable. Because new medications are developed every day and because new side effects to existing medications become known over time, we can be certain that there will be new and different drugs that affect dreams in the future.

At the turn of the twenty-first century, there is one class of medications that is particularly popular and that has profound effects on dreams and on mental state in general. These are the SSRIs (selective serotonin reuptake inhibitors), such as Prozac, Paxil, Zoloft, Celexa, and others. Some of these drugs have become legendary in their own right and have inspired books that bear their names. All of them have significant physiological effects that are sometimes similar to, and sometimes distinct from earlier antidepressants such as tricyclics (TCAs) or monoamine oxidase inhibitors (MAOIs).

Antidepressants' effects on dreams were appreciated long before SSRIs became widely available around 1990. It was well known that tricyclic antidepressants such as Elavil, Tofrinil, and Pamelor suppressed both REM sleep and dreams. But patients who used these medications were rarely aware that such an effect was taking place. Typically, it was not until they stopped their medications that they reported a sudden explosion of very vivid dreams. This phenomenon is known as REM rebound. REM rebound occurs when the REM sleep that had been suppressed springs back, and returns with a vengeance, and temporarily rebounds with greater intensity and frequency after stopping the use of the REM sleep-suppressing drug.

There is a slight twist to the SSRI story. These SSRIs were expected to block REM sleep, just as the more cumbersome and less popular tricyclic antidepressants had done in the past. No one predicted that these REM sleep-blocking SSRIs would increase—rather than decrease—the strange and intense and literal dreams that occur during non-REM (NREM) sleep. This side effect of these new "miracle" medications would require some serious reworking of preexisting, set-in-stone theories about the immutable association between REM sleep and dreams.

What was responsible for the dream changes of SSRIs? Since SSRIs are selective serotonin reuptake inhibitors, they block the brain chemicals that deactivate and reabsorb the naturally occurring neurochemical known as serotonin. They make more serotonin available at nerve endings in the brain, the intestines, and some other parts of the body. So serotonin was the most obvious suspect (but not the only suspect).

Scientists were aware of the role of serotonin in mood and perception and sleep long before the relatively recent invention of SSRIs. Serotonin had long been associated with sleep. Its naturally-occurring chemical precursor, tryptophan, was sold as a nonprescription sleeping pill for the expressed purpose of increasing the synthesis of serotonin. Then a chemical contaminant appeared in a shipment of tryptophan and caused serious side effects that led to its being pulled from the market. Tryptophan abounds in foods such as bananas, avocados, turkey, and dairy but is not absorbed through the stomach when eaten with other proteins. But that is hardly the most interesting part of the serotonin-tryptophan story.

Decades ago, research showed that psychedelic drugs such as LSD flooded the nervous system with serotonin. It seemed that serotonin was somehow responsible for the hallucinogens' bizarre perceptual distortions, although it is still uncertain exactly how this happens. These strange LSD perceptions are mostly visual, but occasionally include olfactory (smell) and gustatory (taste) and tactile (touch) perceptions. LSD-induced hallucinations are quite distinct from the mostly auditory hallucinations of schizophrenia and are closer to dreams than anything else that humans experience.

Sleep laboratory studies revealed another sleep-related neurochemical change that is just as interesting as the increase in serotonin. The change concerns the decrease in—and virtual absence of—the neurochemical norepinephrine during sleep. Norepinephrine (and its chemical cousin epinephrine) are well known for their energizing effects. Norepinephrine is essential to propelling goal-oriented behavior and motivation. Interestingly, logical goals are lost during sleep. The brain's executive functions that set priorities and delegate tasks and arrange sequences are turned off at this time. Dream logic exemplifies a state of profound illogic and differs dramatically from ordinary waking logic. One wonders if the absence of norepinephrine secretion during dreams has a direct bearing on these thought processes.

Any number of other neurochemicals are activated or deactivated during dreams. The importance of acetycholine, GABA (gamma-aminobutyric acid), and several other less-studied substances has been recognized but goes beyond the scope of this study.

ILLICIT DRUGS AND DREAMS

The relationship between drugs and dreams (either waking or sleeping) has fascinated humankind for thousands of years, perhaps since the dawn of civilization. Many, many ancient peoples exploited plant drugs to produce personal or collective "prophetic" dreams. The oracles at Delphi entered trance states through the use of plant drugs such as belladonna. The ancient Assyrian and Babylonian idol worshipers accessed altered states of consciousness through specially-brewed beers and secret incense formulas. The earliest Persians relied upon haoma, while the Indian devotees of the Rg Veda venerated the daytime dreams invoked by the fabled soma plant. The Eleusinian mysteries that Plato partook in revolved around an altered dreamlike oceanic state, brought on by a plant potion prepared from nutritious grain and perception-distorting mushrooms. The list of archaic societies that were aware of these dream and drink links goes on and on and is endlessly intriguing.

Shamanistic societies still exist in various parts of the world. Like their ancestors before them, these people continue to exploit locally grown psychoactive plants to produce socially significant, divinatory dream states. Hashish, "Amanita muscaria, mandrake, and peyote are but a few of the hundreds of different dream-inducing sacramental plants mentioned in scholarly treatises on ethnopharmacology. Schultes and Hofmann's *Plants of the Gods*, or Peter Furst's *Flesh of the Gods*, or Weston LaBarre's *The Peyote Cult* are all excellent sources on this subject.[12]

Not all primitive or ancient societies welcomed the insights provided by plant chemicals. The Hebrew prophets of the Old Testament railed against the hallucinogenic incense and intoxicants that delighted their pagan neighbors. On the other side of the Mediterranean, the bygone mystical Pythagoreans devised ingenious dietary rules to avoid perception-altering and nightmare-producing plants that could interfere with the more serene mental state they sought.

The Pythagoreans gained fame for their mystical approach to mathematics and for their invention of basic geometry principles. They lived in a region where dopamine-rich fava and broad beans grew and entered the daily diet.[13] These beans contain small amounts of the same naturally-occurring chemical that is currently used to treat Parkinson's disease. This plant chemical, as well as these dopamine-based medications, are known to cause horrific nightmares, as well as psychosis and insomnia. By prohibiting the eating of all beans, the meditative Pythagoreans avoided the sleep-disturbing effects of dopamine and paved the path to the calm and contemplative state for which their cult called. (They also protected their members from a genetically transmitted blood disease known as "favisim," which is set off by eating fava beans.)[14]

Drug-induced dreams were not exclusive to the so-called primitive societies nor was this practice restricted to religious sects or artistic iconoclasts. Nineteenth and twentieth century scientists experimented with various dream-inducing (and psychosis-inducing) drugs. We cannot forget that opium was once a popular medicament, before it became the bane of contemporary society. It was available over the counter, mixed with alcohol, and sold as "laudanum." Opium was used to sedate mental patients before anything better became available. It was once as popular as aspirin. Bromine was another early and easily available psychoactive drug, used for the mildly upset and the seriously disturbed before it become known that it, too, was more harmful than helpful in the long run.

Working in the mid-nineteenth century, French psychiatrist Moreau de Tours explored the overlap between the dreams of normal people and the temporary, dreamlike psychosis induced by hashish. His early experiments never attracted a wide following among the medical profession, but his pioneering efforts produced a profound effect on French literary movements that followed. Writer, librettist, and dance critic Theophile Gautier founded the Hashish Club to explore these effects in the company of like-minded authors such as Victor Hugo, Henri Balzac, and Guy de Maupaussant. Moreau de Tours merits little more than a footnote today, but the literary legacy he spawned lives on.

Reserpine was one plant drug that gained wide acceptance among psychiatrists practicing during the early to mid-twentieth century. This medication arrived by way of India, where it grew wild. Its serpentine leaves inspired its formal name, *rauwoulfia serpentina*. In the West, this indigenous plant took the pharmaceutical trade name of reserpine. It was used to treat psychosis or depression and also enjoyed short-lived popularity as an antihypertensive. Reserpine resulted in a florid hallucinosis, punctuated with flamboyant and often frightening dreams. Many patients who survived this disturbing ordeal—and not all did— often found themselves symptom-free afterward. Not all were so fortunate, and more than a few grew more depressed. Some committed suicide.[15] Reserpine's appeal as an antihypertensive agent ended, when equally effective drugs without such severe psychiatric side effects became available.

The history of drugs and dreams and doctors would not be complete without mentioning that Freud himself used cocaine. Like all psychostimulants, cocaine has an intense, albeit indirect, impact on dreams, although cocaine users generally do not seek out this drug for its dream effects. Freud used cocaine for experimental purposes only. He was not known to be a recreational cocaine user. Nevertheless, he presumably reacted to the psychoactive effects of the coca plant and probably incorporated cocaine-induced insights into his psychoanalytic theories, however unwittingly. Freud praised cocaine, in his early *Cocaine Papers*, and vigorously denied that the plant had any potential for abuse or addiction. Once it became known just how wrong these observations were, Freud purged this controversial paper from the official edition of his *Collected Works*.[16]

Freud's ideas pervaded the "collective consciousness" of the American public, parts of Western Europe, South America, and Australia but never took as tenacious a hold in their native territory as they did on foreign soil. Compared to psychoanalysis' long-lasting and wide-reaching influence, the sensationalized psycholytic therapy promoted in the 1960s was little more than a blip on the map of history. Popularized by psychiatrists such as Stanislav Grof and Humphries Osmond, psycholytic therapy used LSD to induce dreams, hallucinatory states, and psychotic insights that would not have occurred spontaneously.[17] It was believed that such states would expedite life change, and shorten the protracted length of psychotherapy, and possibly even cure addictions and criminality. It is unclear as to whether or not this technique worked, because therapeutic trials ended when LSD became illegal in 1966. Before it was banned, LSD had inspired thousands upon thousands of serious scientific studies.[18]

To appreciate what happened with LSD-based psycholytic therapy, one must first look at what happened with LSD itself. The history of LSD and its association with dreams is far more fascinating than the history of the much-publicized Prozac of the 1990s. LSD was synthesized in 1938 by Dr. Albert Hofmann, who was a chemist at Sandoz Labs in Basel, Switzerland. The sample was stored on a back shelf and all but forgotten. Its full potential was not appreciated until Hofmann accidentally dosed himself with the drug several years later. Completely unexpectedly, he experienced florid visions of cathedrals and flowers floating past his eyes, while he rode his bicycle through Basel.

Originally hailed as a way to understand, if not also treat, the hallucinosis of schizophrenia, LSD was preemptively pulled from the market in 1966, after it was linked to protracted psychotic states and suicides and even cult killings, such as the Manson murders. By then, this "wonder drug" had become Albert Hofmann's problem child. LSD became even more popular with the general public after it became illegal. It was the darling of the drug culture. Once illegal, it caused more "bad trips" than ever before, possibly because it was used in an irresponsible and inhospitable and illegal atmosphere that left users anxious and irritable from the start.

By the time that Sandoz Labs ceased manufacture, the overall quality of LSD research had dropped dramatically. Overly zealous investigators such as Harvard psychologist Timothy Leary made many hyperbolic claims about the investigational drug and helped potentiate its diversion from scientific study to ritual and eventual recreational use. Popular songs such as "I had too much to dream last night" hinted about LSD's dream-inducing potential. The drug, with its dream effects and all, became an indelible part of pop culture, but a disposable aspect of scientific study.

Opium is another drug that is inextricably linked to dreams, partly because of fact and partly because of the fiction produced under its influence. The very visionary poem about Kublai Khan was written when Samuel Taylor Coleridge was intoxicated with opium. De Quincey's *Confessions of an English Opium Eater* is another relic of the Romantic Era that remains in print today, after having inspired his generation's literary interest in opium's effects, and in the poppy's role in personal memory. Gustave Doré's dark illustrations of Biblical and literary themes were completed under the influence of opium, as was Mary Shelley's famous science fiction and horror thriller, *Frankenstein,* and many, many other memorable works, whose names are too numerous to list here.[19] Filmmaker, poet, and playwright Jean Cocteau's life and work is linked to opium. His *Beauty and the Beast, Blood of a Poet, Testament of Orpheus,* and other films evoke the dreamy state of opium, but his autobiography makes it clear that he completed his masterpieces after he completed his cure.[20]

Scientific studies do not dispute the psychotropic effects that these writers attributed to opium. Rather, they confirm that this drug's dramatic effects make it dangerously addicting. Science has *not* confirmed that opium can turn an ordinary, unimaginative individual into a literary or artistic or cinematic giant of the stature of Shelley or Doré or Coleridge or Cocteau. Most people find that opiates produce a short-term gain (at best) and a long-term loss. It is far safer to experience the dreamlike states of those "opium eaters" secondhand, simply by reading or viewing the artistic legacy that they left behind.

While the literary, musical, and artistic impact of opium is fairly well known, a lesser-known fact is that some of Freud's famous patients were also opium addicts. One woman used opium to self-medicate painful infections that defied treatment in the days before antibiotics. We can surmise that her analyzed dreams were not nearly so spontaneous as they were made out to be and that her intermittent, on-off use of opium products produced strange dreams during withdrawal. Most likely, these withdrawal dreams were analyzed during her psychoanalytic sessions, just as the artist Christoph Haitzmann's withdrawal dreams were analyzed retrospectively, in Freud's paper *A Demonological Neurosis.*

Given the legacy of opium and literary dreams or LSD and musical dreams, it is striking that the dream-inducing potential of drugs such as Prozac or the other SSRIs has not been exploited to date. But there is a very rational reason for this relative lack of interest in "Prozac dreams." People take Prozac or similar antidepressants to optimize their functioning in the real waking world. People do not seek out

Prozac so that they can retreat to an introspective world or a dreamy disconnected state. Those who seek such otherworldly opportunities are apt to look elsewhere for their pharmacological inspiration.

THE DILEMMA ABOUT DRUGS AND DREAMS

The dilemma about dreams and drugs is far from settled. Most psychiatrists practicing at the turn of the twenty-first century avoid interpreting dreams brought on by drug use or drug withdrawal and refer the chemically-dependent patient to drug or alcohol treatment instead. At the very least, they recommend that the patient avoid such problem-causing plants and products. Most physicians make a point of warning patients about prescription medications that cause such untoward effects. Most people (but not all people) have been taught to avoid basing major life decisions on dreams that are produced by a bottle or a capsule or a blotter. But this sentiment could change at any moment, as it has many, many times in the past.

Such opinions about drugs and dreams can and do change quickly for any number of reasons. Scientific breakthroughs may make us rethink our existing assumptions, or politically-motivated publicity campaigns can impact on attitudes, or clever marketing maneuvers by pharmaceutical companies may shift sentiments, or pop culture icons can switch gears suddenly and fickle fans follow their examples. The powers that be of one decade may deliberately induce dreams through drugs and delight in the secrets that they reveal, while those who assume control in the next decade may denounce drug-induced dreams and maybe even deny that such practices occurred in the first place. The decisions that follow typically reflect fashion, rather than fact.

The overlap between drugs and dreams is an especially sensitive point in America, where zero tolerance for drugs has been the rule since the eclipse of the counterculture. European societies are not nearly so sensitive about this issue, and the British in particular find American preoccupations about drugs peculiar. Yet we need to remember that there has always been controversy about whether drug-induced dreams should be avoided or enjoyed or deified or demonized. The Hebrew Bible tells us that the tribes who inhabited the ancient Near East were just as conflicted about this subject as people are today. The debates of Deuteronomy that took place some 2,500 years ago continue to recur, not just among religionists or warring tribes of old, but also among psychiatrists and scientists and society at large.

Perhaps the most important lesson to be learned from these conflicts about body and brain, psyche and soul, and dream and drug lies somewhere else entirely. It is clear that identifying the source of an experience is not the same as imputing meaning to that experience.

Science's understanding of the physiological sources of dream will change over time, as new information is discovered. At some points in time, serotonin will be considered to be most significant. At other times, REM sleep will be deemed to be primary. In the future, new chemicals and causes will undoubtedly be implicated. Our knowledge of the biological basis of dream will never be static.

But this biological data does not hold meaning for everyone. For those who seek reasons rather than causes, it is the meaning of dream, rather than the dream itself, that is most profound. Human beings have an inherent ability to manufacture meaning out of the most mundane events. What could be more mundane and more meaningful than the sleep and dreams that occur every night like clockwork. It has been said that all humans are mythmakers and that psychoanalysis simply enables them to write their own life-myths better than they could have done on their own.[21] People are rarely content to write their lives off as the by-product of basic biology and nothing but, no matter how hard they try, or how reductionist they wish to be, or how scientifically sophisticated they become.

Civilization persists because people can embroider elaborate lace from thin threads of everyday experience. Given this tendency of the human soul and psyche, it seems that scientific explanations for dreams and daily experience, which revolve around body and brain, will always be present. They will always run along a parallel track with heuristic explanations but will never be the last stop on the train, at least not for very long.

At one point, it seemed as though a market flooded with drugs that induce dreams could convince the public of the biological basis of such sleep perceptions and induce them to abandon their delusions about the meaning of dreams. But, if we examine the long course of history rather than this short stage of pharmacology, it is more likely that these additional dream-inducing drugs will only provide even more opportunities to manufacture meaning from more raw material.

NOTES

1. Noll, Richard. *The Jung Cult*. Princeton: Princeton University Press, 1994.

2. Kuhn, Thomas. *The Structure of Scientific Revolutions*. Chicago: University of Chicago Press, 1996; Popper, Karl. *The Logic of Scientific Discovery*. London, Routledge, 1992.

3. Erman, Milton K. "Sleep Architecture and Its Relationship to Insomnia." *Journal of Clinical Psychiatry* supp. 10 (2001): 62, 9–17.

4. Robinson, Daniel N. *An Intellectual History of Psychology*, 3rd ed. Madison: University of Wisconsin Press, 1995; Murray, David. *A History of Western Psychology*. 2nd ed. Englewood Cliffs, NJ: Prentice Hall, 1988.

5. Ellenberger, Henri. *The Discovery of the Unconscious*. New York, Basic, 1970.

6. Jung, C. G. *Psychology and Alchemy*. 2nd ed. Ed. Herbert Read, Michael Fordham, Gerhard Adler, and William McGuire. London: Routledge, 1953.

7. See chapter 1.

8. Hoffmann, E. T. A. *The Best Tales of Hoffmann*. Ed. E. F. Bleiler. Ontario: Dover, 1967.

9. Foulkes, David. *Children's Dreaming and the Development of Consciousness*. Cambridge, MA: Harvard University Press, 1999.

10. Pincus, Jonathan H., and Gary J. Tucker. *Behavioral Neurology*. 3rd ed. New York: Oxford University Press, 1985, 27–29, 233–234, 269–276.

11. Krakow, Barry, et al. "Imagery Rehearsal Therapy for Chronic Nightmares in Sexual Assault Survivors with Posttraumatic Stress Disorder." *Journal of the American Medical Association* (August 1, 2001) 286: 5.

12. La Barre, Weston. *The Peyote Cult*. 5th ed. Oklahoma: University of Oklahoma Press, 1989; Schultes, Richard, and Albert Hofmann. *The Plants of the Gods*. Maidenhead, U.K.: McGraw-Hill, 1979.

13. Edelstein, Ludwig. *Ancient Medicine*. Trans. C. Lilian Temkin. Ed. Owsei Temkin and C. Lilian Temkin. Baltimore: Johns Hopkins University Press, 1967.

14. Grmek, Mirko D. *Diseases in the Ancient Greek World*. Trans. Mireille Muellner and Leonard Muellner. Baltimore: Johns Hopkins University Press, 1983, 224–244.

15. de Ropp, Robert S. *Drugs and the Mind*. New York: City Lights, 1965; Hardman, Joel G. et al. *Goodman & Gilman's The Pharmaceutical Basis of Therapeutics*. 9th Ed. New York: McGraw-Hill, 1996.

16. Freud, Sigmund. "On Cocaine." Strausbaugh, John, and Donald Blaise, ed. *The Drug User Documents 1840–1960*. New York: Blast Books, 1991, 1151–1164.

17. Aaronson B., and Humphrey Osmond. *Psychedelics*. Garden City, N.Y.: Anchor Books, Doubleday, 1970.

18. Lee, Martin A., and Bruce Shlain. *Acid Dreams: The CIA, LSD, and the Sixties Rebellion*. New York: Grove Press, 1985.

19. Berridge, Virginia, and Edwards Griffth. *Opium and the People: Opium Use in 19th Century England*. New Haven: Yale University Press, 1987.

20. Cocteau, Jean. *Opium*. London: Peter Owen, 1930.

21. Levi-Strauss, Claude. *The Savage Mind*. Chicago: University of Chicago Press, 1966.

14

Foretelling the Future

IMPACT OF PROZAC

The last decade of the twentieth century spawned a sea change in the practice of psychiatry, when a new type of antidepressant medication, the SSRI (selective serotonin reuptake inhibitor), became available *and* acceptable to the public and professionals alike.[1] As other new psychotropic medications appeared on the market, the focus of psychiatry shifted from the mind to the brain.

When the American Psychiatric Association crowned the 1990s as the "Decade of the Brain," it seemed as though the storm of science that waited at the gates of the twenty-first century would eclipse twentieth century metapsychology entirely. The psychoanalytic dream therapies that surfaced at the start of the century were endangered and might disappear completely into the darkness of night, like dreams themselves. Yet it turned out that the public's intrigue with dreams did not vaporize as expected. If anything, dream interpretation was more alive than ever. But it was returning to its religious and superstitious roots, now that standard Freudian psychoanalytic explanations were under siege. Jungian-influenced psychospiritual explanations were particularly prominent in the smorgasbord of New Age spiritual explanations for dreams.

It also turned out that medical (rather than psychological) treatments were not nearly so new as they seemed. In spite of all the fuss made about these "innovative" medical treatments of psychiatric disorders, a little scratching beneath the surface showed somatic psychiatric treatments had been used for centuries. ECT (electroconvulsive therapy), "malaria fever therapy," prefrontal lobotomies and leukotomies, and insulin shock therapy were all products of the twentieth century, as were the mercurial cures, sulfas, and penicillin that halted neu-

rosyphilis, which had been an important cause of "general paresis of
the insane" through the early twentieth century. Some of these somatic
treatments earned Nobel prizes for their inventors.

The real difference between this era and earlier eras revolved around
the fact that medications were being prescribed for all social classes and
were not reserved for the poor, who could not afford more humane care.
With the arrival of the SSRIs, medications became the treatment of
choice for depression. Antipsychotic medications had already become
the first-line treatment for the far less common condition of schizophrenia. Medication was no longer just a second-choice solution, to be doled
out only to those who could not afford time-consuming and cost-inten-
sive talking treatment, that came complete with dream interpretation
and other amenities of the couch cure.[2]

Psychopharmacologists—along with their pharmaceutical spon-
sors—insisted that the SSRIs won such enthusiastic support because
they were safe, effective, and easy to use. They praised these drugs
because they improved upon past generations of antidepressants,
which had too many side effects to make them popular with patients.
Too many patients simply stopped taking those uncomfortable medications before they could reap their benefits. Though it is debatable if the
SSRIs are as side effect–free as their manufacturers claim, it is not
debatable that the public has embraced these drugs wholeheartedly, at
least for the time being. Since their invention, these SSRIs have produced upward of five billion dollars per year in sales, and there is still
no end in sight, as of the year 2001.

Skeptics attribute the success of the SSRI antidepressants to method-
ical marketing techniques engineered by clever drug companies and by
patient-hungry psychiatrists, whose psychotherapy skills were under-
bid by growing numbers of nonmedical therapists. Others say that the
baby boomers themselves shifted their attitudes, without the intervention of Madison Avenue, because this generation had come of age
during the heyday of psychedelic drugs. They spent their high school
and college years hearing tongue-in-cheek slogans about "better living
through chemistry." They had witnessed drug-induced behavior
changes, if not necessarily firsthand, then for sure on television or on
college campuses or in army barracks. Broadcast specials about Love
Street, Haight-Ashbury, and Woodstock educated everyone about
chemical modification of mood.

For all these reasons combined, medications such as the much-celebrated Prozac produced a paradigm shift as profound as the shift
produced by Freud's publication of *The Interpretation of Dreams* nearly
a century before.[3] These SSRI-based antidepressants worked quickly
enough to appeal to our fast-food society and contrasted with the slow
and arduous and nonguaranteed cure that came with years of free

associations, dreamwork, and patient-therapist transference. These medications also rekindled popular and philosophical debates about mind and brain, which had been raging since Descartes postulated his mind-body dualism.

Drugs such as Prozac inspired several novels and memoirs and narratives that bore its name.[4] Dr. Peter Kramer's clinically-based *Listening to Prozac*[5] and Elizabeth Wurtzel's patient-focused *Prozac Nation*[6] soared to bestseller status. Around the same time, Scientologists paid for full-page newspaper advertisements denouncing the dangers of the drug and demanding its recall. It was said (especially by Scientologists and criminal defense attorneys) that Prozac could turn mild-mannered patients into savage mass murderers. Possessing a prescription for this drug could save someone from the proverbial electric chair. Some claimed (unsuccessfully) that psychiatrists conspired with pharmaceutical companies to promote these products for their own financial gain.

Prozac and its cousins pushed the psychoanalytic couch out of the consulting room and into the back room. It was said that SSRIs dealt the final death knell to psychoanalytic practice, which had been withering away for a while. At the same time, the SSRIs did more to destigmatize psychiatric treatment than anything since Freud's publication of *The Psychopathology of Everyday Life*. Publicity about their miraculous cures made almost *everyone* want to take them. This was the drug de jour. This celebrated medication produced a secondary, but less sensational, effect on psychoanalytic approaches to dreams and on the role of dreams in therapy overall. New kinds of talk therapy evolved to accompany new medications, ones that focused on cognition and behavior rather than on meaning and cause and the unconscious. Again, dream interpretation techniques were upstaged by such upstarts as cognitive behavior therapy (CBT) or interpersonal therapy (IPT).[7]

In another unanticipated move, SSRIs also made neuropsychiatrists and sleep physiologists rethink previously solid and stable theories about the association between dreams and REM sleep. These SSRIs suppressed REM sleep—as did earlier antidepressants—but they also induced strange dreams. That should not have happened according to sacrosanct sleep theory, which tied dreams to REM sleep. This curious finding did not attract nearly so much publicity as Prozac's hypothetical homicide potential or its personality-altering properties, but it was an important step in understanding sleep, nonetheless.

The notion that dreams occur during a specific stage of sleep, known as REM (rapid eye movement) sleep, had been a cornerstone of sleep research since 1953. Since then, it had become well known that many drugs interfered with REM sleep. Some of the most flagrant offenders were drugs that were commonly used to induce sleep, such as benzodiazepines (Valium, Librium, Halcion, etc.), alcohol, and barbiturates.

This discovery sent sleep scientists back to the drawing board, or at least back to the laboratory, to figure out why these REM sleep-suppressing drugs also produced dramatic and often disturbing dreams during NREM (non-REM) sleep. But this was not a serious setback for sleep science, because science, by its very nature, is prepared to prove itself wrong and to reinvent itself again, in order to advance. What was more difficult to deal with were the economic changes that occurred around the same time that the SSRIs appeared on the market and that were, in part, made possible by SSRIs.

Managed care appeared on the scene around 1990. This new approach to health care delivery altered financial incentives for psychiatric treatment and produced just as profound an impact as any scientific discovery or philosophical shift. Managed care demanded short, quick, cheap, outcome-oriented solutions and reproducible results. Psychoanalytic-style dream interpretation did not fit this bill, and so insurance companies would not pay the bill. As psychopharmacology advanced, insurance reimbursement rates for talk therapy retreated. Being bankrolled for long, drawn-out Freudian or Jungian-style dream interpretation was less and less likely. Turn-of-the-century-style psychoanalytic dream interpretation headed insurance companies' lists of nonreimbursable medical expenses and was put in the same category as recovered memory therapy, holistic healing, Rolfing, rebirthing, and meditation.

At this very same time, more and more people were receiving prescriptions for medications that increased dreams overall and that induced disturbing dreams in particular. With fewer and fewer "official," financially-affordable opportunities to discuss such disturbing dreams, one had to wonder how people were processing these dreams. Without reimbursement for the time-honored, twentieth century psychotherapy tradition, would people be content to write their dreams off to chemical reactions and forget about anything further, or would they do what people have always done about their dreams, before dreams became medicalized in the twentieth century? It was clear that the growing medical subspecialty of sleep medicine was not diverting such dream discussions. The first edition of the standard sleep medicine textbook did not have a single chapter on dreams, and the second edition literally devoted a single chapter to dreams.[8] According to its table of contents, sleep medicine clinics seemed more concerned with snoring than with sleeping and least concerned of all with dreams.

One look at bookstore shelves made it clear where dream discussions had headed. Without official outlets available, the time-honored tradition of dream interpretation was returning to the realm of religion, where it had begun. Whenever science is not available to answer a question or to provide a service, someone or something else is sure to step in. A subject such as dreams, which has intrigued humankind since the start of history, was not ready to disappear, just because *one* particular approach to dreams was less available and less credible than it had been in the past. Psychoanalytic approaches to dreams could quickly be amalgamated with supernaturalist and spiritualist and even superstitious approaches to produce a vaguely familiar syncretic product tailored to the needs and beliefs of twenty-first-century society.

It is risky to attempt to foretell the future, but it is always necessary to look ahead. Often the best way to do that is to peer into the past. If we were to foretell the future today, we can say one thing for certain. Oneiromancy of one form or another will always persist, as it has in the past. It is simply the form of oneiromancy that changes, but not the intent. People will always have hopes that dreams can foretell their futures, and they will always invent ways to make meaning out of their dreams. The methods may metamorphose, but we can safely say that a new method will always arrive, just in time to replace the last.

ADDENDUM

This book came to completion just before the World Trade Center tragedy occurred. How strange it was, and how sad it was to see the twin towers devoured by flames, like an unreal apocalyptic vision from Bosch, or Brueghel, or Daniel, or Doré. Neither John Martin nor his mad brother Jonathan could have painted a more accurate portrait of destruction.

In the aftermath of this event, some of those who always suffered from doomsday dreams may come to see themselves as prophetic, just as shamans and seers have in the past. There will be many more, who never lost a night's sleep in the past, who will awaken at night, seeing these visions in their dreams and haunted by images of helplessness. Hopefully, this distress will pass quickly for most people, as it usually does. Yet we can predict that some 25 percent will endure the recurring nightmares of PTSD (post-traumatic stress disorder), and that for some of them, the study of dreams will take on new meaning under their circumstances.

In the past, times of distress have typically been accompanied by retreats to religious beliefs and by seeking solace in long-abandoned superstitions and in new religious movements. Political scientists point out that people retreat most into spiritual practices or personal introspection when legitimate political power is not possible, and that is certainly not the case in this situation. While it is still too soon to say what people will do to heal their wounds, or what psychological salves they will turn to, or what kind of political action they will choose, it is not too soon to predict that personal dreams will assume far more importance to each individual than they have in the recent past. It is likely that newer approaches to dream will develop, far sooner than was ever anticipated when the writing of this book began.

NOTES

1. Hardman, Joel, and Limbird, Lee, ed. *The Pharmacological Basis of Therapeutics*. 9th ed. New York: McGraw-Hill, 1996.
2. Porter, Roy. *The Greatest Benefit to Mankind*. London: Norton, 1997; Porter, Ray. *A Social History of Madness*. London: Phoenix Giants, 1987; Shorter, Edward. *A History of Psychiatry: From the Era of the Asylum to the Age of Prozac*. New York: Wiley, 1996.
3. Micale, Mark S., and Porter, Roy. *Discovering the History of Psychiatry*. New York: Oxford University Press, 1994.
4. Slater, Loren. *Prozac Diary*. New York: Penguin, 1999.
5. Kramer, Peter D. *Listening to Prozac*. New York: Viking, 1993.
6. Wurtzel, Elizabeth. *Prozac Nation*. New York: Riverhead, 1997.
7. It is unclear if "imagery rehearsal therapy" will be accepted by public and professionals or how it will compare to accepted psychopharmaceutical techniques. However, in the wake of the World Trade Center tragedy and the expected rise in nightmares accompanying PTSD (post-traumatic stress disorder), it is likely that this new and apparently benign technique will be tested out in far more people than originally anticipated.
8. Shneerson, John. *Handbook of Sleep Medicine*. Oxford, U.K.: Blackwell Science, 2000.

Bibliography

Aaronson, B. and Humphry Osmond. *Psychedelics*. Garden City, NY: Doubleday-Anchor, 1970.

Abrams, M. H. *The Mirror and the Lamp*. New York: Oxford University Press, 1953.

———. *Naturalism and Supernaturalism: Tradition and Revolution in Romantic Literature*. New York: Norton, 1971.

Adams, P. Sitney. *Visionary Cinema*. 2nd ed. Oxford, U. K.: Oxford University Press, 1979.

Allan, Robin. *Walt Disney and Europe*. London: John Libbey and Company, 1999.

Arnhem, S. I. *Film as Art*. Berkeley: University of California, 1957.

Art Institute of Chicago. *Odilon Redon: Prince of Dreams 1840–1916* New York: Abrams, 1994.

Bakan, David. *Sigmund Freud and the Jewish Mystical Tradition*. Princeton, NJ: Van Nostrand, 1958.

Baudelaire, Charles. "The Poem of Hashish;" "On Cocaine." Strausbaugh, John, and Donald Blaise, ed. *The Drug User Documents 1840–1960*. New York: Blast Books, 1991, 36–49.

Bernstein, Richard J. *Freud and the Legacy of Moses*. Cambridge Studies in Religion and Critical Thought 4. Cambridge, U.K.: Cambridge University Press, 1998.

Berridge, Virginia, and Edwards Griffth. *Opium and the People: Opium Use in 19th Century England*. New Haven, CT: Yale University Press, 1987.

Bjork, Daniel W. *The Compromised Scientist: William James in the Development of American Psychology*. New York: Columbia University Press, 1983.

Bourguignon, Erika, ed. *Religion, Altered States of Consciousness, and Social Change*. Columbus: Ohio State University Press, 1973.

Breton, Andre, Paul Eluard, and Philippe Soupault. *The Automatic Message*. London: Atlas Press, 1997.

Bulkeley, Kelly. *Visions of the Night*. Albany: State University of New York Press, 1999.

Campbell, Joseph, ed. *Primitive Mythology*. Harmondsworth, U.K.: Penguin, 1976.

———. *Myths, Dreams, and Religion*. New York: Dutton, 1970.

Carskadon, M. A., ed. *Encyclopedia of Sleep and Dreaming*. New York: Macmillan, 1993.

Castillo, R. *Meanings of Madness*. Pacific Grove, CA: Brooks/Cole, 1998.

Charcot, J. M., and Paul Richer. *Les Demoniaques Dans L'Art*. Paris: Macula, 1984.

Charet, F. X. *Spiritualism and the Foundations of C. G. Jung's Psychology*. Albany: State University of New York Press, 1993.

Cocks, Geoffrey. *Psychotherapy in the Third Reich*. 2nd ed. New Brunswick, NJ: Trans/Action Publishers, 1997.

Cocteau, Jean. *The Art of Cinema*. Trans. Robin Buss. London: Marion Boyars, 1992.

———. *Opium*. London: Peter Owen, 1930.

Cohn, Norman. *The Pursuit of the Millenium*. New York: Oxford University Press, 1974.

Crews, Frederick. "The Memory Wars. Freud's Legacy in Dispute." New York: *New York Review of Books*, 1995.

Dante. "Purgatory" and "Inferno." Almansi, Guido, and Claude Beguin. *Theatre of Sleep: An Anthology of Literary Dreams*. London: Pan, 1981.

DeKorne, Jim. *Psychedelic Shamanism*. Port Townsend, WA: Loompanics, 1994.

Delevoy, Robert L., Catherine DeCroes, and Giselle Ollinger Zinque. *Fernand Khnopff: Reve, Mort, et Volupte*. Bruxelles, Cosmos Monographies, date unknown.

Dement, W. C. *Some Must Watch While Some Must Sleep*. San Francisco: Freeman, 1974.

de Quincey, Thomas. *Confessions of an English Opium Eater*. Oxford, U.K.: Oxford University Press, 1985.

de Ropp, Robert S. *Drugs and the Mind*. New York: City Lights, 1965.

Devereaux, George. *Reality and Dream: Psychotherapy of a Plains Indian*. New York: Doubleday-Anchor, 1969.

Dodds, E. R. *The Greeks and the Irrational*. Berkeley: University of California Press, 1951.

Donn, Linda. *Freud and Jung*. New York: Collier, 1988.

Eberwein, Robert. *Film and the Dream Screen*. Princeton, NJ: Princeton University Press, 1983.

Edelstein, Emma J., and Ludwig Edelstein. *Asclepius: Collection and Interpretation of the Testimonies*. Baltimore: Johns Hopkins University Press, 1998.

Edelstein, Ludwig. *Ancient Medicine*. Trans. C. Lilian Temkin. Ed. Owsei Temkin and C. Lilian Temkin. Baltimore: Johns Hopkins University Press, 1967.

Eisner, Lottie. *The Haunted Screen: Expressionism in German Cinema*. Berkeley: University of California Press, 1969.

Eliade, Mircea. *Myths, Dreams, and Mysteries*. New York: Harper, 1967.

———. *Shamanism: Archaic Techniques of Ecstacy*. Princeton, NJ: Princeton University Press, 1964.

———. *Autobiography. Vol. I 1907–1937. Journey East, Journey West*. Trans. Mac Linscott Ricketts. Chicago: University of Chicago Press, 1981.

Ellenberger, Henri. *The Discovery of the Unconscious*. New York: Basic, 1970.

Erikson, Erik H. *Childhood and Society*. 2nd Ed. New York: Norton, 1963.

Erman, Milton K. "Sleep Architecture and Its Relationship to Insomnia." *Journal of Clinical Psychiatry* supp. 10 (2001): 62.

Fikes, Jay Courtney. *Carlos Castaneda, Academic Opportunism and the Psychedelic Sixties*. Victoria, B.C.: Millenia, 1993.

Foulkes, David. *Children Dreaming and the Development of Consciousness*. Boston: Harvard University Press, 1999.

Freud, Sigmund. "The Uncanny (1919)." *Studies in Parapsychology*. Ed. Philip Rieff. New York: Collier-Basic, 1963, 19–62.

———. *The Interpretation of Dreams*. Trans. Joyce Crick. New York: Oxford University Press, 2000.

———. "On Cocaine." Strausbaugh, John, and Donald Blaise, eds. *The Drug User Documents 1840–1960*. New York: Blast Books, 1991, 1151–1164.

———. "A Neurosis of Demonical Possession (1923)." *Studies in Parapsychology*. Ed. Philip Rieff. New York: Collier-Basic, 1963, 91–125.

Fromm, Erich. *The Forgotten Language: An Introduction to the Understanding of Dreams, Fairy Tales, and Myths*. New York: Grove, 1957.

Gabbard, Glen O., and Krin Gabbard. *Psychiatry and the Cinema*. Washington: American Psychiatric Press, 1999.

Gamwell, Lynn. *Dreams 1900–2000*. Ithaca, NY: Cornell University Press, 2000.

Gamwell, Lynn, and Richard Wells. *Sigmund Freud and Art: His Personal Collection of Antiquities*. Binghamton: State University of New York, 1989.

Gay, Peter. *Freud, A Godless Jew*. New Haven, CT: Yale University Press, 1989.

Gibson, Michael. *Symbolism*. Cologne, Germany: Benedikt Taschen, 1995.

Goetz, Christopher G., Michel Bonduelle, and Toby Gelfand. *Charcot: Constructing Neurology*. Oxford, U.K.: Oxford University Press, 1995.

Goodman, L. S., and A. G. Gilman. *The Pharmaceutical Basis of Therapeutics*. 4th ed. New York: Macmillan, 1970.

Gordon, Cyrus H. *The Ancient Near East*. New York: Norton, 1953.

Gould, Michael. *Surrealism and the Cinema*. London: The Tantivy Press, 1976.

Greenberg, Harvey Roy. *Screen Memories: Hollywood Cinema on the Psychoanalytic Couch*. New York: Columbia University Press, 1993.

Grmek, Mirko D. *Diseases in the Ancient Greek World*. Trans. Mireille Muellner and Leonard Muellner. Baltimore: Johns Hopkins University Press, 1983, 224–244.

Grof, Stanislav. *Birth, Death, and Transcendence in Psychotherapy*. New York: State University of New York Press, 1986.

Grunebaum, Adolph. *The Foundations of Psychoanalysis*. Berkeley: University of California Press, 1984.

Hamilton, Malcomb. *The Sociology of Religion*. London: Routledge, 1995.

Hardman, Joel, and Limbird, Lee, eds. *The Pharmacological Basis of Therapeutics*. 9th ed. New York: McGraw-Hill, 1996.

Harner, Michael, ed. *Hallucinogens and Shamanism*. New York: Oxford University Press, 1973.

Hoffmann, E. T. A. *The Best Tales of Hoffmann*. Ed. E. F. Bleiler. Toronto: Dover, 1967.

Homans, Peter. *Jung in Context: Modernity and the Making of a Psychology*. 2nd. ed. Chicago: University of Chicago Press, 1995.

Huysmans, Joris Karl. *Against the Grain [A Rebours]*. New York: Dover, 1969.

James, Tony. *Dreams, Creativity, and Madness in Nineteenth-Century France*. New York: Oxford University Press, 1995.

Johnstone, Christopher. *John Martin*. New York: St. Martin's, 1974.

Jones, Ernest. *On The Nightmare*. New York: Liveright, 1951.

Jullian, Philippe. *The Symbolists*. Trans. Mary Anne Stevens. London: Phaidon, 1973.

———. *Dreamers of Decadence*. New York: Praeger, 1975.

Jung, C. C. *Memories, Dreams, Reflections*. Rev. ed. Trans. Richard Winston and Clara Winston. Rec. and ed. Aniela Jaffe. New York: Vintage, 1961.

———. *The Portable Jung*. Trans. R. F. C. Hull. Ed. Joseph Campbell. New York: Penguin, 1971.

———. *Psychology and Alchemy*, Ed. Herbert Read, Michael Fordham, Gerhard Adler, William McGuire. 2nd ed. London: Routledge, 1953.

Kaplan, Julius. *Gustave Moreau*. Los Angeles: Los Angeles County Museum of Art, 1974.

Kapur S., and P. Seeman. "The Dream in Contemporary Psychiatry." *American Journal of Psychiatry*. 158:3 (2001).

Kaye, Elizabeth. *American Ballet Theatre: A 25-Year Retrospective*. Singapore: American Ballet Theatre, 1999.

Kirsch, Thomas B. *The Jungians: A Comparative and Historical Perspective*. London: Routledge, 2000.

Klein, Dennis. *Jewish Origins of the Psychoanalytic Movement*. Chicago: University of Chicago Press, 1981.

Kracauer, Siegfried. *From Caligari to Hitler*. Princeton, NJ: Princeton University Press, 1947.

Krakow, Barry, Michael Hollifield, Lisa Johnston, Mary Koss, Ron Schrader, Teddy Warner, Dan Tandberg, John Lauriallo, Leslie McBride, Lisa Cutchan, Diana Chang, Shawn Emmons, Anne Germain, Dominic Melendrez, Diane Sandoval, and Holly Prince. "Imagery Rehearsal Therapy for Chronic Nightmares in Sexual Assault Survivors with Posttraumatic Stress Disorder." *Journal of the American Medical Association* (August 1, 2001) 286: 5.

Kryger, M. H., H. Mair, Thomas Roth, and William C. Demint, eds. *Principles and Practice of Sleep Medicine*. Philadelphia: Saunders, 1993.

Kuenzli, Rudolph, ed. *Dada and Surrealist Film*. Cambridge, MA: MIT, 1996.

Kuhn, Thomas. *The Structure of Scientific Revolutions*. Chicago: University of Chicago Press, 1996.

La Barre, Weston. *The Peyote Cult*. 5th ed. Norman: University of Oklahoma Press, 1989.

Laderman, Carol. *Taming the Wind of Desire*. Berkeley: University of California Press, 1993.

Lavie, Peretz. *The Enchanted World of Sleep*. New Haven, CT: Yale University Press, 1996.

Lee, Martin A., and Bruce Shlain. *Acid Dreams: The CIA, LSD, and the Sixties Rebellion*. New York: Grove Press, 1985.

Levi-Strauss, Claude. *The Savage Mind*. Chicago: University of Chicago Press, 1966.

Lincoln, Jackson S. *The Dream in Primitive Culture*. London: University of London, 1935.

Lucie-Smith, Edward. *Symbolist Art*. London: Thames and Hudson, 1972.

MacGregor, John M. *The Discovery of the Art of the Insane*. Princeton, NJ: Princeton University Press, 1992.

Maidenbaum, Aryeh, and Stephen A. Martin. *Lingering Shadows: Freudians, Jungians and Anti-Semiticism*. Boston: Shambala, 1991.

McGuire, William, ed. *The Freud/Jung Letters: The Correspondence between Sigmund Freud and C. G. Jung*. Princeton, NJ: Princeton University Press, 1974.

Metz, Christian. *The Imaginary Signifier: Psychoanalysis and the Cinema*. Trans. Celia Britton, et al. Bloomington: Indiana University Press, 1981.

Micale, Mark S, and Porter, Roy. *Discovering the History of Psychiatry*. New York: Oxford University Press, 1994.

Murray, David. *A History of Western Psychology*. 2nd ed. Englewood Cliffs, NJ: Prentice Hall, 1988.

Neumann, Erich. "Mystical Man." Joseph Campbell, ed. *The Mystic Vision*. Princeton, NJ: Princeton University Press, 1968. 375–419.

O'Flaherty, Wendy Doniger. *Dreams, Illusions, and Other Realities*. Chicago: University of Chicago, 1984.

Ostow, Mortimer, ed. *Psychoanalysis and Judaism*. New York: Ktav, 1982.

Pincus, Jonathan H., and Gary J. Tucker. *Behavioral Neurology*. 3rd ed. New York: Oxford University Press, 1985.

Popper, Karl. *The Logic of Scientific Discovery*. London: Routledge, 1992.

Powell, Nicholas. *Fuseli: The Nightmare*. New York: Viking, 1972.

Prawer, S. S. *Caligari's Children*. Oxford, U.K.: Oxford University Press, 1980.

Preuss, Julius. *Biblical and Talmudic Medicine*. Trans. and ed. Fred Rosner. Northvale, NJ: Aronson, 1993.

Rice, Emanual. *Freud and Moses: The Long Journey Home*. Albany: State University of New York Press, 1990.

Robinson, Daniel N. *An Intellectual History of Psychology*. 3rd ed. Madison: University of Wisconsin Press, 1995.

Said, Edward W. *Orientalism*. New York: Vintage Books, 1979.

Scholem, Gershom G. *Major Trends in Jewish Mysticism*. 3rd ed. New York: Schocken, 1960.

Schultes, Richard, and Albert Hofmann. *Plants of the Gods*. Maidenhead, U.K.: McGraw-Hill, 1979.

Shamdasani, Sonu. *Cult Fictions*. London: Routledge, 1998.

Shepard, John W. *Atlas of Sleep Medicine*. London: Futura, 1991.

Shneerson, John. *Handbook of Sleep Medicine*. Oxford, U.K.: Blackwell Science, 2000.

Shorter, Edward. *A History of Psychiatry: From the Era of the Asylum to the Age of Prozac*. New York: Wiley, 1996.

Soren, David. *The Rise and Fall of the Horror Film*. Baltimore: Midnight Marquee, 1997.

Strausbaugh, John, and Donald Blaise, eds. *The Drug User Documents 1840-1960*. New York: Blast, 1991.

Tedlock, Barbara. *Dreaming*. New York: Cambridge University Press, 1987.

Temkin, Owsei. *The Falling Sickness: A History of Epilepsy from the Greeks to the Beginnings of Modern Neurology*. Baltimore: Johns Hopkins University Press, 1971.

Torrey, E. Fuller. *Freudian Fraud*. New York: Harper, 1992.

Underhill, Evelyn. *Mysticism*, 12th ed. New York: Signet-Penguin, 1974.

Virgil. "The Aeneid." Almansi, Guido, and Claude Beguin. *Theatre of Sleep: An Anthology of Literary Dreams*. London: Pan Books, 1981.

Waldberg, Patrick. *Surrealism*. New York: Thames and Hudson, 1997.

Weldon, Michael. *The Psychotronic Video Guide to Film*. New York: St. Martin's Press, 1996.

Woods, Ralph L. *The World of Dreams*. New York: Random House, 1947.

Yerushalmi, Joseph Hayim. *Freud's Moses*. New Haven, CT: Yale University Press, 1991.

Index

ABOUT THE AUTHOR

SHARON PACKER is a physician and board-certified psychiatrist who practices psychiatry in New York City and Woodstock. She teaches college courses in both media studies and cultural studies. Her artwork has been exhibited in several museums. She edited the *Bulletin of Judaism and Psychiatry* for some years. She combines her lifelong interests in the human mind and medicine, the visual arts, and philosophy and religion, through this research into the cultural context of dreams and dream theories.